Student Power, Participation and Revolution

STUDENT POWER,

PARTICIPATION
AND REVOLUTION

EDITED BY John and Susan Erlich

ASSOCIATION PRESS • NEW YORK

STUDENT POWER, PARTICIPATION AND REVOLUTION

Copyright © 1970 by John and Susan Erlich

Association Press, 291 Broadway, New York, N.Y. 10007

Standard Book Number: 8096-1792-7 Cloth
8096-1797-8 Paper

Library of Congress Catalog Card Number: 70-129425

PRINTED IN THE UNITED STATES OF AMERICA

11|18|71 E.B.C. 5.95 (3.97)

OCLC 112287

To Lynn, Kathy and Johnny
who are learning early the power of the people

Contents

Foreword

In January of 1962, Tom Hayden recruited me into Students for a Democratic Society. America was another country then. We wanted an end to nuclear testing, integration, sanity about Cuba and communism, and less bureaucracy. I joined SDS because the Young Democrats were opportunists looking for jobs. The YPSL (Young People's Socialist League) was too dogmatic and anti-communist. I wanted something that was activist, open, and beyond liberalism. My heroes were Camus, C. Wright Mills and I. F. Stone. I had never heard of Fanon or ecology, or Mick Jagger or Yippies. I couldn't find Vietnam on a map.

It is now more than eight years later. Dr. King and the Kennedys are gone. I imagine I am on the Plain of Jars all the time. There is a big hole on 11th Street where the bomb killed three radicals. I am not very optimistic about change. I love listening to The Stones when I'm high. And I picket and write articles to keep Tom Hayden out of jail in Chicago.

We have all changed, and we have all remained constant. So has the New Left. The still-brilliant *Port Huron Statement* anticipated the movements for community control, and against top-down bureaucracy. Bob Moses, the SNCC saint, talked about Vietnam at a funeral service for Goodman, Chaney and Schwerner.

But Weathermen, pigs, Women's Lib, the Panthers and the sympathy for Charles Manson are all new. Perhaps even discarded fads by the time this reaches print.

This book captures the Movement in all its wild kaleidoscopic diversity. Most of it I agree with, some of it I don't. But it all makes a helluva lot more sense than reading *Commentary* magazine or the Democratic Party platform.

And behind even the pieces that appall me, is a shared fury against racism, imperialism, militarism, and the middle-class machine. I wish the writing were better, but these are bulletins written in the trenches, not memos crafted for Presidents.

Read it knowing that, as an underground paper recently put it, "Che Guevera is 13 years old, and he has stopped doing his homework."

JACK NEWFIELD

Introduction

Student activists and the power movement of which they are a part constitute a new phenomenon in the history of America. As individuals and in groups, on campuses and in communities, and diffusing their influence throughout the country, they pose a very special problem for those who seek to define and understand them. They strongly resent and vigorously resist neat categorizations or tidy descriptions of themselves. There is a deep and abiding morality about that resistance—a resistance that says "I am the master of my destiny" and "Acting together we shall be the masters of our collective destinies." The political implications of Stokely Carmichael's dictum "To define is to control" have not been lost on this generation of student dissenters.

At the outset of the 1960's, those who took the lead in the civil rights struggle were deeply concerned with the praise or rebuke their actions received, for it was largely through public recognition that these actions were made or broken. But today this is no longer the case. A major focus of protest is centered on the imprisonment of life in words, elegant plans, and accelerating technological innovations. Modern rebels denounce the kind of mechanical competence that restricts and sanitizes that which should remain imprecise and a bit gritty around the edges. They have informed upon the dehumanizing interaction fostered by our increasingly stratified and polarized social system. A virtue of the young activists has been to obstruct, distract and upset this system.

They are not as politically naïve as the radical generation of the 1930's. They recognize that as individuals and as groups we must hang together through common networks of words and definitions that make possible both continuity and meaningful social organization. But these dissenters are seeking networks of a less absolute order; new and more flexible ways of dealing with people and situations. By developing and trying to live out forms of alternative or counterculture, they are attempting to demonstrate (and test out) some of these novel possibilities.

Lately, the forms of student protest have become increasingly violent. It would appear that unless and until a more significant response from the establishment is made to the substantive issues that students have raised—racism, poverty, militarism, environmental pollution, and the like—escalating cycles of violence-repression-violence may be expected.

While there are many varieties and factional disputes within the student movement, two central groupings ought to be recognized as largely autonomous entities—black students and white students. Black students have increasingly dealt only with issues they conceive of as having direct relevance to black people. At the same time, black students have formed alliances with blacks living beyond the boundaries of the schools and the universities to build a broader black unity. White student radicals have come to be more identified with a growing (and virtually all-white) New Left operating both on and beyond the institutional campuses. For the most part, integrated coalitions are temporary and take the form of support for each other's demands.

In a sense, the student power movement is a reaction to frustrated aspirations; a response to an America that cannot keep faith with poor nations abroad or poor people at home; a response to an America whose rhetoric of social justice so far exceeds its social practices that liberal idealists have become increasingly disheartened and immobilized. Condescending, "involved" liberalism of the New Frontier has been discredited. The implications of student protest go far beyond institutions of learning, far beyond the communities in which students live, to the heart of the American "mission." They are a stern reassessment of this mission and the way in which it flows from a more fundamental "American Dream." Essentially, students are asking, "What shall we, as human beings, be to each other?" The answers of the past have proved inadequate. New answers, creative answers, are to be found both in the new participatory forms with which students are now experimenting, and in the places where student activists and the multiple problems of our society come together.

The words of this book are the words of students. This is as it should be. In the final analysis, the student movement must be what the participants make it, not what those of us who analyze and describe it would like it to be. It is a movement built from individual actors and small cadres, a movement of individual schools and campuses, of communities and national constituencies.

The statements and analyses which follow illustrate student con-

cerns ranging from the search for personal identity and self-fulfill-
ment to the need for revolutionary change in America. Some
themes recur throughout the development of the student movement, others are unique to certain times and places. An attempt
has been made to emphasize recent activities and to utilize materials which suggest future directions.

Particular attention is given to the diffusion of the student movement down the educational ladder into the high schools and junior
high schools, and up the same ladder into the professions and the
community.

These young writer-activists speak of hope and despair. We believe it is right to see the student rebellion more as affirmation
than condemnation, more as a faith in the perfectability of man
than a denial of this possibility. Some radical activists have been
accused of an inadequate understanding of the meanings and the
uses of history. Don't they perhaps have a point when they say
with Jerry Rubin, "I am two years old, I was born in Chicago during the Democratic National Convention"? Surely the invasion of
Cambodia, and the response which it evoked at Kent State and
other campuses throughout the country, was for many young people a time of rebirth in a more radical consciousness.

The *Port Huron Statement* was written in 1962 as a founding
document of Students for a Democratic Society (SDS). It was (and
is) an influential specification of the dissatisfactions felt by students
and the objectives of their movement. In many ways, it served as a
contemporary Declaration of Independence for student activists.
Like all idealized statements of human aspiration, it has proved
both difficult to actualize and prophetic of future trends. The following excerpts from the *Port Huron Statement* suggest an agenda
for what follows and illustrate the potential of the student power
movement.

We are people of this generation, bred in at least modest comfort,
housed in universities, looking uncomfortably to the world we inherit.

*   *   *

Our work is guided by the sense that we may be the last generation
in the experiment with living. But we are a minority—the vast majority

of our people regard the temporary equilibriums of our society and the world as eternally functional parts. In this is perhaps the outstanding paradox: We ourselves are imbued with urgency, yet the message of our society is that there is no viable alternative to the present. Beneath the reassuring tones of the politicians, beneath the common opinion that America will "muddle through," beneath the stagnation of those who have closed their minds to the future, is the pervading feeling that there simply are no alternatives, that our times have witnessed the exhaustion not only of Utopias, but of any new departures as well. Feeling the press of complexity upon the emptiness of life, people are fearful of the thought that at any moment things might thrust out of control. They fear change itself, since change might smash whatever invisible framework seems to hold back chaos for them now. For most Americans, all crusades are suspect, threatening. The fact that each individual sees apathy in his fellows perpetuates the common reluctance to organize for changes. The dominant institutions are complex enough to blunt the minds of their potential critics, and entrenched enough to swiftly dissipate or entirely repel the energies of protest and reform, thus limiting human expectancies. Then, too, we are a materially improved society, and by our own improvements we seem to have weakened the case for change.

Some would have us believe that Americans feel contentment amidst prosperity—but might it not better be called a glaze above deeply felt anxieties about their role in the new world? And if these anxieties produce a developed indifference to human affairs, do they not as well produce a yearning to believe there *is* an alternative to the present, that something *can* be done to change circumstances in the school, the workplaces, the bureaucracies, the government? It is to this latter yearning, at once the spark and engine of change, that we direct our present appeal. The search for truly democratic alternatives to the present, and a commitment to social experimentation with them, is a worthy and fulfilling human enterprise, one which moves us and, we hope, others today. . . .

Theoretic chaos has replaced the idealistic thinking of old—and, unable to reconstitute theoretic order, men have condemned idealism itself. Doubt has replaced hopefulness, and men act out a defeatism that is labeled realistic. The decline of utopia and hope is in fact one of the defining features of social life today. The reasons are various: The dreams of the older left were perverted by Stalinism and never recreated; the congressional stalemate makes men narrow their view of the possible; the specialization of human activity leaves little room for sweeping thought; the horrors of the twentieth century, symbolized in the gas ovens and concentration camps and atom bombs, have blasted hopefulness. To be idealistic is to be considered apocalyptic, deluded. To have no serious aspirations, on the contrary, is to be "tough-minded."

In suggesting social goals and values, therefore, we are aware of entering a sphere of some disrepute. Perhaps matured by the past, we have no sure formulas, no closed theories—but that does not mean values are beyond discussion and tentative determination. A first task of any social movement is to convince people that the search for orienting theories and the creation of human values is complex but worthwhile. We are aware that to avoid platitudes we must analyze the concrete conditions of social order. But to direct such an analysis we must use the guideposts of basic principles. Our own social values involve conceptions of human beings, human relationships, and social systems.

We regard *men* as infinitely precious and possessed of unfulfilled capacities for reason, freedom, and love. In affirming these principles we are aware of countering perhaps the dominant conceptions of man in the twentieth century: that he is a thing to be manipulated, and that he is inherently incapable of directing his own affairs. We oppose the depersonalization that reduces human beings to the status of things. If anything, the brutalities of the twentieth century teach that means and ends are intimately related, that vague appeals to "posterity" cannot justify the mutilations of the present. We oppose, too, the doctrine of human incompetence because it rests essentially on the modern fact that men have been "competently" manipulated into incompetence. We see little reason why men cannot meet with increasing skill the complexities and responsibilities of their situation, if society is organized not for minority participation but for majority participation in decision-making.

Men have unrealized potential for self-cultivation, self-direction, self-understanding, and creativity. It is this potential that we regard as crucial and to which we appeal—not to the human potentiality for violence, unreason, and submission to authority. The goal of man and society should be human independence: a concern not with image or popularity but with finding a meaning in life that is personally authentic; a quality of mind not compulsively driven by a sense of powerlessness, nor one which unthinkingly adopts status values, nor one which represses all threats to its habits, but one which has full, spontaneous access to present and past experiences, one which easily unites the fragmented parts of personal history, one which openly faces problems which are troubling and unresolved—one with an intuitive awareness of possibilities, an active sense of curiosity, an ability and willingness to learn.

This kind of independence does not mean egoistic individualism; the object is not to have one's way so much as it is to have a way that is one's own. Nor do we deify man—we merely have faith in his potential. . . .

There are no convincing apologies for the contemporary malaise . . . the felt powerlessness of ordinary people, the resignation before the enormity of events. But subjective apathy is encouraged by the objective American situation—the actual separation of people from power, from relevant knowledge, from pinnacles of decision-making. Just as the university influences the student way of life, so do major social institutions create the circumstances in which the isolated citizen will try hopelessly to understand his world and himself.

The very isolation of the individual—from power and community and ability to aspire—means the rise of a democracy without publics. . . . The vital democratic connection between community and leadership, between the mass and the several elites, has been so wrenched and perverted that disastrous policies go unchallenged time and again. . . .

The first effort, then, should be to state a vision: What is the perimeter of human possibility in this epoch? . . . The second effort, if we are to be politically responsible, is to evaluate the prospects for obtaining at least a substantial part of that vision in our epoch: What are the social forces that exist, or that must exist, if we are to be successful? And what role have we ourselves to play as a social force?

                    *   *   *

. . . The academic life contains reinforcing counterparts to the way in which extracurricular life is organized. The academic world is founded in a teacher-student relation analogous to the parent-child relation which characterizes *in loco parentis*. Further, academia includes a radical separation of student from the material of study. That which is studied, the social reality, is "objectified" to sterility, dividing the student from life—just as he is restrained in active involvement by the deans controlling student government. The specialization of function and knowledge, admittedly necessary to our complex technological and social structure, has produced an exaggerated compartmentalization of study and understanding. This has contributed to: an overly parochial view, by faculty, of the role of its research and scholarship; a discontinuous and truncated understanding, by students, of the surrounding social order; a loss of personal attachment, by nearly all, to the worth of study as a humanistic enterprise.

There is, finally, the cumbersome academic bureaucracy extending throughout the academic as well as extracurricular structures, contributing to the sense of outer complexity and inner powerlessness that transforms so many students from honest searching to ratification of convention and, worse, to a numbness to present and future catastrophes. The size and financing systems of the university enhance the permanent trusteeship of the administrative bureaucracy, their power leading to a shift to the value standards of business and administrative mentality within the university. Huge foundations and other private financial interests shape the underfinanced colleges and universities, making them not only more commercial but less disposed to diagnose society critically, less open to dissent. Many social and physical scientists, neglecting the liberating heritage of higher learning, develop "human relations" or "morale-producing" techniques for the corporate economy, while others exercise their intellectual skills to accelerate the arms race.

The university is located in a permanent position of social influence. Its educational function makes it indispensable and automatically makes it a crucial institution in the formation of social attitudes. In an unbelievably complicated world, it is the central institution for organizing, evaluating, and transmitting knowledge. . . . Social relevance, the accessibility to knowledge, and internal openness—these together make the university a potential base and agency in the movement of social change.

. . . The university system cannot complete a movement of ordinary people making demands for a better life. From its schools and colleges across the nation, a militant left might awaken its allies, and by beginning the process toward peace, civil rights, and labor struggles, reinsert theory and idealism where too often reign confusion and political barter. The power of students and faculty united is not only potential; it has shown its actuality in the South, and in the reform movements of the North.

To turn these possibilities into realities will involve national efforts at university reform by an alliance of students and faculty. They must wrest control of the educational process from the administrative bureaucracy. They must make fraternal and functional contact with allies in labor, civil rights, and other liberal forces outside the campus. They must import major public issues into the curriculum. . . . They must make debate and controversy, not dull pedantic cant, the common style for educational life. They must consciously build a base for their assault upon the loci of power.

As students for a democratic society, we are committed to stimulating this kind of social movement, this kind of vision and program in campus and community across the country. If we appear to seek the unattainable as it has been said, then let it be known that we do so to avoid the unimaginable.

Obviously this book was made possible by the student activists of the 1960's and those who are emerging into the 1970's. Our debt of gratitude to them for trying to force us to make good on national commitments to freedom, justice and equality can never be repaid. Our special thanks must also go to Carol Mutton and Sue Alexander who made possible the emergence of a coherent manuscript. Finally to Barry Bluestone, Larry Gary, Ron Landsman, and Sue Sattel, who guided our search for materials, must go our deep appreciation.

JOHN and SUSAN ERLICH

Ann Arbor, Michigan
August, 1970

THE RISE OF STUDENT POWER: *THE DEVELOPMENT OF STUDENT CONCERNS—AN OVERVIEW*

R‍EADING student newspapers on campuses around the country today is a little like seeing American news on Canadian television. It is "our world" all right, but with a seemingly strange set of biases. College newspapers—especially on the larger and more prestigious campuses—have come increasingly to represent the views of student dissenters. Recognizing the significance of the communications media in publicizing change efforts, the activists chose their own collegiate newspapers as an early target for radical takeover.

The following series of articles—mostly editorials—were taken from the files of *The Michigan Daily,* official student publication at the University of Michigan.* We feel they present an important historical perspective on the changing interests of students during the decade of participation—the 1960's. Similarly, trends are es-

* These articles represent the individual opinions of staff writers and editors.

tablished which suggest some directions that the student movement might take during the 1970's.

The first editorial is particularly interesting because of its reliance on an article in a scholarly journal as a point of departure. In the early 1960's, students looked for example and guidance from older liberal-activists. Given the model of heroic civil rights demonstrations in the South and self-propelled black activism, students began to participate in a broad range of protests and demonstrations.

Between 1962 and 1964, students' actions were primarily directed outward—to involvement with the problems of others. They went to Washington for the Freedom March of 1963 and fought for voting rights and the desegregation of facilities in the South, tutored in the ghettoes and, generally, provided the major civil rights organizations with millions of man-hours of volunteer effort. Many took a hand in political reform movements, went into the Peace Corps, or worked with local social welfare agencies.

By the mid-sixties, students began to recognize that they had hardly made a dent in the problems they set out so valiantly to attack. Not only had some of the leaders in whom they invested so much hope been murdered, but the society at large just didn't seem to be truly interested. Increasingly, students turned toward the issues which affected them personally, issues where the targets of change were much closer to home—like the draft and the war, and a larger and more significant role in the running of the educational institutions which had such a powerful impact on their present lives and future chances. Mark Killingsworth epitomizes a high point of belief in one participatory ideal, the potential for "rational" discourse as the means to reasonable ends.

The final article, published in late 1969, only hints at the events of the previous three years, during which militant students undertook actions that shook the academic world to its core. Hard-won campus freedoms were preceded by platoons of off-campus police and the National Guard, jail sentences and the development of a whole set of elaborate procedures for handling student dissent. The anti-establishment student radical became an American "type." At the same time, the dissenters became increasingly distressed by the intransigence of those in positions of power, and the growing specter of repression.

Thomas Turner

As I See It (*February 5, 1960*)

Students are beginning to take stands on significant issues, Allan Brick of Dartmouth notes in a recent *Nation* article.

He mentions specifically the current furor over compulsory ROTC, dramatized by freshman Frederick Moore's hunger strike at the University of California and now showing itself in student petitions, demonstrations, front-page editorials and other signs of protest by many young people on many campuses.

Concern with moral values lies behind the agitation concerning ROTC, according to Brick.

What is perhaps more significant about Brick's statement, however, is not his observations on the rise of anti-ROTC, anti-military feeling, but his indictment of faculty members (and clergymen) for refusing to take stands on moral questions.

Without leadership, the students who are in Brick's opinion "ready to be challenged" will grope far more than is necessary in trying to relate themselves and their ideas to the world around them.

On this campus, however, and on many others, a more fitting indictment would be of the administration, which—in such an enormously complex institution—is the only single group which could exercise moral leadership of the sort Brick is talking about.

There is, it must be noted, a paradox of sorts in Brick's arguments. While students are reacting to the absence of moral leadership, they cannot do very effectively without some moral leadership.

Pointing out an alternate source of moral leadership is essential if the reaction is not to be wasted energy.

Consideration of "student issues" such as compulsory ROTC and the National Defense Education Act loyalty oath and affidavit presupposes a "student community," with common goals.

Given a series of student bodies across the country, each beginning to overcome the lethargy and self-concern which has characterized the American campus of the past decade, most of them lacking moral leadership from faculty and administration, there is need for a feeling of identity between these student bodies.

This is particularly the case since the administration and faculty members with whom the isolated student bodies come in contact are themselves part of a tight little world.

Faculty members belong to the same societies and read the same publications, administrators are in contact with their counterparts on other campuses regarding the ever-tighter teacher market, the problem of appropriations and so on, and the result of all this is the appearance of a national academic climate. When conditions become restrictive on one campus, this spreads to other schools.

Faculties and administrations, bound up as they are in a relatively tight national community, have two other characteristics which make group-consciousness on the part of students particularly desirable; this community tends to be conservative and at the same time extremely sensitive to publicity. The latter characteristic ordinarily dovetails neatly with the former, making change next to impossible on many campuses. But if students protest actively, either through a national voice such as the National Student Association, or through a spontaneous wave of protest, or both, the administrations and faculties of individual schools may be moved into action. Congress may also heed a protest thus voiced.

The movements to eliminate the oath and affidavit, and to make all ROTC voluntary, may serve to give students a sense of identity which will serve them in good stead in the future, and which will dramatize the extent to which faculties, and particularly administrations, are derelict in their duty.

2

Malinda Berry

Hayden Advocates Unity to Push Student Ideals (*February 25, 1961*)

"Due to the shrinking of the world we have become vaccinated against horror by horror itself." Thomas Hayden, '61, Daily Editor said yesterday at a meeting of the Americans Committed to World Responsibility.

This complacency toward today's horrors has turned most students against their responsibilities for other men's destinies, Hayden continued. The "student movement" has shown, however, that this generation is not dead to its responsibility.

This resurgence of student action is characterized by demonstrations against the House Un-American Activities Committee, Food for Fayette County drive, protests against compulsory ROTC, anti-discrimination in housing, and formation of the Peace Corps.

"The students in the resurgence of activity must recognize that they are held together by a certain unity of purpose—their responsibilities to other men. But why should we accept responsibilities? Why should there be a student movement?" Hayden asked.

"I must value life and, ethically, we must have reverence for man. Reverence for man is to believe that if any man is not free then none of us is free," Hayden said.

"We must fight for an environment where men can be free.

Where there is a lack of reverence endured we must struggle to remove it. That is why I believe in the possibility of a student movement.

"Reverence is why I am opposed to the HUAC. For 22 years
it has operated destructively. Its function is to threaten the thoughts
of some of us, so we are all threatened by it," Hayden charged.

"Reverence is why I support students working for civil rights.
Students can help diminish suffering and they are doing it," Hayden
continued.

"Most of all, reverence for life is why I support ACWR. It is
dedicated to the perpetuation of human life, respect and dignity.
And, like the Peace Corps, it avers that there is an alternative to
destruction and violence."

3

Mary Lou Butcher

Activism and a New Breed (*April 9, 1965*)

The university student leads a life which is both envied and criticized but rarely appreciated by anyone outside the halls of the
academy. Outside observers reduce his world to books and papers
on one hand and parties and athletics on the other. He is not
thought to have pressing interests divorced from the day-to-day requirements of the academic timetable. He is credited with a little
knowledge about a lot of things and commended for pursuing a
liberal education. He is cited for whatever achievement may be
signified by his grade-point average. He is laughed at for his im-
maturity and his idealism, but nonetheless encouraged to learn for
himself. And on the whole, he is exonerated from responsibility.

Such attitudes are responsible for perpetuating the concept of a
student as a member of a substratum of society, sealed off from
life. Paradoxically, it is also assumed that only the college graduate, with degree in hand, is qualified to grapple with the tests
which contemporary society poses and will continue to pose. How
the supposedly alienated student is ever to comprehend and tackle
societal needs after a four- five- or eight-year incubation period is
not considered, but rather is incorporated into the general mystique
of higher education.

Within the framework of these narrowly conceived views, it is no wonder that burgeoning student activism gives cause for surprise and even alarm. Reactions to student demonstrations, petitions, protests and political endeavors range from utter mystification to rank indignation. Activism is just an extra piece which does not fit the puzzle of student life as it has been theoretically carved out and clung to.

What is missing from the outsiders' analyses is the taste of rootlessness which today's student experiences and the consequent acute need for commitment which he senses. Within the last four years the American student has demonstrated within and without the nation. Growing membership within student direct action groups and political parties portends a continuing activist element within the universities and a lifting of the paralysis which so long existed.

Having been reared in a climate of ostensible peace and prosperity, in a society geared to the brightest and the hardest-working, at a tempo prizing urgency and efficiency, the student observes that these factors are debilitating to a large proportion of society. And he finds them hollow insofar as they demarcate the environment in which he is to live, work, love.

When the network of middle-class values is stretched to its limit, it fails the student. It rejects involvement, tolerance, creativity and self-sacrifice out of hand. It promotes in their stead complacency, expediency and isolation.

Perceiving that many of these values are based on fear and insecurity, the student is faced with a choice between the unsatisfying but more comfortable path of quietism or the challenging and demanding road of involvement. To avoid the sterility of the materialist ethic, to escape the limitations of the classroom, to negate the pursuit of a degree for sake of a degree, to break down barriers among individuals—the student must seek commitment, involvement, responsibility.

Impotent though he may be to alter the behavior, convictions or values of older generations, the student yet is accountable for what he purposes to be. And he must bear responsibility for the effect he has both on his peers and on succeeding generations.

Fear and/or cynicism can effectively cripple the student's potential for effecting social change and finding a purpose. The cult of mass education must inevitably reinforce this unhappy prospect.

Competition, anonymity, specialization spell dichotomy—between student and student, student and educator, academy and the Real World.

What, then, of the activist? What motivates him and enables him to surmount the negative aspects of the contemporary ethos? How can he affect his peers?

Above all, the student activist possesses and cherishes a sense of freedom. It is this disposition which liberates him from fear and requires him to engage in responsibility for his own future as well as for his potential contribution to the well-being of others which is also fundamental.

It has been suggested that many a student activist will eventually abandon his present path to return to middle-class origins and institutions—only to subvert them. If this be the sole consequence of his endeavors, it is perhaps the most worthwhile. The best-educated members of our society must not be divorced from the realities of our society—cybernation, illiteracy, poverty, integration, alienation—nor must they renounce their roles in effecting change.

It is reasonable to assume that the student activist will continue to clamor. His vociferousness has progressively intensified since the "freedom rides," the "sit-ins" and the student movement got underway four years ago. It is upon his peers, however, that the real burden of change rests; they must listen, think, accept and act. And from them will come many of the educators who will affect succeeding generations of students.

The activist strain has been fermenting within the university for four years as it has throughout the nation. A new breed of student is emerging. His impact on and off campus should spark much productive thinking—and action.

4

Neil Shister

Parade and Protest on a Friday Afternoon (*October 16, 1965*)

Somewhere in the hoopla of the drums and the blaring of the trumpets, five blocks away from the judging stand in front of the [Michigan Student] Union, the first acts of an ever continuing morality play unfolded, with the floats and the bands of Homecoming serving as backdrop.

Protests don't seem to mean too much anymore, at least not to most of the university's students who seem to have become insensitized to them. Four guys and a guitar, protesting against protests, got the biggest reaction and the most attention from yesterday's "International Days of Protest" rally on the Diag.

But there are some places where a picket line against the government still hits pretty hard, where you don't throw around lines like "End the War" and "Stop the Slaughter" too loosely. There are places not replete with objective intellectuals willing to tolerate dissent but peopled, instead, with work-a-day-world kind of men to whom the United States government, if not always completely good, is never, ever bad.

Downtown Ann Arbor was such a place Friday, and the protestors there, marching in a block-long picket line with their placard signs, needed a pretty thick skin.

A stockbroker stood in the doorway of his office, benevolently looking down as they marched, saying how it was just like when he was in school and "Communist cell blocks were the big thing." But this was no way to express dissent, he said, for "who would listen to those kind of people? Hell, why don't they take baths or get their hair cut first?"

Most of the bystanders just stared, wonderingly at first, resentfully later. To most, to the men in their tired suits as well as those in their blue work shirts and hard hats, to the women who had brought their children down early to get good places to watch the parade, as well as to the off-duty waitresses and the secretaries staring out of their second-story windows, the whole thing just didn't seem to mean much. But after a while they sensed that the status quo, the set of precious absolutes with which they had lived so long and so well, was being challenged by a bunch of "punk kids who have never been in uniform, who don't even know what this country is all about."

One scraggly bearded marcher, proudly pushing a baby stroller in which sat his bewildered young son, sadly smiled as the crowd heaped its abuse on him.

An old man watched. Unlike most of the rest, he agreed with the marchers. In an almost inaudible voice pocked by broken English he murmured, "Enough war. You leave and you're a hero, you return shot up and nobody looks at you."

By then the bands were coming down South Main Street and attention previously devoted to the protest was now directed towards the floats and pretty girls. There was still an occasional cry of "End the war in Viet Nam" but most people were too preoccupied with "downing the Boilermaker" to really listen to it.

A few of the marchers left their circle chain and took positions near the front of the crowd, and then, like everybody else, became engrossed in the spectacle of the moment. Almost everybody else, that is.

There were three to whom the parade was secondary. Two of the three were big, all had moderate sideburns and one of them spoke with a Southern tinge. The biggest of the three had prematurely gray hair and wore a T-shirt uncovering a tattoo on his left arm of the Marine Corps insignia. They were there to challenge, directly and physically, anybody's right to question, and they had found what they wanted, an isolated protestor silently watching the parade.

He said nothing as they called him "kike" and "Commie," but stared back at them with a look of complete defiance, so convinced in his purpose and genuine in his principle that he seemed to know they couldn't hurt him; and they seemed to know it too and it made them bitter.

"Boy, you better take down that sign or I'm gonna flatten you." The sign and its bearer remained unmoved.

Then, suddenly, came the inevitable fight, although three on one is hardly a fight. The sign was snapped and the marcher was bloody before the police, who were stationed ten feet away but took twenty seconds to arrive, had broken it up. And the police, who enforce traffic violations with such unmerciful justice, surrounded the marcher and his molestors, joining hands and encircling them.

"Officer, that kid insulted the U.S. flag, he waved the sign around while the flag passed and started yelling things."

The police took the gray-haired enforcer and the marcher away in a car, still uncertain about what had really happened and evidently not too curious, for the four witnesses who volunteered their stories had to walk all the way over to City Hall before anybody would even take their names and still nobody wanted to listen to them.

One of the witnesses, a college kid who had stepped in the fight to prevent the marcher from being beaten up worse than he was, asked, more to himself than anybody around him, "I wonder if I would do the same thing again?"

The witnesses came back from City Hall, the "Go-Go" girls and their float were jerking their way by, and somewhere in the distance a high school band was playing "Hail to the Victors" [University of Michigan marching song] off-key.

Student Power: Means and Ends
(*December 3, 1966*)

When I went home for Thanksgiving vacation, my mother asked me: "Dear, what is all the uproar about at the University?"

"Student power," I said.

"Oh, goodness, not like that Hoagy Carmichael fellow," she replied in astonishment.

At that point I realized it was time to define student power—and what ought to come with it.

Student power means a student vote in university decisions which affect them. It means that students, as well as faculty and administrators, deserve a chance not only to speak, but to use the power of a vote, in deciding issues which affect them.

An example is the issue of discipline in university housing—rules on who lives in it and how (hours, open-opens, and so on).

Students are obviously affected because the rules govern their behavior. Faculty are affected because the rules ought to be (even if they aren't) conducive to education. Administrators are affected because (for example) if the rules are poorly written, parents won't send their children to the university—which means that the university could default on the bonds which financed dormitory construction.

seem
defining th
voting voice to
A tripartite com
equally represented,
vote—will eventually begin to
"constitution" which gives students such

But student power—which faculty and administrators
accept in principle—isn't sufficient if students are, indeed, going
to become full members of the university community.

Student power means that students have a vote in university decisions. But which students? How many students? It would be
ironic to say that students ought to have a vote in university decisions without—at the same time—saying that as many students as
possible ought to determine what that student vote ought to be and
what it should say.

Just as it is wrong for an elite to dominate university-wide decision-making (something administrators and faculty now con-
cede), it is also wrong for an elite to dominate student decision-
making on how student power in university decision-making should
be exercised.

The teach-in idea, like the "talk-in" at the Administration
Building yesterday, is one way to enable as many interested students as possible decide on what the student voice in university-
wide decision-making will be.

But—as those present at Thursday's teach-in ruefully admit—
such vast, amorphous meetings are often organizationally "messy"
and disorganized.

On the other hand, working solely through Student Government
Council is dissatisfactory for other reasons—SGC may be more
organized (perhaps) but, even though it in theory represents all
students, SGC still is only 17 students sitting around a table. There
ought to be a way for the rest of the 30,000 students here to speak
their minds directly.

SGC is a representative democracy; involving the whole student
body in some direct way is participatory democracy. Both elements
are essential for valid student participation; valid student partici-

pation is essential for student power; and student power is necessary for valid university decision-making.

Therefore, to provide for both participatory democracy and representative democracy, SGC should work to set up a broad-based student union to involve as many students as possible in student decision-making.

6

Martin Hirschman

Unhappy Anniversary for Student Power
(*December 4, 1969*)

Three years old this week, the massive sit-ins and teach-ins of the Student Power Movement of 1966 have had a profound effect on the recent history of the university.

It is difficult, of course, to establish direct causal relationships between the 1966 actions and the reforms of university regulations and structures that have followed; as much as anything, the Student Power Movement represented a rather blunt attack on the draft and, more specifically, on the arbitrariness of the university administration.

But in a very real sense, the achievements and failures of the past three years constitute the legacy of the Student Power Movement. For the 1966 demonstrations were the first actions sufficiently large and dramatic to force faculty members and administrators to begin taking student demands and interests seriously.

And while much remains to be done in the area of increasing the student role in university decision-making, the changes which have taken place over the last three years have been significant.

The social freedoms new students now take for granted are, in fact, only the recent fruits of a prolonged struggle against repressive restrictions on the lives of students. For example, the abolition of curfews for women living in the dormitories and the establishment of the right of underclass students to live outside the dormitory system have taken place only in the last two years.

In a more positive sense, meanwhile, students have gained unprecedented influence in the governing of the university. While faculty members and administrators have yet to surrender their stranglehold on the ultimate mechanisms of university decision-making, inroads have been made in a wide range of areas—curriculum, course evaluation, student services and even university financing.

Students have even won their 40-year struggle for a discount bookstore. Although even more drastic action than that taken in 1966 was necessary to gain an acceptable bookstore setup, the case still proves that students can have their way if they are right and demonstrate some persistence.

Despite these gains, however, one of the most important results of the Student Power Movement remains in a state of limbo. The institutionalization of the role of students in certain decision-making areas continues, after three years of debate and redrafting, to await inclusion in the Regents bylaws. And, ominously, a recent proposal by the Regents themselves threatens the value of the entire work.

Thus far, the task of writing student powers and rights into the bylaws has proven an arduous one. Appointed in the wake of the Student Power Movement, the President's Commission on the Role of Students in University Decision-making (the Hatcher Commission) took over a year to write its lengthy, well-considered report.

Unfortunately, areas of disagreement still remained, and the commission's recommendations were not specifically designed for inclusion in the bylaws. Hasty attempts to draft bylaws on the commission report lead to a controversy between students and the administration and forced another year's delay, as students and faculty members sought to agree on a specific proposal to submit to the Regents.

Finally this summer, such agreement was achieved. With very minor points of disagreement duly noted, a student-faculty approved draft of the bylaws was submitted.

The Regents began considering the bylaws in October, and last month issued a proposed draft of some of the sections under consideration. Unfortunately, the new proposal includes changes which would drastically alter the effect of the bylaws, to the detriment of the university community as a whole.

One of the major recommendations of the Hatcher Commission report was the elimination of rules relating to the nonacademic conduct of students and faculty members. At present, for example, the schools and colleges maintain rules against the disruption of university functions, with suspension and expulsion—normally the response to academic deficiency—as possible penalties.

Members of the Hatcher Commission wisely believed that the disciplining of students for offenses which were not strictly academic (for example, cheating on exams) should be left to the civil authorities. Offenses like disruptions do not, in any way, bear on the competence of a student to continue in his academic program. In addition, there is a serious question of the ability of a university tribunal to give a fair hearing to a student whose actions were directed against the university.

The primary disciplinary mechanism outlined in the proposed bylaws is a student-faculty-administration body which would be called University Council. The council would be empowered to determine, with the approval of Senate Assembly and Student Government Council, conduct standards for all members of the university community.

Thus, University Council could end regulations governing nonacademic conduct, or at least take authority over such regulations away from the schools and colleges.

Unfortunately, under the draft of the bylaws put forth by the Regents, the power of University Council would be significantly impaired. The rules approved by the faculties of the schools and colleges would remain supreme, with council able to enact regulations only in cases where lower-level rules do not apply. And with the destruction of the power of University Council, hopes of ending nonacademic conduct rules would be significantly dimmed.

A second change made by the Regents would have what appears to be the unfortunate effect of giving undue longevity to University Council regulations. Standards of conduct in the university community, have, for at least the last three years, undergone rapid change, and this situation is likely to continue. Yet under the Regents' new proposal, it would be extremely difficult to effect a change in existing conduct regulations.

Students and faculty members had proposed a system under which either SGC or Senate Assembly could "disaffirm" a council regulation thus forcing immediate redrafting of the statute. This provision is unwisely eliminated in the regental plan.

A third change in the bylaw draft is more ominous for its indication of the intent of the Regents than for its actual substance. Under the student-faculty version University Council rules would be in effect unless the Regents vetoed them. The Regents have turned this around by including approval by them as a requirement for passage of a regulation.

Under the state constitution, of course, there is no way to legally eliminate the role of the Regents as the ultimate university decision-makers. But developments in recent years have demonstrated that the internal stability of the university is best promoted by keeping regental action in this area to a minimum. The new bylaw draft is an indication that this is not their intention.

On the whole, progress for students since the Student Power Movement of 1966 has been slow but steady. Indeed, one indication of student influence is the delicate, but satisfactory compromise reached between students and faculty members over the bylaw proposals—a compromise which the Regents now threaten to destroy.

PART I I

WHAT'S WRONG
WITH THE SYSTEM?

T HOUGH they are all critical of the quality of American life, it is difficult to categorize the articles which follow. Some are highly political, others appear almost apolitical or take political considerations into account with reluctance.

However, what these articles do indicate is the broad search for prime causes of the debilitating problems which threaten almost every sector of our society. In thinking about the processes of education, Jesse Bernstein points out the gross indignities which students suffer at the hands of their teachers. A leader of the Columbia rebellion carries this theme forward in describing his personal radicalization. Carl Davidson, in a more analytical and systematic discussion, considers the broader ramifications of the institutional university and the ways in which student movement activities might be built around its inherent weaknesses.

Cathy Wilkerson, Mike Spiegel and Les Coleman suggest that students ought to begin "destudentizing" their lives. Only in this manner, the authors say, can they divest themselves of the "false privilege" which has been bestowed upon them. Experiences with resisting the subtle (and not so subtle) discrimination against women in the university setting are depicted by Molly Jackson. Finally, Laura Derman offers personal reflections on the difficulties of putting thought and action together to combat our fundamental social problems.

7

Jesse Bernstein *

Doing the Assignment:
A Search for Now and Tomorrow (*1970*)

Where do you begin, and why? Why don't you just do the assignment like everyone else? It's so easy to be like everyone else. They don't ask questions. Well, they do, but they are not the right questions. They ask the questions you are supposed to ask. Anyone can ask those. The right questions are the ones you are not supposed to ask. It's cool to ask a teacher to clarify the assignment, but it's a cop-out if you ask why you have to do it.

People talk about games. Someone wrote a book about games (I know his name, I even bought the book). One answer you get when someone thinks you are going to ask a "right" question is that there are many games in life and our society. Some you have to play, others you have a choice on, others you don't have to go near at all. They might even be immoral or unethical (or fun).

Books don't help you ask questions. They make you answer questions. They do that because of the way you have to read them. They also do it because it's a one-way street; you can't answer back a book, or call it out because it insulted your mother. You have to read books for a reason, usually one that is coercive. Even if you say you like to read, like everyone does, that's because it's the right thing to say. It is an approved answer to forestall a whole lot of

* At the time this was written, Jesse Bernstein was a student at the University of Michigan School of Social Work.

unapproved questions. Why do some people like to whip themselves or others? Books are good if they make you ask questions;
or maybe all books are good, it's just that the readers don't know
what to do with them. Sometimes I want to read a book once and
then forget I ever read it so I can read it again to ask questions.
Maybe it's my fault. Maybe I've been unfair to books and teachers. No, let's stick with books. If books are a one-way street,
they . . . The point is that they can't be there to coerce you in any
way. Once you read a book, you can do with it what you want.
The problem is what others expect you to do with it. They expect
you to memorize parts of it, so you can recite them at appropriate
times as proof of your something or other. Sometimes it's like you
can't say what *you* feel or want to say. Sometimes what other people say is more important than if you would say the same thing on
your own, if you really felt and believed it. Do books detract from
you as a person, or do they add to it? Why do Mills, Coser, Field-
ing, Roth make me feel good, and Perlman, Hollis, Caplan make
me feel sick? The first four make me ask questions. Is it make, or
allow? Did I ever give Wilensky and Lebeau a chance? Why did I
go out and buy Zald's *Reader,* when it wasn't required? Mills talks
about biography and structure . . . Do the bad books lack one or
the other? Do the styles of the writers lack one or the other, or
does the material? If all books are bad, why am I using Mills as a
reference point? Who should I read besides the above four?

Norman Sharp and Harriet Graham write high school history
books. They wrote a world history and an American history text.
Sharp taught me American history in high school. I got the highest
mark in the school on the Regents' exam, but got kicked out of
the Honor Society because I wrote some remark on the paper about
the Supreme Court giving a ruling on the question asked two days
before the test was given, and weeks after the test was prepared.
If the Court would have waited a week on the decision, no one in
the whole state would have been able to answer the question. I
quoted the decision, and put in parentheses ". . . lucky thing for
us students" or something to that effect. Sharp was a great guy. I
liked him, and he liked me. I read his book from cover to cover.
But he is a racist. He left out about the American concentration
camps on the west coast. He left out the parts about the people
who go hungry in this country, and on and on and on. He is a nice

guy, but he's a racist. American history didn't make me ask questions, it stuffed the answers down my throat. For some reason, it gave me colic.

I can't seem to separate books from people. Maybe books that *I* can't relate to people are the bad ones? Maybe books that don't relate to me are bad? But what am I? How much of me is Dr. Spock, the Bible, Freud? How much of me is my grandfather(s), grandmother(s), father, and mother? Why is it important to separate books and people? Because you can't punch a book in the mouth? Coser put out stuff I never dealt with, but is crucial to my whole life; Hollis put out stuff that's either so simple or so far from people, that it is only crucial to social work professors.

Simple sociology, status and role. All those "others" that fuck-up books and me. They got a million ways of saying it, but it's still the same thing. The feeling of disgust that goes upward toward the "top" . . . the feeling of contempt you are supposed to have toward the bottom is now one of confusion about what to do. And those around you. *Peers* . . . how lonely is an oasis, its friends come and go. It's like if you take each status and role at a time, you are playing the game, even if you are saying how this is screwing everything up. Then Henry Meyer asks, "Are we freer within a structure, or without" but tells you not to think about it for too long (because it's one of those "right" questions that just happened to slip out). There has to be some kind of relationship between people. Maybe if I looked at education.

What is the difference between a student and a teacher? When am I a student, and when am I a teacher? Don't teachers learn? If they do, then they are students. If they learn from a student, then the student is the teacher, and the teacher is the student. What difference does it make who is who? The difference is who you are inside, not outside. The difference is how you think, not even what you think. Can a good teacher teach any subject, no matter how much he knows about the subject? Sorry, Eugene (I knew he'd be here sooner or later). That's one thing I'm willing to accept as a temporary hypothesis. *Differential expertise.* If he don't know, how the hell am I supposed to know? But, maybe I should go about finding out about it in a different way than he does? Maybe the question is what or where is *my* expertise? How can I answer that, when I have to answer all those other ridiculous questions?

I got a memorandum today from P. Martin, M.D. Dr. Cotten is going to give a talk . . . is Dr. Cotten going to give a listen? Is this going to be another breast-feeding of professional milk that's going to turn to shit in my mouth? How much longer do I have to play this game, or put up with this political rationalization for doing things? But everything will be all right when people listen to me. When I'm a Dr. and they have to come to meetings because Dr. Bernstein will talk on. . . . But that sucks too. What difference does it make if I have to shovel it or eat it? Will people ever be able to listen to me, and will I ever be able to listen to people? Once in a while, someone asks this question. Sometimes, people talk about picking up cues from others. Sometimes we get awfully close to this question, but that's when the weekend is over, or the solutions are unfeasible, or we have more staff meetings to improve communications (shovel more shit), and you get punished for getting so close to the question.

*   *   *

I was more upset yesterday. I felt my stomach reacting. Today, my head is calmer, but I feel my stomach again. It's not like yesterday. Today, I'm farting like a backfiring Ford with no muffler. Gas is flowing like from a pump (or what ever the hell gas does). I sat at a meeting of students and faculty (university-wide no less) for almost 1½ hours before it all hit me again. It turned to shit before my eyes. I'm becoming like that ass-hole rat with his approach-avoidance neurosis. I cover the questions up so I can rest, even sleep, and the 21 years of forced contentment, the eons of developing mental energy that has reached a pinnacle of repressing and denying itself—reality—begin to do their dirty deed. I ask again why I just don't do the assignment. And something down inside makes me want to try just one more time before I give up, and die a living death.

8

The Education of a Radical (*1968*)

This is an excerpt of a tape made at the Conference of Revolutionary Students held at Columbia University in the fall of 1968. "Joe," who asked to remain anonymous, was one of the leaders in the previous spring's rebellion.

A real experience (tutoring children in Harlem) propelled me to try to understand things much more concretely than I had. It propelled me to try to come to grips with an understanding of the educational system in this society. It propelled me to try to come to grips with an understanding of the role of the teacher in the society. Education comes from the Latin word *educare* which means to lead outward, but this certainly isn't what the schools are doing here. They're trying to press things inward. If there's any way in which they're trying to lead things out, it's to pick people out and move them from their social environment instead of turning them against it. They've seen black men trying desperately to disassociate themselves from the neighborhood in which they were born and raised and grew up. And turning against their own people. This is the way they've been led out, educated. My exposure to the school system was the first thing; my attempt to come to grips with the role of schools, the role of teachers. From that I became much more political. This was in my freshman and sophomore years here. From that I became much more attuned to problems of my own university. I began to try to address myself to the fact that somehow this learning experience for me was much more important than the stuff I was learning in my classes. Somehow this was something real, something tangible. It led me into a whole series of very intellectual, very analytical approaches but nonetheless it had something tangible. It wasn't abstract though it let me raise some abstract questions. It had real social significance and social relevancy. . . .

You define yourself not in terms of your essential reason for being in the university but a sense of extracurricular activities. You define yourself in terms of your fraternity, service associations you join, social relationships you establish. Your essential reason for being at the university is very discrete. You're coming here to take advantage of resources, it's assumed that for four or five years you define yourself in terms of that university. But what you find is that you don't ever. You always define yourself in terms of extracurricular, extrauniversity activities. And that itself was a great shock to me when I became conscious of that process having taken place in myself. Why it was that when I came to Columbia, hopefully, one would assume that I would define myself in terms of activities that Columbia offered. I couldn't—I had to define myself in other terms. . . .

We (SDS) began to try to find a localized source of oppression. You localize your oppression in a cop, in a mayor, in a law, in a particular governor, and what you find is that this localized source of oppression is not the answer. You can get rid of the cop, the mayor, reverse the law. You know, toss out the governor and the oppression remains and you begin to see it as something much more systematic and much less personal. You begin to go further and try to find the systematic social structure that produces this type of individual or that elevates this kind of personality to positions of leadership. The same thing with the war, the war was first seen as an aberration and nobody questioned the basic assumptions of American foreign policy or American compassion. What we said was that the war was wrong and it was a mistake. At first, we were going to educate Lyndon Johnson, so we held teach-ins. But Lyndon Johnson didn't come. So we never educated Lyndon Johnson, and we set up marches. We took half a million people to Washington and with a half a million people he couldn't ignore us, but we found he wasn't there. There was no response. So we began to

look a little deeper. And what we began to see was that this was
not an aberration, but rather in some sense the inevitable result of
American foreign policy, of American economic structure—in effect the inevitable result of American corporate capitalism. And we
begin to analyze the nature of the society's disintegration. We begin
to analyze the meaning or sense of our culture. We begin to try to
relate systematically the superstructure of cultural forms and mechanisms of cultural integration to a substructure of economic relationships. . . .

Yes, Columbia is a part of American capitalist society. Now
that's the most essential aspect, it's a point that's most overlooked
by professors, by commentators, by analysts, and presently by large
numbers of students. . . . What we were doing basically was coun-
terposing an entirely different system of values, a terribly different
idea of what we thought the role of the university should be. What's
happened at Columbia and what's happened at most major universities in this country is that after Hiroshima the government felt
the necessity for a kind of sophistication in research, in develop-
mental techniques, in managerial and methodological techniques
that their usual sources of manpower could not meet. So what happened was that they began to turn to the universities. . . . What
we've begun to see is that the university serves the same role as a
service center, like driving along the highway and whenever you
need something you jump in and get it. What we began to realize
was that this, bad as it was, this was not entirely accurate. That it
is not that the university stands aside and provides manpower, but
rather it's an integral part, an integral part of the relationships in
this society. The fact that Columbia's School for International Affairs sends over 80 percent of its graduates to the CIA and to the
State Department is no accident. It's clear that there are government contracts here we've got to expose, that show that the government has the right to oversee the hiring and firing of professors,
has the right to oversee the use of university laboratory facilities for
these projects. There are contracts here, there is research being
done related directly to the war in Viet Nam for instance, related
directly to the war against the ghettos. . . .

What we began to see was the profound contradictions behind
the liberal rhetoric of value neutrality, of free speech and the values
of political decisions that were being made every day in the halls of

this university. Value neutrality is in itself a political judgment. . . .

I take for granted that we've shaken (through the Columbia rebellion) the structure of American education, we've seen that the university is not invulnerable. We've seen that students can and will unite around issues of common concern. . . . We demanded three things: 1) an end to Columbia's involvement in the Institute for Defense Analysis—which is a Pentagon think tank; 2) an end to the Columbia construction of the gymnasium on land they'd taken from the Harlem community, the land from a public park; and 3) the demand for amnesty. I think things focus on three demands. There are a couple of very important things about these demands. One was the specificity. We were no longer talking in vague terms about stopping American involvement in the war, about American imperialism, about university racism. We were very specific. Stop the gym, get out of IDA, amnesty for all involved. . . . Of course they were talking about end the gym, but what we were really also talking about was the existence of institutional racism in this country. Yes, we said get out of IDA, but what we were really talking about was university complicity in the Defense Department and, by extension, in American foreign policy. Specifically with the war in Viet Nam. And certainly the demand for amnesty is an attempt to bring into question the power structures both within the university and within the society as a whole.

9

Carl Davidson

Campaigning on the Campus * (*1967*)

The Present Malaise of Education

"Happiness Is Student Power" was the most catching slogan em-
blazoned on the many banners and picket signs during the Berkeley
student strike in December 1966. But, as most college administrators know only too well, Berkeley and its rebellious students are
not an isolated phenomenon among the vast variety of American
campuses. Far from being an exception, Berkeley has become the
paradigm case of the educational malaise in the United States; and,
in the last few years, that malaise has been transformed into a
movement. Indeed a specter is haunting our universities—the specter of a radical and militant nationally coordinated movement for
student power.

Students began using the slogan "student power" soon after black
people in the civil rights movement made the demand for "black
power." Are students niggers? After studying the history of the
Wobblies and labor syndicalism, students started thinking about
student syndicalism. Are students workers? Power for what? Just
any old kind of power? The university is a clumsy and uncoor-

* Reprinted from a Students for a Democratic Society pamphlet. Carl
Davidson was a student at Pennsylvania State University.

dinated machine, engulfing and serving thousands of people. Do students want to be administrators?

Obviously the cry for "power" in and of itself is a vacuous demand. Student power is not so much something we are fighting *for,* as it is something we must have in order to gain specific objectives. Then what are the objectives? What is our program? There is much variety in the dispute on these questions. But there is one thing that seems clear. However the specific forms of our immediate demands and program may vary, the long-range goal and the daily drive that motivates and directs us is our intense longing for our liberation. In short, what the student power movement is about is *freedom.*

But aren't students free? Isn't America a democracy, even if it is a little manipulative? To answer those kinds of questions and many others that are more serious, it is important to look more closely at and come to an understanding of the malaise motivating our movement.

What do American students think of the educational institutions in which they live an important part of their lives? The most significant fact is that most of them don't think about them. Such young men and women made up that apathetic majority we called the "silent generation" in the 1950s. While the last few years have shown a marked and dramatic growth of a new radicalism, we should not forget that the apathetic and the cynical among the student population are still in the majority. But this need not be discouraging. In fact, we should view that apparent apathy among the majority of students with a certain qualified optimism.

What makes people apathetic? My feeling is that apathy is the *unconscious* recognition students make of the fact that they are *powerless.* Despite all the machinations and rhetoric used by hotshot student politicos within administration-sponsored student governments, people's experience tells them that nothing changes. Furthermore, if and when change does occur, students fully recognize that they were powerless to effect those changes in one way or another. If this is in fact the case, then why shouldn't students be apathetic? The administration rules, despite the façade of student governments, of dorm councils, and of student judicials. And when *they* give us ex-officio seats on *their* academic committees, the result among most students is that deeper, more hardened kind of apathy—cynicism.

The apathetic students are correct *as far as they go*. They are powerless. The forms given us for our self-government are of the Mickey Mouse, sandbox variety. I would only be pessimistic if a majority of students really accepted the illusion that those institutions had meaning in their lives, or that they could significantly affect those institutions. But the opposite is the case. The apathy reflects the reality of their powerlessness. When that reality confronts the lie of the official rhetoric, the contradiction is driven home— and the apathetic become the cynical. What that contradiction— that daily living with a lie—all adds up to is a *dynamic* tension and alienation. And that, fellow organizers, is the necessary subjective condition for any revolution.

It is important to understand that students are alienated from much more than the social and extracurricular aspect of their education. In fact, their deepest alienation is directed at the educational process itself. . . . Irrelevancy, meaninglessness, boredom, and fragmentation are the kinds of attributes that are becoming more and more applicable to mass education in America. We are becoming a people required to know more and more about less and less. This is true not only for our students, but also for our teachers; not only in our universities, but also in our secondary and primary schools—private as well as public.

What should education be about in America? The official rhetoric seems to offer an answer: education should be the process of developing the free, autonomous, creative and responsible *individual*—the "citizen," in the best sense of that word. Furthermore, higher education ought to encourage and enable the individual to turn his personal concerns into social issues, open to rational consideration and solution. C. Wright Mills put it clearly: "The aim of the college, for the individual student, is to eliminate the need in his life for the college; the task is to help him become a self-educating man. For only that will set him free."

But what is the reality of American education? Contrary to our commitment to individualism, we find that the day-to-day practice of our schools is authoritarian, conformist, and almost entirely status oriented. We find the usual relationship between teacher and student to be a disciplined form of dominance and subordination. We are told of the egalitarianism inherent in our school system, where the classroom becomes the melting pot for the classless society of America's "people's capitalism," where everyone has the opportunity to climb to the top. Again, the opposite is the case. Our schools are more racially segregated now (1967) than ever before. There is a clear class bias contained both within and among our public schools—not even considering the clear class nature of our private schools and colleges. Within the secondary schools, students are quickly channeled—usually according to the class background of their parents—into vocational, commercial, or academic preparatory programs. Concerning the class differences among our public schools, James Conant remarks in *Slums and Suburbs:*

> One cannot imagine the possibility of a wealthy suburban district deliberately consolidating with other districts to achieve a truly comprehensive high school in which students of all abilities and socio-economic backgrounds will study together.

Even if they did consolidate, the problem would only be rationalized, rather than solved. Who knows? Maybe the class struggle would break out on the playground.

Finally, what about that traditional American ideal that we were all taught to honor—the legend of the self-educated and self-educating man? It seems to me that rather than enabling an individual to initiate and engage himself in a continual and coherent lifelong educational process, our public programs are of the sort where an individual is merely subjected to a random series of isolated training situations.

From individual freedom to national service, from egalitarianism to class and racial hierarchical ossification, from self-reliance to institutional dependence—we have come to see education as the mechanistic process of homogeneous, uncritical absorption of "data" and development of job skills. But it is something more than that. The socialization and acculturation that goes on within America attempts to mold and shape American youth. This is mainly the result of the declining influence and, in some cases, the collapse of other traditional socializing institutions such as the church and the family. The schools, at all levels, end up with the job of maintaining, modifying, and transmitting the dominant themes of the national culture.

Quantitatively education has been rapidly increasing in the last few decades; but, as it grows in size, it decreases *qualitatively*. Rickover states in *Education and Freedom:* "We end up where we began a hundred years ago—with an elementary vocational education for the majority, and a poor college preparatory course for a minority of students." Conant, who is quite concerned with the plight of the 80 to 85 percent of urban non-college-bound high school students who are "social dynamite," places as a primary goal of education, giving these students "the kind of zeal and dedication . . . to withstand the relentless pressures of communism."

What about our schoolteachers? How is the nation faring on that front? Over 30 percent of the students in U.S. colleges and universities are going into primary and secondary education. However, despite the quantity, Mortimer Smith remarks in *The Diminished Mind,* "the teacher-training institutions . . . are providing us with teachers who are our most poorly educated citizens." While the job of teachers should command the highest respect in any society, many of us are well aware of the fact that in relation to other parts of the university, the college or school of education is considered to be the intellectual slum of the campus.

It seems clear that bourgeois education in the U.S. is in its historically most irrational and decadent state. Primary, secondary, and university systems are fusing together, thoroughly rationalizing and dehumanizing their internal order, and placing themselves in the service of the state, industry, and the military. Clark Kerr is quite clear about this when he speaks of the "multiversity" making a common-law marriage with the federal government. John Hannah, president of Michigan State, was even clearer in a speech given in September 1961, "Our colleges and universities must be regarded as bastions of our defense, as essential to preservation of our country and our way of life as supersonic bombers, nuclear-powered submarines and intercontinental ballistic missiles." The fact that none of the three weapons systems Hannah mentioned could have been designed, constructed, or operated without college-educated men proves that this is not just Fourth of July rhetoric.

Despite the crass attitudes of so many of our educators, or the dehumanization of the form and content of our educational institutions, it would be a mistake to think the problems are only within the educational system. While it is true that education has been stripped of any meaning it once had, and Dr. Conant is reduced to defining education as "what goes on in schools and colleges," our system of schools and colleges is far from a point of collapse. In fact, it is thriving. The "knowledge industry," as Kerr calls it, accounts for 30 percent of the Gross National Product; and it is expanding at twice the rate of any sector of the economy. Schoolteachers make up the largest single occupational group of the labor force—some three million workers. Twenty-five years ago, the government and industry were hardly interested in education. But in 1960, the aggregate national outlay, public and private, amounted to $23,100,000,000. As Kerr says, "The university has become a prime instrument of national purpose. This is new. This is the essence of the transformation now engulfing our universities." In short, our educational institutions are becoming appendages to, and transformed by, U.S. corporate capitalism.

Education is not being done away with in favor of something called training. Rather, education is being transformed from a quasi aristocratic classicism and petty-bourgeois romanticism into something quite new. These changes are apparent in ways other than the quantitative statistics given above. For example, we can examine the social sciences and the humanities. The social and psychological "reality" that we are given to study is "objectified" to the point of sterility. The real world, we are to understand, is "value-free" and pragmatically bears little or no relation to the actual life-activity of men, classes and nations. In one sense, we are separated from life. In another, we are being conditioned for life in a lifeless, stagnant, and sterile society.

For another example, there is more than a semantic connection between the academic division of labor and specialization we are all aware of, and the corresponding division of labor that has gone on in large-scale industry. But it is important to understand what that connection is. It does *not* follow that because technology becomes diversified and specialized, then academic knowledge and skills must follow suit. André Gorz makes the relevant comment:

It is completely untrue that modern technology demands specialization: quite the reverse. It demands a basic "polyvalent" education, comprising not a fragmentary, pre-digested and specialized knowledge, but an invitation—or, put more precisely, a faculty of self-initiation—into methods of scientifico-technological research and discovery.

If it is not the new technological production that deems necessary the kind of isolated specialization we know so well, then what is responsible? Gorz spells it out again, "Capitalism actually needs shattered and atomized men" in order to maintain its system of centralized, bureaucratized and militarized hierarchies, so as "to perpetuate its domination over men, not only as workers, but also as consumers and citizens."

From this perspective, we can begin to understand that the educational malaise we as students and teachers have felt so personally and intensely is no aberration, but firmly rooted in the American political economy. In fact, the Organized System which Paul Goodman calls "compulsory mis-education" may miseducate us, but it certainly serves the masters of that system, the U.S. ruling class, quite well. As Edgar Z. Friedenberg wrote: "Educational evils are attributed to *defective* schools. In fact, they are as likely to be the work of *effective* schools that are being directed toward evil ends by the society that supports and controls them." Furthermore, he continues later in the same article, "Schools are a definite indication that a society is divisible into a dominant and a subordinate group, and that the dominant group want to teach the subordinate group something they could not be trusted to learn if left to themselves." Clark Kerr would accept this, both for the society in general, which he divides into the "managers" and the "managed," and for the university. Kerr states: "The intellectuals (including university students) are a particularly volatile element. . . . They are by nature irresponsible. . . . They are, as a result, never fully trusted by anybody, including themselves." But Kerr doesn't dismiss us. Even if we are by nature irresponsible (perhaps because we can perceive the contradictions?) he considers us essential. "It is important who best attracts or captures the intellectuals and who uses them most effectively, for they may be a tool as well as a source of danger."

I think we can conclude that the American educational system is a coherent, well-organized, and—to the extent that the rulers are still ruling—effective mechanism. However, it has turned our humanitarian values into their opposites and, at this same time, given us the potential to understand and critically evaluate both ourselves and the system itself. To that extent the system is fraught with internal contradictions. Furthermore, the events comprising the student revolt in the last few years demonstrate the likelihood that those contradictions will continue to manifest themselves in an open and protracted struggle. As Kerr predicted, we are a source of danger and incipient revolt. And the fact that Kerr was fired and the police used in the face of that revolt only goes to prove that those contradictions are irreconcilable within the structure of corporate capitalism. As Quintin Hoare remarked in the *New Left Review* 32, "A reform of the educational system involves a reform of the educators as well, and this is a political task, which immediately ricochets back to the question of transforming consciousness and ideology throughout society." The central problem of radically transforming the educational system is that of the transformation of the teaching and the learning body—the faculty and students. And this transformation, while it *begins* with the demands of the students' and teachers' work situation, cannot take place unless it occurs *within* and is organically connected *to* the practice of a mass radical *political* movement.

Work and Alienation Within the University

To begin, I will make a number of qualifications for the purpose of resolving disputes with other radicals before they happen. First of all, much of the work done in American education is irrational. Both the learning and teaching of many (but not all) of the manipulative techniques of bourgeois political economy that goes on in our schools of business administration, education, and social science can in no sense be considered productive work. However, while this is true of the university in part, it does not follow that it is true of the university as an *objective whole*.

Second, I am not trying to say that students are workers in the strict sense. At best, so long as he, his family, or his friends are paying for his education, his learning activity results only in the production of *use value;* i.e., the potentially socially useful increase in the *future* productivity of his labor power. However, to the extent to which the student is *paid* by private or state institutions to engage in *specific* kinds of intellectual work, his activity *might in some cases* be seen as commodity production; i.e., the development of the productivity of his labor power as *an actual exchange value,* rather than as a potential use value. This small number of students might be called workers. However, the position of most students is that of workers-to-be, i.e., trainee or apprentice. But as a trainee, it is important that we recognize that many students share many of the social relations and conditions of production with many of the skilled workers of large-scale industry.

Finally, it is true that many faculty members are becoming more entrepreneurial and developing many interests that are objectively bound up with the ruling and sub-ruling classes. However, to say this is true of all faculty members fails to take into account a kind of class division that is occurring within the faculty in American universities. Clark Kerr distinguishes three functional types within the faculty of the multiversity. The top-level faculty—the heads of departments, intellectual administrators, research promoters, and paid consultants—should be seen as petty bourgeoisie and managerial sector constituents who have their interests tied up with the ruling and sub-ruling classes. The second group, the traditional academics, should be seen as middle-class professionals in the classic sense. However, the third and largest group, the lower-echelon faculty who are primarily engaged in teaching in the mass production line of large classes should be seen as members of the new working class. Their objective interests are with the students and the working class in general, despite the significant problem of their false consciousness. . . .

So much for the qualifications. What is the nature of the teaching-learning activity within our educational institutions that might permit us to call them "knowledge factories" in other than an analogous sense? First of all, we need to take into account a few historical factors. The growth of the American political economy in the last thirty years has been facilitated in part by the development of a new technology. The development of the new technology itself, the job displacements it created, and the increase in job skills required for its operation, created tremendous pressure on the state for the training of a highly skilled sector within the labor force. The working class, recognizing the need for the new skills, both for themselves and their children, also made demands of the government for both more and better education. Even at present, skill levels are rising at perhaps the highest rate in history. The government responded and is continuing to respond. According to Kerr, "Higher education in 1960 received about $1.5 billion from the federal government—hundredfold increase in twenty years." However, while the demand for expanding education comes from both the needs of a developing technology and from the demands of working-class parents, it is the needs of the industrialists that *structure* the form and content of the educational expansion. According to Gorz, the state responds to capital rather than people, "since the development of education falls under the general head of growing collective needs produced by monopolistic expansion." In the last few decades, the expanding reproduction and accumulation of a continuing increase in the *productivity of labor power* is an *objective necessity* of contemporary corporate capitalism. Kerr remarks: "Instead of waiting outside the gates, agents [of the industrialists] are working the corridors. They also work the placement offices."

The colleges and universities have gone beyond their traditional task of socialization and acculturation. They are deeply involved in the production of a crucial and marketable commodity—labor power. Again Gorz comments, "The work of learning (and teaching), of extending and transforming professional skills, is implicitly recognized as socially necessary and productive work, through which the individual transforms himself according to the needs of society (and industry)." It is this aspect of the university that is most crucial for the political economy. The production of an increase in socially useful and necessary labor power is the new historic function of our educational institutions that enables us to name them, quite accurately, knowledge factories. In this process of historical change, liberal education has been transformed into its opposite and what we are witnessing is the advent of training and indoctrination. The core of the university with its frills removed, has become the crucible for the production, formation, and socialization of the new working class. . . .

The machinery of knowledge production pervades the university. And, despite its invisibility, it is no less real or tangible. The productive apparatus consists of grades, exams, assigned books, papers, and reports, all the curriculum and scheduling requirements, non-academic *in loco parentis* regulations, scientific equipment and resources, the mechanics of grants and endowments, disciplinary procedures, campus and civil police, and all the repressive and sublimative psychological techniques of fear and punishment. Most, if not all, of this machinery and the purposes it is used for are beyond the control of the students and faculty who work with it. All government, all control, all the parameters of decision-making have fallen into the hands of the administrative representatives of the ruling class. At best, handpicked "representatives" of student and faculty "opinion" are prearranged. For example, female students are permitted to determine how strict or "liberal" their dorm hours might be; but the underlying assumption of whether they should have curfews at all is beyond question. Or, while some (but not all) college professors are free to teach *what* they please, they are not "free to decide *how* to teach—whether in large numbers or small, in departmentalized courses or others, one day a week or five."

Like any good training program, the knowledge factory accurately reproduces all the conditions and relations of production in the factories of advanced corporate capitalism—isolation, manipulation, and alienation. First the teaching and learning workers of the knowledge factory are alienated from each other, isolated and divided among themselves by grades, class ranks, and the status levels of the bureaucratic hierarchy. Secondly, they are alienated from the product of their work, the content and purpose of which have been determined and used by someone other than themselves. Finally, they are alienated in the activity of education itself. What should be the active creation and re-creation of culture is nothing more than forced and coercive consumption and distribution of data and technique. Throughout the educational apparatus, the bureaucratic mentality prevails. History and ideology have come to an end. Science, the humanities, even philosophy have become value-free. Politics are reduced to advertising and sales campaigns. Finally government and self-determination become matters of administration and domination.

The Meaning of the Student Revolt

Our manipulators have overlooked one fundamental factor; there is one facet of human history to which the bureaucratic *Weltan-*

schauung is blind. Men are not made of clay. Despite all the official pronouncements asserting the end of this or that, the wellsprings of human freedom still run deep. All the attempts to teach ignorance in the place of knowledge have come to naught. The student revolt is an historic event. Someone (the Berkeley students?) let the cat out of the bag. The emperor has no clothes.

Our rulers are aware of this. The bureaucrats of corporate capitalism must cut back and control the quality of and content of "liberal" education. They know only too well that a widespread culture rising out of critical thought might challenge, during a crisis, the existing relations of production and domination. The CIA control of the National Student Association and other "cultural" organizations proves this only too well.

But the corporate ruling class is not primarily interested in containing and pacifying us *as intellectuals.* Their real concern with us lies in our role as the highly skilled members of the new working class. As Gorz points out, "skilled workers . . . possess *in their own right* . . . the labor power they lend." Their skills are an attribute of *themselves* and not just the material means of production. Gorz continues:

> The problem of big management is to harmonize two contradictory necessities: the necessity of developing human capabilities, imposed by modern processes of production and the political necessity of insuring that this kind of development does not bring in its wake any augmentation of the independence of the individual, provoking him to challenge the present division of social labor and distribution of power.

From this analysis, we can understand the student revolt in its most strategic and crucial sense. What we are witnessing and participating in is an important historical phenomenon: the revolt of the trainees of the new working class against the alienated and oppressive conditions of production and consumption within corporate capitalism. These are the conditions of life and activity that lie beneath the apathy, frustration, and rebellion on America's campuses. André Gorz predicted a few years back: "It is in education that industrial capitalism will provoke revolts which it attempts to avoid in its factories."

Nevertheless, the "student power" movement is still vague and undefined. Its possibilities are hopeful as well as dangerous. On the one hand, student power can develop into an elitist corporate monster, mainly concerned with developing better techniques of "co-managing" the bureaucratic apparatus of advanced industrial society. On the other hand, a student power movement might successfully develop a revolutionary class-consciousness among the future new working class, who would organize on their jobs and among the traditional working class around the issues of participatory democracy and worker control. The character of the future movement will depend to a great extent on the kind of strategy and tactics we use in the present. The struggle will be protracted, that is certain. There is no certain or predetermined victory. We should not forget that 1984 is possible. And not many years away. But we have several years of experience behind us from which we can learn a great deal.

Reform or Revolution: What Kinds of Demands?

Fighting for reforms and making a revolution should not be seen as mutually exclusive positions. The question should be: What kind of reforms move us toward a radical transformation of both the university and the society in general? First of all, we should avoid the kinds of reforms which leave the basic rationale of the system unchallenged. For instance, a bad reform to work for would be getting a better grading system, because the underlying rationale—the need for grades at all—remains unchallenged.

Secondly, we should avoid certain kinds of reform that divide students from each other. For instance, trying to win certain privileges for upper classmen but not for freshmen or sophomores. Or trying to establish nongraded courses for students above a certain grade-point average. In the course of campus political activity, the administration will try a whole range of "divide and rule" tactics such as fostering the "Greek-Independent Split," sexual double standards, intellectuals *vs* "jocks," responsible *vs* irresponsible leaders, red-baiting and "non-student" *vs* students. We need to avoid falling into these traps ahead of time, as well as fighting them when used against us.

Finally, we should avoid all of the "co-management" kinds of reforms. These usually come in the form of giving certain "responsible" student leaders a voice or influence in certain decision-making processes, rather than abolishing or winning effective control over those parts of the governing apparatus. One way to counter administration suggestions for setting up "tripartite" committees (one-third student, one-third faculty, one-third administration, each with an equal number of votes) is to say, "OK, but once a month the committee must hold an all-university plenary session—one man, one vote." The thought of being outvoted 1,000–1 will cause administrators to scrap that co-optive measure in a hurry.

We have learned the hard way that the reformist path is full of pitfalls. What, then, are the kinds of reformist measures that do make sense? First of all, there are the civil libertarian issues. We must always fight, dramatically and quickly, for free speech and the right to organize, advocate, and mount political action—of all sorts. However, even here, we should avoid getting bogged down in "legalitarianism." We cannot count on this society's legal apparatus to guarantee our civil liberties: and, we should not organize around civil libertarian issues *as if it could*. Rather, when our legal rights are violated, we should move as quickly as possible, without losing our base, to expand the campus libertarian moral indignation into a multi-issues *political* insurgency, exposing the repressive character of the administration and the corporate state in general.

The second kind of partial reform worth fighting for and possibly winning is the abolition of on-campus repressive mechanisms, i.e., student courts, disciplinary tribunals, deans of men and women, campus police, and the use of civil police on campus. While it is true that "abolition" is a negative reform, and while we will be criticized for not offering "constructive" criticisms, we should reply that the only constructive way to deal with an inherently destructive apparatus is to destroy it. We must curtail the ability of administrators to repress our *need to refuse* their way of life—the regimentation and bureaucratization of existence.

When our universities are already major agencies for social change in the direction of 1984, our initial demands must, almost of necessity, be negative demands. In this sense, the first task of a student power movement will be the organization of a holding action—a resistance. Along these lines, one potentially effective tactic for resisting the university's disciplinary apparatus would be the forming of a Student Defense League. The purpose of the group would be to make its services available to any student who must appear before campus authorities for infractions of repressive (or just plain stupid) rules and regulations. The defense group would then attend the student's hearings *en masse*. However, for some cases, it might be wise to include law students or local radical lawyers in the group for the purpose of making legal counterattacks. A student defense group would have three major goals: (1) saving as many students as possible from punishment, (2) desanctifying and rendering dysfunctional the administration's repressive apparatus, and (3) using (1) and (2) as tactics in reaching other students for building a movement to abolish the apparatus as a whole.

When engaging in this kind of activity, it is important to be clear in our rhetoric as to what we are about. We are not trying to *liberalize* the existing order, but trying to win our *liberation* from it. We must refuse the administrations' rhetoric of "responsibility." To their one-dimensional way of thinking, the concept of responsibility has been reduced to its opposite, namely, be nice, don't rock the boat, do things according to our criteria of what is permissible. In actuality their whole system is geared toward the inculcation of the values of a planned irresponsibility. We should refuse *their* definitions, *their* terms, and even refuse to engage in *their* semantic hassles. We only need to define—*for ourselves and other students*—our notions of what it means to be free, constructive, and responsible. Too many campus movements have been coopted for weeks or even permanently by falling into the administrations' rhetorical bags.

Besides the abolition of repressive disciplinary mechanisms within the university, there are other negative forms that radicals should work for. Getting the military off the campus, abolishing the grade system, and abolishing universal compulsory courses (i.e. physical education) would fit into this category. However, an important question for the student movement is whether or not positive radical reforms can be won within the university short of making a revolution in the society as a whole. . . .

What then is open to us in the area of positive anti-capitalist reforms? For the most part, it will be difficult to determine whether or not a reform has the effect of being anti-capitalist until it has been achieved. Since it is both difficult and undesirable to attempt to predict the future, questions of this sort are often best answered in practice. Nevertheless, it would seem that the kinds of reforms we are looking for are most likely to be found within a strategy of what I would call "encroaching control." There are aspects of the university's administrative, academic, financial, physical, and social apparatus that are potentially, if not actually, useful and productive. While we should try to abolish the repressive mechanisms of the university, our strategy should be to gain control, piece by piece, of its positive aspects.

What would that control look like? To begin with, all aspects of the nonacademic life of the campus should either be completely under the control of the students as individuals or embodied in the institutional forms they establish for their collective government. For example, an independent Union of Students should have the final say on the form and content of all university political, social and cultural events. Naturally, individual students and student organizations would be completely free in organizing events of their own.

Second, only the students and the teaching faculty, individually and through their organizations, should control the academic affairs of the university. One example of a worthwhile reform in this area would be enabling all history majors and history professors to meet jointly at the beginning of each semester and shape the form, content, and direction of their departmental curriculum. Another partial reform in this area would be enabling an independent Union of Students to hire additional professors of their choice and establish additional accredited courses of their choice independently of the faculty or administration.

Finally, we should remember that control should be sought for some specific purpose. One reason we want this kind of power is to enable us to meet the self-determined needs of students and teachers. But another objective that we should see as radicals is to put as much of the university's resources as possible into the hands of the under class and the working class. We should use campus facilities for meeting the educational needs of insurgent organizations of the poor, and of rank-and-file workers. Or we could mobilize the universities' research facilities for serving projects established and controlled by the poor and workers, rather than projects established and controlled by the government, management, and labor bureaucrats. The conservative nature of American trade unions makes activity of this sort very difficult, although not impossible. But we should always be careful to make a distinction between the American working class itself and the labor bureaucrats. . . .

From this starting point, how does SDS see its relation to the rest of the campus? I think we have learned that we should not look upon ourselves as an intellectual and political oasis, hugging each other in a waste land. Rather, our chapters should see themselves as organizing committees for reaching out to the majority of the student population. Furthermore, we are organizing for something —the power to effect change. With this in mind, we should be well aware of the fact that the kind of power and changes we would like to have and achieve are not going to be given to us gracefully. Ultimately, we have access to only one source of power within the knowledge factory. And that power lies in our potential ability to stop the university from functioning, to render the system dysfunctional for limited periods of time. Throughout all our on-campus organizing efforts we should keep this one point in mind: that sooner or later we are going to have to strike—or at least successfully threaten to strike. Because of this, our constant strategy should be the preparation of a mass base for supporting and participating in this kind of action. . . .

What should come out of a student strike? First, the development of a radical consciousness among large numbers of students. Secondly, we should try to include within our demands some issues on which we can win partial victories. Finally, the organizational form that should grow out of a strike or series of strikes is an independent, radical, and political Free Student Union that would replace the existing student government. I have already dealt with the general political life of radical movements. But some points need to be repeated. First of all, a radical student union must be in alliance with the radical sectors of the under class and working class. Secondly, the student movement has the additional task of radicalizing the subsector of the labor force that some of us in SDS have come to call the new working class. Thirdly, a radical union of students should have an anti-imperialist critique of U.S. foreign policy. Finally, local student unions, if they are to grow and thrive, must become federated on regional, national, and international levels. However, we should be careful not to form a national union of students lacking in a grass-roots constituency that actively and democratically participates in all aspects of the organization's life. One NSA is enough. On the international level, we should avoid both the CIA and Soviet Union sponsored International Unions. We would be better off to establish informal relations with groups like the Zengakuren in Japan, the German SDS, the French Situationists, the Spanish Democratic Student Syndicate, and the Third World revolutionary student organization. Hopefully, in the not too distant future, we may be instrumental in forming a new International Union of Revolutionary Youth. And even greater tasks remain to be done before we can begin to build the conditions for human liberation.

10

Cathy Wilkerson, Mike Spiegel
and Les Coleman

The False Privilege * (*1968*)

For most of our lives the university has been offered to us as a special opportunity, a chance to get ahead in the traditional American fashion. How often have we heard that we are privileged—we personally or even we as a nation of Americans—to go to college. As a result, many of us have worked our way through that "privileged" institution. Many others have gone on the wages of parents who worked to give us what society has called "a better chance" than they had or than many thousands of other Americans now have.

An Anti-Human Contract

Partly we are told that our supposed privilege comes at the expense of others—those who must work while we are free to develop ourselves—and partly we have had to find out what expense was involved. Through the sixties, more and more students have learned that our supposed privileges have come at the expense of black people and the populations of Vietnam and other Third World countries. We began to see that the wealth and opportunities of-

* Reprinted from the *New Left Notes* (October 7, 1968). Cathy Wilkerson was a student at Swarthmore, and Mike Spiegel and Les Coleman were students at Harvard.

fered us were built upon an American empire that involves the suppression of millions of people. And further, we have seen that the university, through its research and its training, is institutionally a direct participant in military and counterinsurgency policy. We as students did enter into a contract with the university when we went there—we were there to get ahead, and in return we were to serve the System's ends. As we understand those ends, and understand how we are to achieve them, we begin to understand also that not all of the fine print in the contract was legible. Not only is the contract anti-human, dehumanizing to us and destructive to others, but the so-called privilege is no privilege at all; the promise of the university is false.

A False Privilege

What is the reality of the promise of success we've been offered? What jobs should we take? Do we want to join the managerial staff of some corporation and look into the empty faces of fellow businessmen eight hours a day, drink their faces out of our minds all night, and play the game of competing to have the best job in the biggest corporation that exploits the most people? Or would it be better to join America's research and action team and help destroy the world? Still better, why not just stay on in the university, teach the same irrelevancies we've learned, and slip gradually through boredom into death? At any rate, make enough money to buy more televisions, plastic food, monster car machines, and other contrived necessities to keep from thinking or living a human life. . . .

So the promise is false. In its function as trainer and socializer for future participants in the society, the university seeks to perpetuate values at the core of which is the acceptance of (false) privilege. These are the values of individualism—being one-up, individual recognition for social accomplishments, being in a position to control other people's lives to one's own advantage. And with them comes the attitude that "not everyone can make it, but if a few do on the backs of the rest, if I do, I like the system."

The structure of student life—life at the expense of others— leads to a characteristically American situation. The abstracted education of the university is so divorced from the practice of everyday living that nothing is learned out of recognition of need—human need—and there is no recognition of the interdependence of people's lives in society. What results is that the student reacts either by spending all his life compulsively deciding how to best spend his time and money (when there is no decent way to do that in the atmosphere of the university), or he makes a conscious decision to waste his time and money, just as absurdly and publicly as he can, lest the situation blow his mind altogether.

But the miseducation of the college and the creation of such antihuman values and relationships are not peculiar to the university. Capitalist institutions, by nature exploitive, depend on fostering those values to maintain themselves. America has a whole history of this particular evil.

America the Beautiful

The possibility of making a large individual fortune—the private-enterprise system—has never existed in a vacuum. From the beginning, America was founded and controlled by businessmen who built their empires by exploiting the slave or indentured labor they contracted from Africa and Europe, and by expending their control over lands that belonged to the American Indian. The pioneer spirit took forms which should look familiar to the American student. The pioneer went west to compulsively and brutally control the land, the people, and the resources he found: or he went west to slaughter the race of the American Indian, destroying the farmland by carelessly laying waste to it with profitable crops, and brag like the fool he was that he never got a damn thing from it and would die without owning anything but his boots. Behind the myths of the history books lies evidence of the persistent practice of racism, genocide, suppression of women, and exploitation of other men's lives and labor.

Economic history reveals that our early tradition flowered—into a monster. Individual capitalists like Rockefeller and Gould built enormous economic empires based on ruthless wage oppression and the military suppression of labor organizations. The individually controlled empires became corporations, staffed by men who mindlessly followed the maxim: the best position in the biggest corporation. Meanwhile, the capitalists and corporate capitalists dabbled in the financial control of foreign trade and foreign industries. But the great push to show corporate growth—so that stockholders invest more and make possible further corporate growth—led to the production of more goods than minimized wages can buy.

The solution was found increasingly in control of foreign markets and foreign labor. The corporation, if it got political control of foreign markets, could dispose of its overproduction at great profits. If the corporation controlled foreign industry, it could afford to pay (and so buy off) domestic workers the wages it didn't pay foreign workers. Everybody was kept in control. From time to time the exploited peoples of other countries have revolted—struggled for their liberation—but you know, that is what the military production center is for.

Just as capitalism, the private-enterprise system led to exploitive employment and consumption, a power elite, and world economic and military imperialism, the individualist Horatio Alger fuck-the-other-guy values of a free-enterprise culture have led to the dehumanizing and destructive lives of today's Americans.

Shut It Down!

We must attempt to make clear the historical role of those values, and politically attack the university for its role in the perpetuation of those relationships. As well as attacking the university for its participation in war research and exploitation of surrounding working-class communities, we must also challenge the other main function of the university, which is to turn out corporate morons to take up the task of administering the world. The university is not a place devoted to human development which "makes a few destructive mistakes." The university is a place *dedicated* to the perpetuation of class exploitation and class oppression. It is dedicated to making us identify with the exploiters and the oppressors, catching ourselves in the stupid chains of individualism.

Our strategy therefore must be an attack on the entire institution of the university, a challenge to its purpose and to its right to exist. Wherever possible, we must strive to shut it down—shut it down rather than "reform" it, because as long as the society exists in its present form the university can only function to achieve the aims we have just discussed.

Not all campuses, in fact probably very few, can achieve a Columbia. To say we should shut it down is only a reflection of our understanding of the role of the university and its educaton in our society.

"De-studentize"

We should begin to speak to students about "de-studentizing" their lives. We must break students away from their identification with the university and its structure of values, as well as break their identification with the university as corporate/government researcher. We must call for the stoppage of that institution, for an end of that old identity of the student.

We can call instead for a new identity—an identity with the exploited class, the working class. That class must be in struggle if it does not accept the false privilege and anti-human contract that binds it in its own exploitation. In struggle the values of that class are the values of the collective, of a lived understanding of collective human need and collective human survival. It is struggle to end the existence of a privileged class, to proletarianize the society.

Tactically we will find that there must be methods for expressing this analysis at some level other than the actual closing of the university. Both the internalized values of the university and the force which stands behind them will make it difficult to carry such a program out. But imaginative tactics of confrontation should be our method, not academic round tables on how to restructure the university.

Suppose a group of five people in a course decided to do a required paper together. And on top of that, they made copies and all handed in the same paper (or only a single copy with all their names on it). At that point they explained that their desire was to do a paper which they thought was interesting, and that their concept of education included people learning how to learn together; that they condemned the values of individualism implicit in grade competition and held that the value of an educated society meant that people learned in a social context, together, not merely being educated apart and bringing that individual education together through competition to achieve an irrational and anti-human end.

Perhaps even an "outside agitator" could help on this paper, with the explanation that he or she also was interested in what you students were working on and had some things to offer from his or her experience. This could work as well in high schools, and could also be applied to exams. It is just one method of attacking education's role in inculcating the values of individualism. Also it would probably produce severe reaction from the authorities around an issue which is easily explained to students.

These kinds of principles and tactics should be substituted for the reformist approaches we have often taken: using student government referendums instead of challenging the legitimacy of the student government and proclaiming academic critiques of courses that show they make a few mistakes on their own terms. We are not and will not be on their terms.

In addition we should continue to educate about and disrupt those functions of the university which are immediate functional parts of this country's capitalist system: its racist policies, its corporate exploitation of the community surrounding the university, its participation in research and training for clear imperialist or militarist enterprises. But in attacking around those issues, we must make it clear that we are also attacking the institution and what those issues mean to people's lives within the institution— within the false privilege and the anti-human contract.

In all the ways we attack on issues we should keep the problem of destudentizing in mind. That means we see much of the problem we face, in organizing, as one of delegitimizing the university as an institution. Instead of building all year around one or another issue—like IDA or ROTC—chapters should divide into as many groups as there are good issues. Each group should do its canvassing and educational work on its issue, but try to pull in new people to frequent confrontations: small demonstrations; "stump speeches" given in lots of different parts of the campus, during classes, et cetera; and guerrilla theater. Our job is to challenge the institution in our tactics as well as our rhetoric—frequently and imaginatively.

We must link our struggle with off-campus struggle in any concrete ways we can. In doing so we must again stress our rejection of the imposed concept of "student." People who are not students should be welcomed into our struggle against the university, and those of us in the university should take an active part in off-campus struggles, as well as attacking the university for its role in the society which the struggle is against. Still, our main emphasis must be on organizing a youth movement on the campus, because that is where our power lies.

Once again, saying that we want to shut the university down is not the whole of our program, it merely concretizes our analysis. It says we reject the false privilege and the anti-human contract that characterize the university as an integral part of American capitalism. We do not want to participate in the control of that kind of an institution, as long as that is the kind of institution it is. We know we can not change it until the whole System can be changed. Therefore we want to control the university as students controlled Columbia—in order to change America, not to participate in the System the way it is.

11

Molly Jackson

The New and the Newer:
Women on Campus * (*1970*)

It seems impossible to me that only two years ago I had never really thought about the constant oppression of women as women. I had had plenty of personal affronts on the job, but never connected a fraction of the elements of male chauvinist society with my experiences. I was a political person, "knowing" to look for the new forces of revolution in our time, but not really understanding why, at its formation in 1955, *News and Letters* designated women, along with workers, blacks, and youth, as a revolutionary category.

I first thought seriously about Women's Liberation about the time the new movement was starting, when a Puerto Rican friend told me about the treatment she and other women were receiving in some black and Puerto Rican leftist groups at the time: Women not only limited to certain nonthinking work, but formally excluded from many meetings; a boyfriend telling her to shut up in public when she tried to express an idea; one CORE office at which, if you called up with anything but a simple factual question, you were told by a woman that she couldn't answer it, that you should call

* Reprinted by permission of *News and Letters* (January 1970). At the time of the events described, Molly Jackson was a student at the University of Chicago.

back "when a man is here." What was going on? It was part of the authoritarian tendencies blossoming in the New Left, but it was much more—it was the result of the lack of self-conscious, organized voices of women to fight the discrimination against them which so thoroughly saturate the dominant culture that we are *all* infected with it.

About a year ago, I became involved with the W.L. group at the University of Chicago. It was during the occupation of the Administration Building by several groups, including WRAP (Women's Radical Action Project). In a spring in which there was little new in the student movement, a reflection of the New Left's approaching dead-end, the voice of W.L. was very new and very strong during that demonstration. The WRAP women were an organized, cohesive group. They met regularly on their own, formulated their own actions and ideas, and took part fully in the mass meetings with the men. For many women, it was the first time they had chaired a meeting, written a leaflet, or expressed their own ideas in front of a large group. Part of the impetus, of course, came from the fact that the event which triggered off the sit-in was the firing of Marlene Dixon, a radical woman professor who was active in W.L. But the women, including many who originally entered the building only because they liked Mrs. Dixon as a teacher, went beyond the single issue: they wrote and distributed analyses of male chauvinism in the university and the society, and convinced the larger group to add demands for more women professors and students, courses on women's history, and free child care to the rather standardized demands for student control and open admissions. They raised the issue of W.L. among *everyone* on that campus for the first time.

The Columbia University women had sparked an idea the year before, when they suddenly balked at being on the food committees during that occupation, and demanded that there be equal numbers of men and women on them. Now the University of Chicago women effectively applied the concept that women are equal to men in the realm of ideas. The women also shook up the "radical" men on a personal level. In addition to the women's example of self-organization and their full participation in every aspect of the occupation, from strategy to "sitting security," they also confronted the men with their male chauvinism during the long period of close contact.

The following exchange, for example, must today be standard in such situations: Man—"If you're so liberated, how come you won't sleep with me?" Woman—"That's exactly the kind of thinking I'm liberated *from!*"

After the sit-in, large numbers of women began to attend the weekly WRAP meetings—often more than 60. Almost every meeting consisted of several elements. There would be a business part to discuss requests for speakers around the city, demonstrations, other W.L. groups, etc. In a "personal" part we talked about our daily problems as women. I was surprised at the strength this gave many of the women to participate in the other activities, as well as giving them a whole new view of society when they discovered that *their* problems were common, and thus the fault of the society, not of themselves. Often, there was a "political" discussion. Again, I was surprised at the sophistication of the women. Most quickly stated, matter-of-factly, that capitalism oppresses women by using them as a reserve of cheap labor, that it uses men against them to prevent workers' solidarity, that part of women's mistreatment by their husbands is an outlet for the husbands' anger and frustration at *their* dehumanized jobs. Not so explicit, but surely in our attitudes, was the idea that women must be a force for liberation that will combine with other movements to tear down the existing society and create a totally new one, and must assure by our movement that the new one will be free of all aspects of male chauvinism.

We were fortunate to have a concrete women's struggle that crossed class and racial lines taking place on our own campus. The idea of a free child care center provided by the university for its employees and students was spreading among the employees. It became particularly important with the low-paid, unskilled university hospital workers, most of whom are black women. In the early spring these workers wildcatted against both the university and their corrupt, do-nothing union. Among their demands was the child care center. Students helped man the picket lines, and after it was over the wildcatters formed a permanent organization to try to change the union leadership and to press for the child care center. Shortly after that, another group of employees—secretaries and other office workers—formed a third group to fight for the center. These women did important research into the nonavailability of child care in the city and country, the cost and setup of good child care, etc., although they were later to be scorned by some SDS-WRAP women for lacking "militancy." I think it was good that any organization took place among these women, who are extremely isolated from each other and are trained to think of themselves as a part of their bosses, not as exploited employees.

The WRAP women took the lead in calling open mass meetings, coordinating, organizing, and arranging demonstrations. Some good ideas for the center, including the demand that it be controlled by the parents who use it, resulted. The university became scared enough at the thought of a joint movement by students and employees to send officials to rallies and set up a committee to "look into the feasibility" of the center. But the movement fizzled out by the end of the school year. One reason was that WRAP failed to press for a permanent steering committee or some body composed of both employees groups, who should have been leading the campaign, and who would have kept it up over the summer when the students were gone. Another—and related—reason was that the "most political" WRAP women abandoned work on the campaign to concentrate on the faction fights in SDS.

By this time, WRAP had ceased having the "personal" parts of meetings, and many women had dropped out as a result of that and of what it reflected about the leadership, the "most political" women. The women who dropped out said they "weren't ready" to do without the personal sessions and to "take the step into political work." What nearly all of the politicos failed to tell them is that you develop, *both* "personally" and "politically," through your own actions. This idea had been implicit earlier in the year, when one experienced and one inexperienced woman would always write a leaflet, go to speak to a new group, etc., together. But the vanguardist, authoritarian lines developing in SDS caused many SDS-WRAP women to begin to scorn their "less developed" sisters. WRAP shrank rapidly, and the women who were left stuck their heads in a cloud of rhetoric and no longer had time for what might have been a real movement of workers and students. (I might add that, from what I hear about compulsory group "love-making" in the Weathermen these days, some of the "political" women needed those personal sessions at least as much as the nonpoliticos needed help in organizing.)

A couple of illustrations of mistakes made by WRAP leadership are interesting to contrast with what their "constituency" was saying. For example, WRAP called a rally about the child care center and few people came. They proceeded with the speeches anyway. One of the women in the "secretaries" group turned to a few of us and said that if the hospital workers wouldn't come to a lunchtime rally across campus, we should go to them. She took her baby out of its carriage and carried it, and stuck a megaphone under the blankets. We wheeled the carriage right into the middle of the hospital cafeteria floor. She took the megaphone out of hiding and gave a whole speech about the center and a mass meeting at night before the campus cops came and threw us out. Another example was the WRAP meeting at which many politicos were saying we couldn't organize the students around the child care issue because they weren't thinking about having children. A student who had never been to a meeting before got up and said, "I haven't had any political experience, but I think you're wrong. *You* may not be thinking about having children, because you are the kind of woman who goes on to graduate school and a career, or is so active in organizations that you don't want children soon. But most of the women in college were sent there to get just enough education so they can make a little conversation with the professional husbands they will have. After these four years we may be stuck in the house for the next twenty. We are *very* interested in good, free child care."

It is no wonder, after being involved in or observing the mess the New Left is in, that many W.L. groups became so afraid of dogmatism that they spurned theory. Or after looking at the state powers that call themselves Marxist and the youth who want to repeat the same mistakes, that they spurned Marxism. Women have been told by men "theorists" of both the bourgeoisie and the Left that Marxism is purely materialism. What is *really* new about the W.L. movement, I think, is its rejection of simple economic solutions to women's discontent. We are saying, not that we want to be like men, even rich men, in this society, but that we want to be whole human beings called women—beings who have many choices of how to live, many opportunities to create—beings who cannot exist without a total restructuring of society.

It is this Humanism that makes this movement different from

the Suffragette or any other movement for equal rights with men in the past. And this Humanism *is* Marxism. Marx combined materialism and idealism to create a philosophy of liberation that can end class, racist, and sexist society. He scorned "vulgar communism," such as the change from private to state capitalism in Russia and China, as much as capitalism. He explained that it is who *controls* the means of production that determines all human relations in the society, the relation of person to person including man to woman. If the end of your philosophy is not freedom for everyone, it is not Marxism.

Marxist-Humanism has been bursting out in the last two decades—in this country, in the mass black and student movements, and now it is a potential of the W.L. movement. This is the even newer in the brand-new women's fight. I can see a change even since last year, when W.L. stressed statistics on job discrimination to spread their cause. Now they are talking about redefining *all* relationships in society. Even the "grandmother" organization of W.L., N.O.W., an organization of professional women itself only a few years old, is considered too conservative and too centralized in authority. And, I think, a serious search for theory—for a key to the self-development of our *own* movement—is starting. Hopefully, W. L. will overcome its fear of structure and philosophy, and meet up with *all* the different women in the country, so it can form a mass movement that will link up with the other forces for liberation and create a society in which women can be *whole women.*

12

Laura Derman *

A Failure of Imagination (*1970*)

The question of what I would like to do but am unable to do is answerable in terms of the severe restrictions placed on me by the institutions of society. I've been precluded from even conceptualizing satisfying alternatives to my present life-style.

The educational system has taught me the "art" of rote learning and memory. Educators conceive the purpose of education as a means of enabling the student to criticize the present society and to posit alternatives for the future. Not only have I been unable to do this for the society, but I can't even posit alternatives to my own dreary existence.

It's not that imagination has been eliminated in a technological society, but it has been limited to possibilities within a certain framework. It asks "how," not "why." For example, when one wants to build a road or fly to the moon, it answers *how* not *why*. It is traditionally the *why* questions which have puzzled and stimulated people. The *why* questions are at the root of religion (in its broad sense) and the *how* questions are at the root of technology. The limitations of imagination make themselves felt most obviously in the creative arts. How else are we to explain why America has not produced first-rate art? It's also made itself felt in political

* At the time this was written, Laura Derman was a student at the University of Michigan School of Social Work.

criticism. Even those members of society like myself who consider themselves radically opposed have their analyses crippled by a lack of imagination. For instance, I know of no New Leftist who's been able to define a comprehensive alternative structure. This stands in clear opposition to the nineteenth century which saw all kinds of comprehensive schemes for alternative societies. So I'm left in the position of having escaped enough to see the crap but not far out enough to posit serious alternatives to it and thus while I seem to have copped out of the question, I really haven't.

From the courses I've taken, the implicit assumption, instead of being the outright tripe of "what is ought to be," is the sophisticated tripe of "what is" ought to be slightly modified. This is especially true in some of the more directly relevant social science courses, i.e., political science and sociology. Instructors feel that time spent framing alternatives which are not possible under the present framework is time wasted. This kind of attitude is not only anti-educational but also inevitable and is probably not the fault of the instructor. This has developed in me a kind of schizophrenia. On one level I act and on a completely different level I think and my thinking and acting can never coincide. Intellectually I recognize the awful futility of organizing a welfare rights group. Even were the group functioning at its optimum level, i.e., a large, cohesive group fighting and winning its rights, a group functioning will without an organizer—it would be an exercise in futility. The powers-that-be in this society need the poor and will do all that is necessary to preserve poverty. Yet I work on. I spend long hours in a struggle that I know will go nowhere. This vision of futility has not yet affected my organizing (at least I'm not aware that it has) but it seems inevitable that it will.

The duality between thought and action will hinder me in my work all the more so because my alternatives are not thought out. Were they I could perhaps begin working toward them. It's clear that not only is my ability to select existing alternatives limited but even more limited is my ability to create alternatives. To a large extent this is the result of my experiences in school.

In my early education, the idea of students freely choosing options was somewhat subversive. As demands for educational reforms grew, students were allowed to choose one out of several slightly different alternatives. Instead of having to take sociology and economics and psychology, you had the option of taking three of five courses in the social sciences. While this is a step in the right direction, it hardly allows the student to pick his own alternatives. Thus when it comes to developing and framing an alternative, be it economic, social, or political, I am incapable.

My creative thinking has also been stifled by the demands of time. Having to memorize class notes and assignments left little time for creative thinking. In addition, innovative thoughts were rarely praised. That's not what most teachers were interested in. And now, when I have some time for creative thinking, I have great trouble in doing so.

I'm further restrained by living in a society where I benefit from its material wealth. As Marcuse points out, the society not only co-opts alternative proposals, but saps the strength of its potential opposition. The material well-being which the society is able to provide to most, "sells" the political system, the economic system, the whole ethos of the society. How does one resist the constant stream of goodies which shower down? How can a society which produces for our every material want be opposed on a twenty-four-hours-a-day basis? (And isn't this what revolutionaries are all about?) A silver-studded wood-grained technomatic razor castrates us.

Being a woman in this society places a further handicap on me. In overt and subtle ways I've been taught that I must dress attractively, think what "my man" thinks, raise a family and, if I must work, be a teacher or social worker. My work must not be an important part of my life. It's something to do before children are born and after they are grown so as to occupy my time. My values, my dreams, and my thoughts are not the important ones. Even my parents' friends, whom I have always viewed as somewhat more enlightened and politically sophisticated, can't fathom my wanting work to be as significant a part of my life as marriage. Their response to my frustration, in crude terms, is find yourself a good man and be a school social worker. Just being aware of my position as a woman and hating its subservient aspects doesn't make it very much easier to deal with. All these factors—the educational system, overbearing societal pressures, and my position as a woman —combine to make it difficult to find satisfying life-style alternatives.

PART III

CONFRONTATION: *BLACK, WORKING CLASS AND IVY*

WITH inflammatory rhetoric and tactics ranging from those inspired by Saul Alinsky's Industrial Areas Foundation to those initiated in the civil rights movement to those gleaned from Third World guerrilla tactics, student rebels have confronted dismayed university trustees, administrators and, often, faculties with a broad range of demands. Along with certain value elements, the strategy and tactics of student protest have increasingly taken on identifiable forms of their own. From campus to campus, there are divergent analyses of the dimensions of the problems which gave rise to more extreme forms of rebellion, just as the activists themselves differ greatly on the ideology and tactics of their protest. Similarly, there continues to be wide disagreement about the appropriateness of a broad spectrum of "solutions" which, even within university confines, vary from a notion which suggests that students ought to take what they are offered and like it (or go elsewhere) to a system which would permit students to give courses, assign grades and grant degrees. While there are clearly limitations to both of these extreme models, almost everyone thoughtfully concerned about the student power movement agrees that it has helped to throw a public spotlight on areas in which changes in American higher education (as well as in a wide range of American social institutions) are urgently needed.

How does one gauge the success or failure of a major confrontation on a university campus? There are no simple answers. Some analysts have argued that in the long run the gains would have been achieved anyway, and that the rebels only succeeded in undermining the "community of scholars" that was in large measure responsible for the most meaningful parts of their education. For others, success has been a measure of the degree to which major student demands were met in some significant way. The single perspective which has probably been most neglected is that of the students' own assessment of their rebellious actions.

The three articles which follow describe major confrontations in widely dispersed areas of the country—Tuskegee Institute, Alabama, San Francisco State College and New York's Columbia College. Precipitating incidents, the response of various student factions, the reaction of administrators (including the use of off-campus police), and the involvement of the surrounding community are very different from one situation to the next. The Tuskegee experience signals a new level of black student consciousness. A sense of immediacy is captured in the description of San Francisco State through an exploration of the feelings of a strike participant. Mark Rudd utilizes the Columbia rebellion as a framework for analyzing the potentials for future actions.

However, the commonalities among them should be carefully noted. Surely, students may be seen as trying to take a hand in affairs which they felt most immediately relevant to their own lives. The sense of power, excitement and community in each protest effort can hardly be denied. Underlying all three protests is a feeling of exhilaration that seems to come of grasping some piece of your own freedom in your own hands.

13

Stephanie Mines
and Phil Frazier

Bringin' It All Down Home * (*1969*)

At Tuskegee Institute in 1968, black students staged a seizure for power. They demanded not merely educational reform but a total restructuring of the school in the interests of the black community. The mandate which they issued and the form that their demonstration took established an irreversible precedent in the history of student-university-community relations. In times of extreme flux, it is difficult to make definitive historical connections, but it can be said that the Tuskegee revolt initiated trends that were to be repeated again and again across the country.

Tuskegee Institute in Macon County, Alabama, is an isolated town within a town—a scene of apparent affluence with an atmosphere of neatness and calm. The homes surrounding Tuskegee Institute are owned by "black professionals" all of whom are tied, in one way or another, to the college. Tuskegee proper is owned and controlled by white businessmen as are the large and prosperous farms surrounding the town. The residents of Tuskegee Institute rarely have to come in contact with the black sharecroppers who comprise the major portion of the population in this Black Belt county.

Established in 1880 by Booker T. Washington as the Tuskegee

* Reprinted from *The Movement* (April, 1969, issue). Stephanie Mines and Phil Frazier were staff writers for *The Movement*.

State Normal School, Tuskegee Institute was, and continues to be, a training center for blacks which makes it possible for them to become an unobtrusive part of society. Under the direction of Booker T., and later George Washington Carver, the school was essentially geared toward agricultural, mechanical and nonprofessional work. Today, it offers training in engineering, agriculture, veterinary science, nursing, home economics and "mechanical industries" such as construction.

There is a token "School of Arts and Sciences" where courses in the Humanities are taught by a few transient white teachers. The Philosophy Department, for instance, has a faculty of two and the Political Science Department, at its peak, had a faculty of three. The only Ph.D. offered is in Veterinary Science. Master's degrees are available for only a few majors, like Sociology and Education. Many of the departments employ outdated equipment and methods, insuring that blacks who study to be engineers, for instance, will not be competitive for top-level positions.

Clearly, then, the nature of Tuskegee has not changed since the days of Booker T. Washington and George Washington Carver (it is only recently that young black people have begun to outspokenly question the fact that they do not control the enormous profits made from Carver's development of hundreds of products utilizing peanuts and sweet potatoes). While purporting to be a model of progress and self-advancement, Tuskegee, in fact, simply perpetuates the racist division of labor by training blacks for jobs white society feels suits them best. Even more importantly, Tuskegee Institute was seen by black people throughout America as a "promised land"—the one place where their sons and daughters can learn "respectable" trades and become a meaningful part of society. So, when the black students of Tuskegee challenged the nature and function of Tuskegee Institute, they also challenged a religious faith in the dream of racial assimilation and slow, steady progress.

The students that led the Tuskegee insurrection were part of a dialectical process that summarizes the growth and development of the black student movement. For the most part, they were middle-class blacks who came to Tuskegee in the early 1960's to fulfill their parents' dreams of self-improvement. In a few cases, such as Sammy Younge's, they were the children of the bourgeois "professional" blacks who were a part of Tuskegee's privileged, college-tied, black community.

They arrived in Tuskegee in the midst of campaigns for desegregation and voter registration, and given the singularly uninteresting and meaningless quality of the college curriculum, many soon became involved in civil rights generally, and in SNCC more specifically. In March of 1965, Tuskegee Institute students marched to Montgomery, Alabama, to protest the denial of voting rights to black people and the brutal beating of civil rights demonstrators in Selma on the previous Sunday. For most of the Tuskegee students, this was the first organized demonstration against white supremacy. James Forman, describing the charge by the sheriff's posse on the marchers and the internal disagreements between SNCC and SCLC, calls the incident "the students' cram course in civil rights."

After the Montgomery march, a number of Tuskegee students began to work closely with SNCC, often leaving school to work as organizers or spending more time in the Movement than in the classroom. Among them was Sammy Younge, Jr.

Sammy Younge, Jr.

Sammy is important because his life and death contain the essence of the first half of the process of political and personal development that the student activists at Tuskegee experienced. In addition, his death signaled the end of an old era of compromise and reconciliation and the beginning of a period of aggressive, forthright and outspoken demands for human dignity.

Born into the Tuskegee community that was bound physically, materially and philosophically to Tuskegee Institute, Sammy's decision to join SNCC entailed a total transformation of values—a complete rejection of the benefits and life style of the middle class that was reflected in a revitalization of his person, even down to his appearance.

His fellow students saw him change from an "Ivy Leaguer" who wanted to succeed in school to a young man who refused to accept hypocrisy in any form, including a degree from an institution that was clearly irresponsible and nonfunctional from the perspective of the black community. It is impossible to say exactly what generated this metamorphosis in Sammy—there were probably a multitude of experiences on a number of different levels—but his participation in the Montgomery march and his contact with SNCC workers who came to Tuskegee to organize voter registration were certainly contributing factors. Through SNCC Sammy was able more clearly to conceptualize his identity—to realize himself as a man with a community to which he was responsible and a history of which he was proud. SNCC helped Sammy define his origins and his direction, but he did not stop there. He continued to search for his specific role in the Movement—to develop himself as a human being and to define himself in terms of the world around him.

Like many of his fellow students, Sammy became intensely involved in the Freedom Democratic Party, and worked on organizing voter registration campaigns, in rural Mississippi. The students were detaching themselves more and more from Tuskegee Institute and hardly considering it, even when they worked to desegregate Tuskegee's public accommodations.

The image one gets of Sammy Younge, Jr. from talking to his friends is one of extreme energy—movement—like a flashing light that cannot be contained. A friend of his, seeing the intensity of feeling in the midst of chaos at Berkeley the other day, said, "Sammy's here, baby, Sammy Younge is in town."

Despite the strong commitment of students to the civil rights movement it became clear in late 1965 to the SNCC-oriented student leadership of Tuskegee that voter registration, boycotts, marches and attempts to desegregate public accommodations were not having their anticipated effect. Minor, legal victories were won but there was no substantial change in the quality of people's lives. In Tuskegee, for instance, voter registration resulted in the election of a black sheriff who acted white.

Death of an Era

Despite this growing awareness, it is not easy to change direction in midstream. In January 1966, Tuskegee students were engaged in a voter registration campaign in Tuskegee. They had brought 118 people to the courthouse for that purpose. Sammy and a number of other SNCC workers had been threatened at knife point because they refused to be intimidated by the registrar's attempts to cancel voter registration on that day. The threats were reported to the

FBI who declared that the situation was "out of their jurisdiction" and in the hands of the local authorities. That night Sammy Younge, Jr. was shot dead by service station owner Marvin Segrest, who is now alive and free in Tuskegee, having been acquitted by an all-white jury in Lee County, Alabama.

It is not sufficient to say that Sammy's death had a radicalizing effect on the Tuskegee students. It was one of the final arguments necessary to convince them that the old methods were dying—that Sammy's death could not be vindicated by marches and boycotts and nonviolent demonstrations. His death also bound more closely together the leadership cadre of Tuskegee students who had been with Sammy since his freshman year at Tuskegee. They became committed to completing the process that Sammy had begun—to actualizing his unfulfilled and possibly unrealized objectives in their own outspoken, uncompromising actions. There was a brief and predictably unsuccessful attempt to memorialize Sammy's death in marches and boycotts, particularly after Segrest's acquittal. But, that was like the funeral service for the end of an era.

Sammy's death redirected student attention to Tuskegee Institute. The school, along with the black civic and social organizations, refused to join with the students in protesting Sammy's murder. When added to the general failure of nonviolent tactics in gaining social change, this unwillingness of the school administration to recognize the significance of Sammy's death forced some students to reconsider their attitudes and objectives. They began to reevaluate the school itself, not in terms of their own dissatisfaction with the curriculum, but in terms of the black communities where they had been working.

Sammy's friends returned to Tuskegee as students—drawing a circle of experience that began in college, led them to the community around the college and then returned them to school, with apparently very little changed. But, a great deal had changed. Suddenly, their former dissatisfaction with the content of college life began to take on substance when understood in the light of their work as SNCC organizers. Given the conditions of life in Macon and Lowndes counties, how could Tuskegee stand isolated, bearing no relation to the lives of the people it was supposedly built to serve? In what specific ways did Tuskegee function in the interests of black people? Was the training students received there instrumental in making life better for black people? Was the curriculum geared toward advancement or repression? Why was the school controlled by white trustees? Why was it that the Tuskegee curriculum caused the students to despise their heritage rather than celebrate it? What did it mean that the head janitor at the school was a Tuskegee graduate? The war in Vietnam added depth to these questions—would young black men continue to die in Vietnam while Sammy's murderer ran free in Tuskegee? Why had Sammy died—wasn't it time to resurrect his power, his vitality?

These were the questions being asked by the SNCC-educated vanguard. Simultaneously, the majority of the students were noting Tuskegee's inferior quality of education on a narrower, departmental level. The school was not turning out qualified, trained workers who could compete on the job market. Students in the department of engineering and the school of mechanical industries complained about the outdated equipment being used. Students in other departments wanted more majors available to them—there was no music major, for instance, and the nurses wanted to establish a "Community Outreach Program" so that they could get college credit for work done outside the school. Athletic scholarships were not offered at Tuskegee and the students resented this denial of prestige in an area where black people excelled.

While these grievances were esentially bourgeois in content, they led to the conclusion that Tuskegee was not fulfilling its supposed objective—training black people to function in a white society. The real nature of Tuskegee was thus revealed to the majority of students in a very specific way. If Tuskegee did not serve them, then who did serve them? If a degree from Tuskegee did not get them a good job, then what was it worth?

The Black University

At this point the students who had been in SNCC were able to politicize these complaints and give them wider scope. Because of their experiences in the black community and their confrontations with both the white and black establishments, they could understand how and why Tuskegee Institute did not function in the interests of black people and that, in fact, it was instrumental in the suppression of black people. The dialectical process that had first led them out of the school and into the community and then forced them to return to the college was now having its effect.

From this combination of demands for specific departmental reform and the political perspective supplied by the SNCC-educated vanguard came an organization called Unity and the formulation of a mandate which contained, as its introduction, the concept of the "black university"—the college controlled *by* black people *for* black people, autonomous in its decision-making power and concerned primarily with serving the community which surrounds it.

On February 29, 1968, a State Department official was scheduled to speak at Tuskegee about Vietnam. Unity decided that this speaker was antagonistic to the real interests of black people and that Tuskegee must be made into a place where black ideas are realized. The students took over the podium and threw eggs at the State Department officials. The Tuskegee Institute administration immediately began to take punitive action—and the students responded by rejecting the entire judicial procedure.

This incident provided the setting for the presentation of the mandate to the president of the college (Luther H. Foster). The mandate, with its "black university concept," was the explanation for the students' rejection of the State Department official as a suitable speaker for their campus. But the president declared that he did not have the power to implement changes as extensive as those called for by the mandate. So, the students withdrew pressure until April 5 when all the trustees were scheduled to arrive at Tuskegee to commemorate Founders' Day. On April 4, Dr. Martin Luther King, Jr. was assassinated. The students decided to go ahead with their plans to present the mandate to the trustees the following day. It may appear strange that Dr. King's death did not alter the students' plans. One of the leaders of Unity explains this by saying that the mandate was so important that most of the students could not conceive of halting its presentation to the trustees. It might also be suggested that while Dr. King's death meant the end of nonviolence to most Americans, for the Tuskegee students who had been in SNCC that death had occurred two years earlier with the murder of Sammy Younge, Jr. They were finally paying tribute to Sammy—conducting their own memorial service on the Tuskegee campus.

Trustees Held Captive

The trustees arrived with their wives and families for a weekend of patronizing leisure with the darkies on the plantation (see Ralph Ellison's description of Founder's Day in *Invisible Man*) and found instead that the students had some serious work for them to do. With the purpose of communicating to the trustees the seriousness of the demands and the necessity for an uncompromising and speedy implementation, the students locked all exits from Dorothy Hall (the building where they were to reside during their stay at Tuskegee), took over the communication system and established a picket line around the building. Of the 3,000 member student body over 2,000 students were actively participating in the demonstration. The trustees and the president were told that they would be permitted to leave only when the demands contained in the mandate were met and implementation assured.

The trustees were held captive for two and a half tense days during which the apparently strong alliance of diverse political elements in Unity began to show signs of strain. As might have been anticipated, the most discernible split was between the students who had experienced that dialectical process of political education and those who had not.

With the knowledge that Tuskegee's black sheriff had a court injunction against the students and that they could be charged with kidnapping, the students released a trustee who claimed he would die of a heart attack if not permitted to leave. Shortly after his release the National Guard arrived and was stationed around the campus.

Those who still believed that educational reform was the issue argued with those who emphasized the "black university concept" about whether or not to accept an offer from President Foster. Foster claimed that the trustees had granted him full power to implement the demands and agreed to remain in Dorothy Hall if the students would release the trustees. Tired and pressured by the threatening nearness of the National Guard, the students released the trustees.

The National Guard, restrained only by the fact that the students could get to the trustees before the Guard got to the students, informed Unity that they would not hesitate to charge the building now that the students had only a Negro president for security. Recognizing that their seizure for power was now a failure, the students began to leave the building, and eventually, with kidnap charges hanging over their heads, to leave Macon County and scatter throughout the country, temporary exiles from the place that had given them their birth as political revolutionaries.

The incident at Tuskegee, flowing as it does directly out of the struggle of black people for control over their lives, must be seen as a wellspring of current developments in the black student rebellion. Whether or not the SNCC vanguard at Tuskegee were the sole originators of the concept of the "black university" is really unimportant. What is important is the growth of this theory of educational self-determination from direct contact with the southern black community and the dialectic of political education epitomized, in part, by the life of Sammy Younge. It is the interaction of the college-community-college-community process that draws our attention to Tuskegee 1968 and causes us to consider its historical impact on places like San Francisco State College.

14

Louie Patler

San Francisco State College: An In-depth Historical Analysis * (*1969*)

S.F. State is an urban commuter college. Because of exorbitant rents students usually live some distance away from the campus. Unlike many California colleges and universities, S.F. State students tend to be more working-class, self-supporting, and a bit older than the average student.

Going to San Francisco State College is a relevant educational experience. I had such an experience for two years (September, 1966–June, 1968). As is usually the case, the mass media have made it very difficult to get a grasp of the issues surrounding the strike and their historical roots. What I shall attempt to do is give historical information based on my two years there, and some inside information taken from letters written to me by students currently active in the strike.

Student Organizations

CAMPUS ACTIVISTS. There are two basic types of activists on campus. On the one hand are institutional reformers committed to

* Reprinted by permission of *The South End* (January 9, 1969). At the time this was written, Louie Patler was a graduate student at Wayne State University.

revisions in the curriculum, changing grading standards and experimenting with new forms of teaching techniques. On the other hand you have the campus revolutionaries committed to confrontation and the eventual overthrow of the college as it currently exists. Into the former group fall the Experimental College (EC), the Community Services Institute (CSI), parts of the Black Students Union (BSU), and Third World Liberation Front (TWLF). In the latter group of more radical persuasion fall Students for a Democratic Society (SDS), Progressive Labor (PL), and the rest of BSU and TWLF.

Prior to the strike of November 1968, the groups had been operating quite autonomously. The leadership of these student groups tend to be in their late twenties, and the general membership in their early twenties. Almost all the major leaders got "radicalized" through the civil rights movement where they tried their hand at organizing in the South. Most such leaders are pragmatic, verbal, and have a communication hookup all over the United States. (For example, the chairman of the JOIN Project in Chicago was staying with the leaders of the Community Services Institute last spring; and I was given nine names of Detroit leaders to look up when I arrived.) Let's look at the activities of a sample of these groups to give you some idea of their links with the community and their basic orientation.

THE EXPERIMENTAL COLLEGE. The EC started in the spring of 1966 under the philosophy that any individual who wanted to explore any topic, and could get one other person to work with him, constituted a "classroom." The old differentiation between "student" and "teacher" was abolished. It soon became clear however that this kind of "free university" was a bourgeois luxury. To allow for the masses to participate the EC arranged for credit in many of its "courses." From an initial enrollment of a few dozen, the EC last spring had had over 2,500 enrolled in its classes.

COMMUNITY SERVICES INSTITUTE. Formerly called Work-Study, this group has two major thrusts. First they have many ties with the community and supply—on request—community organizers, and resources to various agencies and groups. They are organizing in the high schools, have been training radical teachers in public schools, have initiated a B.A. in work-study, etc.

BLACK STUDENTS UNION. The BSU has so many projects working that it is difficult to explain each (e.g., Black Draft Counseling; Black Tutorial; black cultural programs on and off campus). Their thrusts have been directed at getting black students into S.F. State, getting students out of S.F. State with a B.A. which is relevant to black people, working in the black communities surrounding San Francisco.

STUDENTS FOR A DEMOCRATIC SOCIETY. SDS came into its own during the last school year with major demonstrations against Dow and ROTC on campus. After ironing out some of their differences with the Progressive Labor people, SDS organized the May demonstration along with the BSU and TWLF. This demonstration led to the departure of John Summerskill as president and was a vital coalition which has formed the backbone of the current strike.

Underlying Issues

S.F. State is far ahead of most universities in the extent of "student power." Yet students realized that their power had serious restraining forces from the administration, the Board of Trustees and Governor Reagan. The EC was investigated by Sacramento (the state capital) because it offered controversial courses (e.g., urban guerrilla warfare). The BSU was investigated because some of its alleged members had beaten the editor of the campus paper. SDS was investigated because it is SDS and had received much negative publicity. CSI was being watched because of the activities of some of its community organizers.

Being "watched" or "investigated" is one thing, but being RE-PRESSED is quite another. It is this repression that was a precipitating ingredient to the current strike.

During the last student body elections, a slate of officers was elected by an overwhelming majority of votes. The reason for this was that all of the officers were leaders of the EC, BSU, CSI, etc. Winning the election meant controlling (so they thought) $150,000 in student "incidental" and "activity" fees. They immediately refused to give any money to athletics—which normally received $40–70,000. They then gave large sums of money to the "Programs" (EC, CSI, BSU). This was too much for the politicians to take and steps were taken to "relieve students of the burden of disbursing funds." Steps were also taken to relieve the student body president of the power of appointment of work-study NDEA jobs. All of this action took place during the summer when student protest and mobilization was difficult to organize.

The final precipitating act took place when George Murray [a black teaching assistant in the English department] was fired because of an "inflammatory" speech made in Fresno, California! Campus leaders knew George Murray and they had heard him speak often—usually putting America down as a racist, imperialist nation (he is famous for his use of the word "bullshit," e.g., "American is bullshit"). Hence, Murray joined Huey Newton and Eldridge Cleaver as political prisoners who, because of their adverse publicity, were denied due process. Students realized this and the strike was on. What follows is a letter from a campus reformer actively involved in the strike. It explains far better than I could what happened in the strike prior to Christmas (1968) recess:

> I don't know where to begin about the State thing. It's really hard to get a handle on it. I hardly need to tell you that the press has done an incredibly poor job of reporting but it seems to be getting better. The single most important issue, and the one that has been completely ignored by the media, is the offensive Sacramento was launching under Title V against *all* student financial aid run programs from Associated Students to B.S.U., C.S.I., Experimental College, etc.
>
> This started in the summer, Murray's firing and the present Attorney General's investigation into Associated Student funds are only specific instances of a general trend.
>
> It has come down to a bare power struggle between the militant right in Sacramento with their representatives on Campus (Hayakawa, etc.) and the militant left coalition of B.S.U., S.D.S., Programs people and Faculty.
>
> AFT has been gaining strength and is getting more involved. Community support and support in High Schools, Junior Colleges and Colleges is *much* stronger than the press has indicated. If AFT goes out, the entire State College system could be paralyzed. This is why Hayakawa closed the Campus a week early. All of this support would have been evident for everyone to see if school had remained open.

I don't know how to tell you just how deep the cleavages are and how extremely volatile the situation is. People on both sides see this as an all-or-nothing situation and I think they are right. There are a number of levels to this conflict and I can't hope to explain them all to you. Right now there seems to be a very strong position developing which centers on opposition to Hayakawa's police state rather than unqualified support for B.S.U. and Third World demands. *All* civil liberties have been suspended and due process is a joke. The last three days of school there was absolutely *no* violence on the part of students. Still, club-wielding police could charge any group of students who appeared to be supporting the strike. Peaceful, legal pickets are attacked without any order to disperse. At least half of the 130 people who have been arrested are completely innocent of anything other than being on the campus at the wrong time. *Anyone* arrested will have at least two and usually five charges lodged against him. Several ministers and community people, including Carlton Goodlet [editor of a large black newspaper], have been arrested on trumped-up charges of inciting to riot, assault, theft, and resisting arrest. Try to take down a badge number (if the cop is wearing one—most don't) and you get clubbed and charged with interfering with an officer, resisting arrest, etc.

Anyone identified as a strike leader, that is anyone who speaks to any group, has a warrant issued for his arrest and is picked off at the first opportunity. Ecumenical House [religious affiliated organization] has been surrounded and searched at least three times *without* a search warrant.

All of these tactics are pre-planned and have the active support of Hayakawa, Alioto, and Sacramento.

So you see, there is a hell of a lot more going on than meets the eye. . . . I'm seriously considering doing my thesis on this whole thing and have already been encouraged by some of the people in my department. At this point, I haven't been to a class in six weeks and I will probably have to drop six of my twelve graduate units. The classes I had were a drag anyway but the instructors will allow anyone to drop without an F up to the last day of the semester which helps. I was going to get my Masters in June but now it looks like August at the earliest.

In the midst of all this conflict there has been some real community developing. Many Faculty are really beginning to see that they are in the same boat as the students. Tragedy and triumph are collective.

You can see from this letter that the strike has been very successful. Student groups have coalesced and are learning more every

day about power, the press, civil liberties, "third world" administrators (Hayakawa) and relevant educational experiences. But an
interesting new development has taken place: the faculty is getting
the same kind of education. Hence the new thrust in the strike is a
coalition of students and faculty.

Faculty have seen that academic freedom is a cliché when they
are employed by a Board of Trustees like California has. They
have been forced to face the reality that the campus is no longer a
sanctuary from the realities of the community (police come on
campus to solve on-campus issues). They have realized that many
of their peers are reactionary, authoritarian, and not particularly
objective in their analysis of the problems and in suggested solutions (remember that only about ⅓ of the faculty is actively supporting the strike—the 350 American Federation of Teachers
members). And they have realized that the student strike leaders
are among the brightest and most sophisticated on campus, rather
than brushing them aside as "hippie types."

How much longer the strike lasts, how many more arrests there
will be and how many more students and faculty will be clubbed
depends on the speed with which the opposing forces can agree
upon the *issues*. It seems unlikely to me that this kind of understanding will occur very soon. Students and faculty are seeking expanded power and the administration, Board of Trustees and the
governor want to retain control. Just as the repression of Batista,
not the charisma of Fidel Castro, precipitated a revolution in Cuba,
so too may Hayakawa and Reagan be the catalysts of a continuing
student revolution. We shall see.

¡Viva la Huelga!

15

Mark Rudd

Notes on Columbia * (*1969*)

Before and during the Columbia rebellion, the SDS chapter faced situations very similar to those encountered by other chapters around the country. Questions of militancy vs. isolating yourself from the base, questions of relating to a black students' movement, questions of student power vs. a radical position on the university, questions of how to work as a radical within mass political situations, all came to the forefront in our experience at Columbia. They also became the key questions at places like Brooklyn College, Kent State in Ohio, San Francisco State, Brandeis and literally hundreds of other campuses where the movement is at various stages of building itself.

This article is being written with the belief that our experiences can be absorbed and used, and, what is most important, the movement can go on to higher levels, evading old mistakes in order to commit the mistakes of the future. . . .

New Left Notes this fall reported a split which had occurred in the Ann Arbor, Michigan, chapter of SDS, between advocates of a liberal-radical position on student power and "base-building" (called "The Radical Caucus"), and advocates of struggle and ag-

---

* Reprinted from *The Movement* (March, 1969, issue). At the time this was written, Mark Rudd was a student at Columbia University.

gressive action in exposing the imperialist and racist university and building a radical movement ("The Jesse James Gang").

A roughly parallel split in the Columbia chapter in March had prepared the way for the militant and aggressive stance of SDS which led to the blowup of April 23. For years SDS nationwide has been plagued by the "base-building vs. militant action" debate—revolution in the chapter at Columbia and the subsequent mass student rebellion to show the essential unity of the two lines, and the phoniness of the debate. (Recently Progressive Labor Party has pushed this stupid debate to discredit the "right-wing, anarchist, debrayist, mindless activists" it sees everywhere. The only result of this, based especially on the experience of Columbia, should be to discredit PL as the real right wing).

From April, 1967, to March, 1968, the SDS chapter had been led by a group of people who tended to stress "organizing" and "base-building" above action and "confrontation." Though possessing a "Marxist" analysis, they believed that the way support is gained is by going out to people and talking to them about our analysis. Various pieties about the necessity to build the base before you take action, and the dangers of isolating yourself from the base were incessantly pronounced in the name of the "Marxist analysis." The word "politics" was used as a bludgeon with which to beat unruly upstarts into place and to maintain control over the chapter. One example will illustrate this point.

In early March, at a meeting of the SDS Draft Committee (which had been doing something called "political draft counseling"—a total dud as far as building a radical movement goes), the question of what to do when the head of the Selective Service System for New York City came to speak at Columbia came up. Someone suggested that SDS greet the Colonel by attacking him physically—which would clearly define the fact that we consider him to be an enemy. The idea was defeated by a vote of 30–1 after the old leadership of the chapter argued that an attack on the Colonel would be "terrorist, apolitical and silly," and especially would not communicate anything to anyone (since the action had "no political content"). It was decided that the draft committee would be present at the speech to "ask probing questions."

Several SDS members and nonmembers then organized clandestinely the attack on the Colonel. In the middle of his speech a

mini-demonstration appeared in the back of the room with a fife
and drum, flags, machine guns, and noise-makers. As attention
went to the back, a person in the front row stood up and placed a
lemon-meringue pie in the Colonel's face. Everyone split.

Only two groups on campus did not dig what became known as
the "pie incident." First was the administration of Columbia University. Second was the old leadership of Columbia SDS, which
disapproved because the action was terroristic and apolitical and
would jeopardize our base on campus.

Meanwhile almost everyone on campus thought this was the best
thing SDS had ever done (though we disavowed any part in it and
said it was the NY Knickerboppers who had done the job). People
understood the symbolism in the attack and identified with it because of their own desires, often latent, to strike back at the draft
and the government. This was in symbolic miniature form, the
same dynamic of militant action by a vanguard and then mass identification which worked so well during the rebellion a month later.

In a criticism session held after the pie incident, members of the
chapter began to learn the difference between the verbal "base-
building," nonstruggle approach of the old leadership (now called
the "Praxis Axis") and the aggressive approach of those who saw
the primacy of developing a movement based on struggle. This latter group, centered around myself and John Jacobs, as well as
others in and out of SDS, came to be known as the "Action-Faction" due to the never-ending search for symmetry.

Subsequent to the ascendancy of the ideas of the Action-Faction
the chapter began engaging in more and more militant confrontations—an illegal demonstration on March 27 against IDA, in
which we chased 2 vice-presidents around the campus; the disruption of a memorial service for Martin Luther King in order to expose the fact that while Kirk and Truman were eulogizing King,
their university was completely racist toward the community and
toward its employees. . . .

This prominence of militancy and the aggressive approach
should not be interpreted as a victory for the action side of the
action vs. base-building dichotomy. In fact, action and education
(verbal and otherwise) are completely united, two aspects of the
same thing (call it "base-building," "organizing," "building the
movement," whatever you like). A leaflet or dorm-canvassing is no

less radical activity than seizing a building—in fact both are necessary.

At Columbia we had a four-year history of agitation and education involving forms of activity from seminars and open forums on IDA to confrontations over NROTC and military recruiting. All went into developing the mass-consciousness that was responsible for the Columbia rebellion. The point is that we had to develop the willingness to take action, vanguard action, before the tremendous potential of the "base" could be released. In addition, the vanguard action also acted as education for many people not yet convinced. The radical analysis never got such a hearing, and a sympathetic one, as during the rebellion.

There are no sure ways to know when the base is ready to move. Many militant actions which expose the participants will result only in an educational point entering the consciousness of the people, without developing mass support. An example of this is the sit-in against the CIA which took place at Columbia in February, 1967, involving only 18 people (led by Progressive Labor Party, before it turned right). This seemingly isolated action (even the SDS chapter did not participate) helped ready people for the direct action to come one year later by making a first penetration into students' minds that direct action is both possible and desirable.

We had no way of knowing whether the base was ready at Columbia: in fact, neither SDS nor the masses of students actually were ready; we were spurred on by a tremendous push from history, if you will, embodied in the militant black students at Columbia.

Before April 23, the Students' Afro-American Society and Columbia SDS had never joined together in a joint action or even held much cross-group communication. SAS had been mostly a cultural or social organization, in part reflecting the class background of its members (SDS' position on campus likewise reflected its members' middle-class background—the tendency toward over-verbalization instead of action, the reliance on militant, pure, revolutionary rhetoric instead of linking up with people).

It was only with the death of Martin Luther King SAS began to make political demands—though still mostly about the situation of black students at Columbia. Another important factor in the growing militancy of SAS was the struggle of the Harlem community against Columbia's gym in the form of demonstrations, rallies, and a statement by H. Rap Brown that the gym should be burned down if it somehow was built.

The push to the whites and Columbia SDS I spoke of came in its first form from the assassination of Martin Luther King, which spurred SDS on to greater militancy. Secondly, and more immediately, was the speech at the sundial at noon April 23, by Cicero Wilson, chairman of SAS, at which we were honkey-baited, but also at which people developed the anger and the will to engage in direct action—i.e., tearing down the fence at the gym site. This one symbolic act opened the floodgate of anger and strength and resolve against the racism and pro-war policies of the university, and set the stage for the occupation of Hamilton which followed.

The pivotal event of the strike, however, was the black students' decision to barricade Hamilton Hall the night after the joint occupation began. In this decision, the blacks defined themselves politically as members of the Harlem community and the black nation who would fight Columbia's racism to the end. It was also this action that gave the whites a model for militancy and, on a broader scale, forced the whites to wake up to the real world outside themselves.

At the time that the black students in Hamilton Hall announced they were going to barricade the building, SDS' goal was the same as it has always been—to radicalize and politicize the mass of white students at Columbia and to create a radical political force of students. This self-definition, however, led to the conclusion that we did not want to risk alienating the mass of other white students by confronting them, say, from behind a barricade. Part of our decision not to barricade must also be seen as a remnant of the earlier timid and nonstruggle attitudes so common in the chapter.

The blacks, for their part, had decided that they would make a stand alone, as a self-conscious black group. This decision was also prompted undoubtedly by the lack of militancy on the part of the whites in Hamilton and especially our lack of discipline and organization.

After leaving Hamilton, a change came over the mass of white students, in and out of SDS. People stayed in Low Library "because we can't abandon the blacks." Not only did people see the model for militancy in the black occupation of Hamilton, but they also began to perceive reality—a world outside themselves—and the necessity to fight, to struggle for liberation, because of the situation in that world.

It was the action of the black students at Columbia—a group outside the individual fragmented "middle-class" students at Columbia—that woke up these students to the fact that there is a world of suffering, brutalized, exploited people, and that these people are a force willing to fight for freedom. Especially important to this realization was the power of Harlem, both manifest and dormant. Now the liberal universe—the isolated self—was shattered, and the mass occupation started by a handful of whites, the 23 who stayed in Low, grew to be the natural response of well over 1,000 people who wanted to fight back against the oppression of blacks, Vietnamese and themselves.

From another point of view, the militancy of the SDS whites forced others to reconsider their position and eventually to join the occupation. But the SDS occupation itself hinged on that of the blacks, and the overwhelming presence of the black students and Harlem itself forced us to keep the image of the real world clear and bright in our minds. Because of the blacks, we recognized the immediacy and necessity of the struggle: Vietnam is far away, unfortunately, for most people, and our own pain has become diffuse and dull.

This point about the example and vanguard role of whites vis-à-vis other whites must also be stressed. When neutral or liberal or even right-wing students see other students, very much like themselves, risking careers, imprisonment, and physical safety, they begin to question the political reasons for which the vanguard is acting, and, concomitantly, their own position. Here, education and propaganda is essential to get out to people the issues, and also the rationale for action. At no time is "organizing" or "talk" more important as before, during and after militant action.

One of the reasons why people joined en masse was the fact that white students, with the same malaise, alienation, unhappiness about this society and their lack of options in it, and the same hatred for the war and racism, saw a way to strike back at the enemy in the actions begun by a few. This was the same enemy, the ruling class and their representatives, the Board of Trustees of Columbia, that had been oppressing blacks and Vietnamese. So, with a little class analysis, articulated by SDS, hundreds of whites saw how they had to move for their own liberation as well as that of others.

This is not to deny the importance of black militancy, but only to emphasize the complex and dialectical relationships existing between blacks, white militants, and "the base." In struggle after struggle on campuses and in shops, the blacks have been taking the initial and even vanguard role. San Francisco State, where the direction and militancy of the struggle has been given by the Black Students' Union and the Third World Liberation Front, is the best example of the most oppressed taking the vanguard.

Kent State in Ohio, Brandeis, the high school students' strike in New York City, and numerous other cases, similarly show the importance of black vanguards. This is not an empirical fact peculiar only to schools, but in shops and in the army, too, blacks have been taking the lead and whites following—e.g., the Dodge Revolutionary Union Movement, which gave rise to a white insurgent caucus in the UAW, and the Fort Hood 43.

The implication of the primacy of the black movement is not that whites should sit back and wait for blacks to make the revolution. It is, rather, that we should study and understand the roots, necessity of, and strategy of the black liberation movement in order to understand how our movement should go.

At Columbia, our understanding of the dynamics at work was at best intuitive: we knew that whites and blacks had to organize their own, but we didn't know how this worked in practice—separate tactics, separate organization. At some schools, such as Kent and San Francisco State, the white militants did as well or better than we to the extent that they were conscious of their own role in relation to black militants.

This question "in relation to" has at least two clearly different pitfalls. First, because of the intensive and all-pervading racism in the United States, white radicals are sometimes unwilling to follow black leadership. . . .

The second pitfall "in relation to" the black movement is a passivity based on the opposite side of the traditional white leadership syndrome. Blacks are often unwilling to take the leadership or vanguard position in a struggle, having had white leadership thrust on them for so long, or else feeling isolated (as they, in fact, are at many white schools), or else having assimilated traditional middle-class values of success.

White radicals at many places feel that blacks must initiate anti-racism struggles, and that they will follow in support. The origin of this feeling is both the desire to see blacks taking leadership positions, a good thing, and also the attitude that racism is a "black problem" and cannot be raised legitimately by whites as a "white issue."

But any anti-capitalist or "revolutionary" program must fight in the interests of the most oppressed—the blacks and the Vietnamese—as well as in the interests of the working class in general. Thus our movement must be consciously anti-racist if it is ever to advance beyond short-term self-interest or economism or reformism or any of the myriad other liberal errors.

Racism must become a conscious "white problem," and must be fought at every point. This was our belief at Columbia, when Columbia SDS took independent action against the administration for its racism by disrupting the Martin Luther King Memorial service. The black students did not take part in this disruption, but the disruption did help shock SAS into action, along with other factors, especially the demonstrations of the Harlem community against Columbia.

Similarly, at Kent State in Ohio, the demonstrations against the Oakland Pig Department recruiters, as anti-racist demonstrations, were initiated by the white SDS chapter and picked up by the black students. At both Kent and Columbia, the black students then went on to take dominant and even decisive roles.

At school after school, white radicals are waiting for black students to take the lead. Since racism must be combated, they are in error in not taking the initiative, giving both black students and the mass of whites the impetus to carry the struggle forward. They must also, however, know when to follow the lead of blacks, and when to work parallel. At Columbia, inadvertently sometimes, we did all three.

One of the things we learned at Columbia is that the old SDS dictum, "People have to be organized around the issues that affect their lives," is really true. Not in the way it has always been meant, i.e., student-interest-type demands like dorm rules, bookstores, decisions over tenure, etc., but in the broadest, most political sense.

That is to say, that racism and imperialism really are issues that affect people's lives. And it was these things that people moved on, not dorm rules, or democratizing university governance or any of that bullshit.

The general public, and the movement in more subtle ways, have been subjected to a barrage of propaganda trying to show conclusively that the rebellion at Columbia (as well as other rebellions) was due to campus unrest over archaic administrative procedures, lack of democracy in decision-making, and, above all, an immense failure of communication among students, faculty and administration. It is unnecessary to document this beyond referring the reader to any article about Columbia in *Time* magazine.

In general, the Left itself has understood the primacy of revolutionary anti-imperialist politics present in the core of the rebellion, but few have had access to our arguments concerning student power and "restructuring" of the university, and thus many have believed either 1) We admitted the necessity for reform and at least partially worked toward it; or 2) The failure of the movement this fall was due to the failure of Columbia SDS to respond to the mass movement for restructure and reform. In other words, we were co-opted by the new liberal administration and Students for a Restructured University. Neither is the case.

Every militant in the buildings knew that he was there because of his opposition to racism and imperialism and the capitalist system that needs to exploit and oppress human beings from Vietnam to Harlem to Columbia. It was no accident that we hung up pictures of Karl Marx and Malcolm X and Che Guevara and flew red flags from the tops of two buildings. But there was some confusion over our position toward the university itself.

We were engaged in a struggle that had implications far beyond the boundaries of the campus on Morningside Heights—and, in fact, our interest was there, outside the university. We did want to stop the university's exploitative, racist and pro-imperialist policies, but what more? This unsurety over program toward the university reflected a political confusion that only became solved as the radicals discussed more among themselves and were faced with a greater number of self-appointed liberal reformers who wanted to "save the university."

Given that the capitalist university serves the function of production of technology, ideology, and personnel for business, government, and military (we had hit at these functions in our exposure of IDA and expansion), the question of "saving" the university implies capitulation to the liberal mythology about free and open inquiry at a university and its value-neutrality.

Whatever "good" function the university serves is what the radical students can cull from its bones—especially the creation and expansion of a revolutionary movement. The university should be used as a place from which to launch radical struggles—anything less now constitutes a passive capitulation to social democracy and reformism, whatever the intention of the radicals involved.

This position on the university leads to a clear position on "restructuring." It is irrelevant. Tremendous pressure on the coalition strike committee was brought by liberals who proclaimed the creation of a "new, just, democratic Columbia University" as their goal. Professing revolution as another one of their goals, they saw reform of the university as one of the many "steps" toward revolution. Behind this conception, of course, was the traditional liberal view of reform of institutions, one by one, which would through evolution lead to enough humanistic reform, somehow called revolution. Also present was a healthy fear of both the personal and social effects of struggle.

Demands about democratizing the university are *procedural*—a form which of necessity will be empty and early co-opted by an extraordinarily powerful ruling class and its representatives, the Board of Trustees and administration. What we are after is *substantive* change—such as was embodied in the six demands, and especially the demands on IDA and the gym. This is where our fight for power is located. . . .

We see the goal of the student movement not as the creation of an eventual power base, involving all students around all their concerns, radical and otherwise, which is a very old conception of what we're up to, but rather, building a radical force which raises issues for other constituencies—young people, workers, others—which will eventually be picked up on to create a broader, solider revolutionary movement.

Since the working class will be the agency of change, it is these people who must be addressed by any action initiated by students. This is very different from "creating alliances." It means the entire

110 Student Power, Participation and Revolution

content of our movement must be radical—i.e., anti-imperialist, anti-capitalist—not concerned with the parochial, privileged needs of students. This use of the student movement as a critical force is exactly what began to happen at Columbia—no power base was carved out; rather, good, solid radical issues were raised for the community, the city, and, in fact, the entire nation. To the extent that our issues lacked a focus and a target outside students, they were not consciously "revolutionary."

After the police bust which cleared over 1,000 people from five buildings, the rebellion faced a critical turning point. The mass of students, faculty, community people and others demanded spontaneously a strike against classes, shutting down the university. But the political basis for this strike—its demands, tactics and organization—were still unclear. Radicals wanted the strike to maintain the original six demands, as a means of keeping the political focus on racism and imperialism, while liberals pushed for as broad a strike as possible—"You've got a good thing here, don't blow it, everyone's with you, but don't force your politics onto people" was a typical liberal remark.

The real danger despite the chorus of liberal warnings, was in watering down the politics and the tactics of the strike. This the radical strike committee knew (this was the same strike committee that had been established during the liberation of the buildings, with two representatives from each building), and yet the result of the expansion of the strike committee, even with the politics of the six demands, was the eventual weakening and loss of mass base which occurred in the weeks after the bust.

In brief, the story of the expansion of the strike committee is as follows. The original committee called for a mass meeting for Wednesday night, the day following the bust. This meeting was attended by over 1,300 people, all vigorously anti-administration, and most of whom were ready to follow radical leadership. At that meeting, the strike committee proposed a two-part resolution:

1) Expand the strike committee to include representatives of any new constituency groups to form on the basis of 1 rep to 70 members. Groups could join if they supported the original six demands.

2) Restart the university under our own auspices by run-

ning liberated courses, and eventually establishing a provisional administration.

Debate centered around the question of requirements for joining the strike committee: the radicals thought it was absolutely necessary in order to maintain some political coherence, while the liberals, centered around the graduate-faculties student council grouping, wanted, as usual, the broadest base possible and no requirements. A full description of the political and psychological vicissitudes of this meeting is given by Eric Mann in his article, but in brief, through a misunderstanding, I capitulated the strike committee position to the liberal one, establishing an apolitical strike committee.

This error in itself did not have to be fatal; nor was it, since the radicals did go out and organize like hell the next day, both in the constituent groups which were being formed and in the new strike committee itself. The new committee passed almost unanimously the six demands, plus a seventh on being able to participate in restructuring, so it looked to us (the radicals) that we had "reinjected" politics back into the committee. One good aspect of the error, which should not be underestimated, was that the liberals were prevented from organizing themselves into an opposition for two whole weeks. They had had plans to walk out of the original meeting described above and form a rump strike committee, but those plans were blocked by my "co-optation."

The failure to deepen and expand the radical base which had formed during the occupation of the buildings, however, lay at the root of our problems. Instead of maintaining the communes as the bodies with effective power, they became only the left wing which sent delegates to a coalition strike committee organized much like a student council. Not only political sharpness, but also the militancy which defined our strike by struggle was lost.

The people in the buildings had fought. Many were new to the radical movement, many were just learning—this was a time of openness, of new experiences and life-situations. If ever the phrase "practice outran theory" was true, this was such a time. People seizing buildings, yelling "Up Against the Wall, Motherfucker," fighting cops, committing their lives and careers to a movement for liberation—this was all new and unexplained in political terms. During the liberation of the buildings, too, the frantic pace had kept discussion on too much of a tactical level (should we barricade?, should we negotiate with the cops?), often focused away from the broader questions that would tell people why, where this is all going, how it fits into a broader, world-wide struggle. . . .

The confusion over the radical position on the university, and the function of a student movement in building a revolutionary movement has begun to be cleared up by the Revolutionary Youth Movement proposal passed by the Ann Arbor Winter NC. The ideas in this resolution have not been completely clarified in SDS, but the departure from both student-movement-in-itself and also worker-student alliance politics is clear to most. This proposal is, in a sense, the ideological successor to Columbia.

The victories of the Columbia struggle, however, were great. It was the most sustained and most intense radical campus struggle up to that time, around the clearest politics.

At a time when the radical movement was the most disheartened and dispirited due to the gains of McCarthy, the Columbia rebellion broke through the gloom as an example of the power a radical movement could attain. It is no coincidence that the McCarthy movement at Columbia, starting off with over 600 members the first day, has never been able to revive after the rebellion of the spring. Liberal politics were exposed as just so much shallow verbiage and wasted effort when compared to the power of a mass radical movement, around significant issues such as racism and imperialism. The radical "base," for the first time ever at one campus, attained a number in the thousands.

At Columbia, our two principle demands, the ending of construction on the gym in Morningside Park, and the formal severing of ties with the Institute for Defense Analyses, were, in fact, met. This laid the basis for broadening the demands this fall to ending all defense and government research and stopping all university expansion into the community.

Perhaps the most important result of the rebellion, in terms of long-term strategy for the movement, was the creation of new alliances with student, nonstudent, community and working-class groups throughout the city. A chapter that had been mostly inward-looking and campus oriented suddenly opened up and began to realize the tremendous importance of the various types of hookups—

support, tactical alliance, coalition—which would broaden the radical movement beyond its white "middle-class" student base.

First of all was the tactical alliance with the black students in Hamilton Hall, sometimes close, sometimes more distant, but always working parallel toward the same goal. This was described at the beginning of this article, but it's worthwhile reiterating the tremendous importance of the experience as a model for the different types of relationships possible with militant black students.

Backing up the black students as a source of power, and to some extent behind the whites as well, was the Harlem community, sometimes mobilized, sometimes lying in wait. This force proved not only the greatest single deterrent to a police bust, but also provided *all* demonstrating students with support in the form of mass rallies and demonstrations, manpower, money, food donations and morale boosting. Black high school students sparked the militants in Fayerweather Hall, then returned to their own schools and within two weeks had created the most militant high school anti-racist strikes New York City has seen in recent times. A Strike Committee member spoke at a rally at 7th Avenue and 125th Street in Central Harlem, the first white person to do so in anyone's memory. After the rebellion, the relationship between N.Y. SDS and N.Y. Black Panther Party has grown increasingly closer.

As a result of the liberation of the buildings, anti-Columbia organizing activity in the mostly white Morningside Heights neighborhood revived to an all-time high. The Community Action Committee, organized completely by community residents, provided support to the students in the form of demonstration and even a rent strike of tenants in Columbia's tenements. On May 14, the CAC liberated an apartment in a tenement on 114th St. in an effort to dramatize the decimation of the community by Columbia's racist expansionist policies. The CAC led numerous actions over the summer, all working closely with students at the Liberation School. The work of the CAC was not all a bed of roses, problems developed over the fact that the organizers were mostly middle-class young people who were estranged from both white working-class residents who were threatened and the middle-class residents whose buildings were not in jeopardy.

As a direct result of the strike, cafeteria workers, mostly Spanish-speaking, ended their 30-year battle with Columbia, one of the most repressive employers in the city, with the formation of a local of Local 1199 of the Drug and Hospital Workers' Union, one of the few anti-war unions in New York City. Student organizers, all SDS members, did most of the work for Local 1199, and red-baiting by the bosses was effectively turned against Columbia since the workers knew the students would be on their side if the union was denied.

Internal changes in the chapter took the form of the wealth of experience absorbed by hundreds of individuals. It is almost a truism at this point to cite the incredible changes in consciousness that took place through the action ("Revolution is the best education for honorable men"—Che). The rebellion trained new leaders, some of whom have left Columbia to provide other local movements with leadership.

Our strength was greatest at the time of our greatest militancy. It was also the time that we resolved to fight—to disregard all the liberal Cassandras warning us of the horrors of the police bust and the right-wing reaction. In a sense it was a time when we overcame our own middle-class timidity and fear of violence. We, of course, were following the lead of the blacks, but we were also forging new paths where elite white students had never been before. At that time nothing could defeat us, not the police, not the jocks, not the liberal faculty, so treacherous and yet so important, only our own (we found out later) weakness and bad political judgment. The liberal world was paralyzed; radicals had a vision of what victory seems like.

Of course we made mistakes, dozens of them. At the lowest points, feeling that the movement itself had erred in irreconcilable ways (such as leaving Hamilton Hall, which we at that time did not understand as inevitable and even a source of strength), we found the strength to go on in the knowledge that somehow history was carrying us forward. Also important was the observation that after making 43 mistakes, 44 wouldn't make any difference, so we threw ourselves into the next crisis.

Above all, we learned almost accidentally the great truth stated by Chairman Mao Tse-tung, "Dare to struggle, dare to win."

PART IV

DIFFUSION: *RADICAL*

CONSCIOUSNESS AND ACTION

> *you never*
> *think of death*
> *until your children*
> *have been dragged off*
> *to war* *

PERHAPS it has been the war in Vietnam more than any other single factor that has led to the rapid diffusion of the impact of the student movement to the high schools, graduate schools and professions. It offers something for every kind of radical—from the ideologically sophisticated veteran of multiple confrontations to the irate fourteen-year-old whose brother has just been busted for obstructing an Army recruiter. It is the epitome of American militarism and a colonial mentality from which we seem unable to extricate ourselves. Racism is evident both in the treatment of black soldiers and in the racial inferiority with which many Americans view the enemy. No land in the history of the world has been

* From a poem by Roger Tazwell, "This Can't be the Way," *Chicory,* New York: Association Press, 1969, p. 27.

so impoverished, ravaged as totally as Vietnam. The war has consumed the resources necessary to even begin a *real* war on poverty in America. The unparalleled horrors wrought by our modern weapons of destruction will be carried in the conscience of this generation of young people. From this perspective, "Hell no, we won't go!" seems a modest proposal. Clearly high school students facing the draft (or with friends and brothers facing the draft) are ready to listen to information about what kind of a government it is, what kind of society it is, that can force young people to fight in this most unpopular war.

Beyond the war itself, the criticisms of an educational system that supports militarism, racism and poverty have reached receptive ears among high school (and junior high) students. Still, most have continued to look for evidence of the democratic processes, equal opportunity, and justice in their own schools and community. But like the collegians before them, they have come away frustrated, disappointed and angry. Our ideals, they find, are honored mostly in the breach. Older dissenters have been quick to capitalize on this profound disenchantment.

For the "aging" radicals who are completing (or have completed) college, the prospects for a productive and happy life appear similarly dim. They see the cities as well as the entire physical environment being destroyed by greed and avarice. These dissidents view material success which offers no accompanying interpersonal warmth and sharing as destructive of the human spirit. So they have set out to rebuild old realities and create some new ones. In the graduate schools and in a broad range of occupations, the activists have sought to establish new bases of power and mutual support for each other. As it reaches beyond the colleges, the student movement is more and more an enterprise aimed at the creation of a new and very different society.

Les Coleman of SDS sounds one of the keynotes by describing the building of an action program around specific grievances of high school students. Following are two group interviews which bear vivid testimony to the ability of teen-agers to think through their own life situations and see clear implications for direct action. The "Mission Rebellion," originally an offshoot of the strike at San Francisco State, quickly developed a character of the high school students' own making.

A group of social work students offer a statement which is but a small indication of the enormous pressures being built up within a wide spectrum of graduate schools for more relevance to the external environment and sweeping reform within. The end of this trend is not yet in sight. Finally a piece about the Radical Education Project explores a novel program for maintaining and building a radical consciousness, a new Left, throughout all segments of American life.

16

Les Coleman

The Schools Must Serve the People * (*1969*)

We live within a monster—a monster of imperialism and racism that necessitates war, permanent militarization, the subjugation of women, the brutal oppression of the people of color of the world, and the inhuman exploitation of all working people. The cause of this monster is the class and colonial structure of the empire: the majority of people are maintained producing wealth they never share in and the nations of the third world bear the constant oppression and colonization of the white oppressor nation—U.S. imperialism. Within this country there exist both class and colonial divisions—class divisions exploit working people of all colors and colonial divisions are at the basis of the special oppression of black and brown sectors of the population. It is this class and colonial basis of the system that we must challenge.

Schools Maintain Class Structure

The whole education system now—from grade schools on up—is used to tie the allegiance of youth to the capitalist system by building an ideological army for the ruling class. It functions to maintain the class and colonial divisions in the society. SDS opposes this and

---

* Reprinted from *New Left Notes* (April 4, 1969, issue). Les Coleman was a student at Harvard.

takes its stand against the class and colonialist functions of the education system. Schools cannot be made to serve the people, or be prevented from serving the capitalist class, without a fight against that class. The capitalist class has never given up anything it needed to make the system function to their advantage unless they were forced to by the struggles of the people. This is still true today. The function of the education system cannot really be changed and the system made to serve the people, until the power of the whole capitalist class is challenged and destroyed. What we present here, in the following ten-point program, is a summary of our general objective for the educational system. Our struggle to win these demands is only part of the whole class struggle unfolding in this country and throughout the world and must contribute to the fight to end the monster and the state power which maintains all its aspects of class and colonial domination.

Ten-Point Program

1. We demand an end to the track system in the schools. The track system, the classification of students into "different levels" of study by racist, anti-working-class tests and teachers, is nothing but a way of maintaining class and colonial divisions in the society. Consignment to the lower tracks is nothing but a ticket to the army and then to low-paying jobs or unemployment in the ghetto. This unjust consignment falls systematically on working-class youth and heaviest on black and brown youth. We are committed to fighting and exposing the more subtle and hidden forms of tracking throughout all the schools in every way we can.

2. We demand an end to flunkouts and disciplinary expulsions. We want all who have been flunked out or kicked out to be readmitted, because school standards and authorities which are responsible to the power structure in this country have no legitimate human right to judge the people. Flunkouts and expulsions are again systematically a way of maintaining working-class and especially black and brown youth as the fighting force and lowest-paid labor force in the society. We want an end also to the regimentation— the school behavior rules, the dress codes, the cut system—which is meant to keep us from challenging the kind of education the system sees fit for our indoctrination.

3. We demand the teaching of history and social conditions of the people in this country which exposes the true injustice of this racist capitalist society and the just struggles of colonized and exploited working people against injustice. We are more concerned that there be teachers who know peoples' history and know what is actually going on among the people than that we have teachers with fancy degrees. We demand an end to the political firing of teachers who do give us a true perspective.

4. We want the schools to directly serve the people where they now function like all corporations in this society to exploit and oppress the people. We demand that schools end cooperation with recruitment for those American corporations which rule and exploit the people, that they end the exploitation of surrounding communities through their control of real estate and urban renewal programs, and that they end the brutal and unhuman wage and working conditions oppression of school employees.

We support with the full power of our movement the struggles of the black community for control over their schools. This control is of primary necessity for the self-defense of the black people against the colonial nature of the day-to-day brutalization of their children in the schools. We must see our job as one to unite with the people and serve them in struggle. We must give this form of support of this just demand.

5. In all schools we call for the unlimited admission of black and brown students because we see that the special colonial oppression involved in their exclusions, and its acceptance by the majority of whites, is the foundation on which this corrupt system maintains itself.

6. We want decent truthful education paid for by the wealth of this country. Three percent of the population controls 90 percent of the wealth of this country, and yet the labor of the majority of the people is what makes the country run. If a man works for a wage all his life he should be guaranteed that his children will have an education paid for by the wealth he has helped to produce. Tuition increases tend to keep working people (especially black and brown people) from getting a decent education, and maintain the inequalities in the society. We demand free education and we oppose all tuition increases.

7. We call for an end to military recruitment in the schools, and

an end to training and research institutes that serve the American military, including the internal occupation force—the police. We don't want any more police in the schools; we want ROTC and police institutes stopped immediately. The permanent militarization of this country—having its effects on all aspects of American life—on employment, on women, especially on youth—has been accomplished only to protect an empire based on the exploitation and colonization of the laboring people of the world. This militarization, therefore, cannot be said to serve the people, since it maintains the main enemy of the people of this country and the whole world—American imperialism.

8. We want an end to all forms of male supremacy in the schools. This ranges from the male supremacist content of courses and perspectives of instructors to the way women are counseled or tracked into the worst jobs and the most submissive roles in the society. The inequality of women, perpetrated throughout the entire education system, is a principal division of the power of the people to get what they need in the whole country and the source of the misery of over half the population.

9. We want a real understanding of the movement of national liberation and of communist countries which the U.S. government has committed us to life or death opposition against. We believe that anti-communism has been preached to us in order to maintain our participation in and allegiance to an empire which benefits a very few and oppresses the people of the world. We want an end to these lies. We want courses taught accurately on Vietnam, Cuba and China. We want teachers who hold the point of view that wars like the war in Vietnam are fought, not in the interests of the American people, but in the interest of a small class of businessmen to maintain an unjust and inhuman empire.

10. We support the ten-point program of the Black Panther Party for BSA's on the campus. These demands, which summarize the struggle for survival and self-determination of the black people are just demands which this racist country has never supplied to black people. While some of the demands raised by the Panthers would be incorrect if raised by white students, the special colonial nature of black oppression makes demands for black self-determination and community autonomy a matter of survival for blacks and should be supported. The black liberation struggle, of which

the Black Panther Party is the true anti-capitalist leadership, is the struggle to which all working people must be won if the oppressor class is to be defeated.

Strategic Understanding of the Ten-Point Program

We must be clear about the nature of this program. We raise demands which are necessary for the survival of the people—just struggles which they are in fact fighting. We fight to win these struggles knowing that we will win some partial victories—resulting in concrete gains for the people and thereby winning their confidence—but that complete fulfillment of their demands requires the destruction of capitalism. We become a vanguard force when we educate the people that fulfillment of their demands requires a socialist revolution.

Our campus work has been marked by our failure to do extensive mass education. In most cases a small core in the chapter is responsible for the "analysis," and it does not get taken to the people except during periods of action where it is tacked onto the issue at hand—a firing, a suspension, a demand of the BSA—in an abstract way which the mass of the people do not grasp. Therefore, we must establish ourselves on the campus as fighting for a series of clear objectives and with general support for them before this or that action comes up.

Counterposed to these 10 points which challenge class and colonial privileges are the waves of so-called student power issues, which in content aim to maintain false class privilege. Demands for more participation for students in school administrative committees may simply mean that students want more power to maintain their false class privilege: the "privilege" to stay out of the army while working-class youth, especially black and brown youth, are forced to fight; their "privilege" of access to higher-paying jobs because of a meaningless college degree, and so on. While students may have been moved to student power fights in the past out of a genuine militancy and anger at the system, it is our task to draw the issues more sharply. The idea that students can be brought into a sustained struggle on a student power basis and then brought along to fight against the class and colonial nature of the university has proved overall to be wrong. If students come into a struggle in the interests of accepting false class privilege they will not very quickly change to a struggle against that false privilege. The ones who will fight class privilege would have done so initially if the issues had been correctly stated.

The "student power" strategy of establishing joint student-faculty-administration committees never gets us anywhere and creates the illusion of power which prevents us from building a movement. Because the schools oppress all the people, they must be made to serve the people, not just the students. Our principles should be clear! We don't demand power, we demand what we want and need and what is just and we show our real power in getting it. Our real power is to refuse those who control the schools something they need. Since they need the schools to go on functioning—serving as corporate enterprises, service stations of imperialism, and perpetrating class and colonial divisions in the society—our power is to be able to keep the schools from functioning. If the schools won't give us what we justly demand, we will strike.

We do not say that the school should serve the students: we say that the schools should serve the people!

The key fight today is against white supremacy: this fight has been raised primarily by the black liberation movement, and for the most part still is. Because we incorrectly understand the nature of this fight we have sometimes talked about adding "white" demands onto the demands of black groups and attacked black student demands as "middle-class" etc.

All the objectives in this program are both anti-colonial and anti-capitalist. Clearly not all these demands would be raised in the same struggle. There is no more need to raise "other" demands in the context of a struggle around demands raised by black or Third World students. There is not only not a need, it is often incorrect 1) because loading issues on a struggle is often opportunist, and 2) because it fosters the wrong idea that the demands of black people for self-determination and equality are not demands in the interests of all working-class people.

The black movement has a dual nature. Black people, kidnapped from their homeland and brought to this country, were the first victims of U.S. imperialism. Still, today, they are oppressed as a people, because they are black. Yet since the great majority of black people are workers, they are also an advanced component of U.S.

working-class struggles. The resistance of black people embodies elements of both external and internal confrontation with American imperialism. But both aspects of the black struggle are in the class interests of all working people, just as the struggle of the Vietnamese is in the class interest of all working people. Unless whites can be won to the support of black struggles in their national aspect, white national chauvinism—white support for the imperialist oppression of colored peoples—will not be overcome.

Finally, we see that as a revolutionary youth movement, we are fulfilling our revolutionary function in the schools through the ten-point program. We are raising the class antagonisms in the society. We are trying to articulate the just class and anti-colonial demands of the youth in the schools and of the people that these schools exploit and oppress in the immediate school community and throughout the empire. We are trying to use our strength to advance these demands, these aspects of the class struggle. At the same time, we must prepare the people for the necessity of revolution. We must make it clear at every juncture that the education system cannot be made to serve the people while the capitalist class maintains state power and that it is only a unified working class that can make this country belong to and serve the people.

17

The United Student Movement (*1969*)

The following interview appeared in the Penninsula Observer *(April 21, 1969). The United Student Movement is an organization of socialist high school students, most of whom attend Palo Alto ("Paly") or Cubberley high schools in California. Several students discussed the history and activities of USM.*

PHIL: In its formative stages (in early 1967) the USM was a very liberal, mild group.

RANDY: It was a lot of little girls. Then a couple of radicals came along, and we started the "period of activism" over the war. We handed out leaflets, organized people to go to the April 15th (1967) march in San Francisco. We did a vigil at the napalm plant in Redwood City. That was the period of activism; it was a good thing at the time. But we tried to do a free high school in the summer, which failed. It didn't correspond to objective reality at all. Who wants to go to school after school?

PHIL: That takes us to the beginning of the last school year (1967–68), when several USM people had begun to call themselves radicals. We considered ourselves SDS types, started a big student-power push at the high schools, got people elected to the student government at Cubberley on a student-power platform.

We thought Cubberley was going to collapse, we were going to win. We thought seriously of tactical plans for taking Cubberley, stuff like that. Then along came Oakland Stop the Draft Week (October 16–20, 1967).

JOHN: We came back from that, and lots of people got involved with USM. USM started at Paly High School that year.

PHIL: We had a rally during Stop the Draft Week at Paly that outdrew a football rally.

RANDY: That fall we had speakers come—Terry Cannon, David Ransom, Dave Harris. And people came, hundreds of people would come and listen. The school at that point had no real rules about that sort of thing; they just let it happen. For a while we had a lot of people. The meetings were in great big rooms and there were all these teen-agers and all these parents. But nothing happened.

PHIL: This was also the "period of anarchism" in the organization. There *was* leadership, but we believed in "anarchism." In fact, we weren't sure what we believed in.

RANDY: We figured any trouble we made was good trouble.

JOHN: We spent months trying to decide "What is the USM?" and "Who are we?"

RANDY: People kept passing out leaflets, and then they got suspended. We struggled with the free speech issue, but people said, "Forget it, I don't want to hear about it, make it go away, I want to get high."

JOHN: Then Paly had its own little ego trip, the "Day of Conscience" (against the war), last April 26th. It was supposed to be a student strike. At Cubberley it got smashed before it even started, but at Paly two girls were suspended for passing out leaflets. Ray Ruppel, the principal, made that blunder—it finally cost him his job—and sixty or seventy people went out on strike. We thought we were going to set up a high school for suspended students. We drew up a student bill of rights, passed out leaflets, collected a lot of money and so on.

The bill of rights disappeared into a "study committee," the kids went back to class, and we were all suspended for five days. Nothing really ever came out of the strike.

PHIL: This led us to realize that we had to have a concrete analysis of concrete conditions, a realistic idea of what we were trying to do and an analysis of the people we were trying to deal with.

JOHN: What happened was some of us started reading, expanding our awareness, realizing the relationships—who was oppressed and who did the oppressing and why. Well, we refounded the USM, got a sponsor, kicked him out a week later.

PHIL: We set up a cell system and study groups. We tried to get lots of people into the cells far too rapidly, without making any ideological agreements. It just collapsed. But our statement of principles came about as a result of the cell system failing.

JOHN: By that time a lot of people had become convinced that the power elite in the U.S. could not be "voted out of power," but had to be forced out of power. People emerged from an infatuation with McCarthy to an understanding of how Vietnam, economic oppression at home, and student oppression tied together.

PHIL: So we started trying to set up collectives in each school, and started the newspaper, *Serve the People*.

OBSERVER: What is it like to be a high school revolutionary? Are you isolated? Do you get hassled much?

PHIL: Any revolutionary in this society feels isolated.

JOHN: People can talk to me about other things than the fact that I'm a "socialist" or "radical." I'm friends with a lot of people who aren't. I tend to merge pretty well with the masses. I haven't got too much of an identity problem. But the pigs at school are hassling all the time, suspending people for being radicals. They don't exactly want to kick you out, they want to save you.

PHIL: They want to get you in line.

RANDY: In extreme cases they just don't want you to be in contact with anyone else. They define you as sick, want you to leave everyone else alone. They try to minimize your influence over "their" student body. The high schools accuse outside agitators of doing all this stuff.

JOHN: Millar, Paly principal, is a liberal. He passed around a circular to all the teachers saying "We don't think the paper *(Serve the People)* is going to make instant communists or instant revolutionaries. Here we have a textbook case, here's what a certain section of our student body thinks. We should study this as an object lesson, to encourage dissent." But then the thing on Don

Guidoux came out, the pig-page thing, and they confiscated our papers.*

RANDY: But you can use the administration's free speech claim against it. You can say, "They have a statement of principles themselves, higher education and all that crap. Okay, we'll have speakers saying resist the draft, have a demonstration, so on." Then all of a sudden the school says "This organization, they're communists and they're running amok and there's a law against this sort of activity in our schools, and there are outside people, of course, controlling it, and they are trying to subvert our whole school system." Then they smash you. Then it becomes an issue that you don't really have free speech. You'll never win that, you'll never get free speech, but you can make people in high school realize that it's a fraud.

OBSERVER: Then what?

RANDY: Hopefully, they'll become more aware, learn more, become aware of the radical perspective, that there is something wrong here.

JOHN: Eventually they will do what we've done. We all went through all of this. In the Palo Alto high schools most people are going to go on to college and become what their class position dictates—middle class. But a growing number are going to be sifted out along the way, maybe five percent are going to drop out of college. Some will become hippies, but there's going to be a certain number who fall out and become revolutionaries.

OBSERVER: Who is going to make the revolution?

PHIL: Your friends are the working class and the lumpen. They have to be your friends, or you aren't going to have a revolution in this country. They have to be made revolutionary. In the last analysis the working class is going to make the revolution, led by the black working class. Also the petty bourgeoisie, the new working class, some elements of that.

RANDY: Some of our best friends are also in other countries, the oppressed people of other countries. They are going to rise up first and weaken America until conditions will be much better

* The second issue of *Serve the People* was confiscated by high school authorities, reportedly because of a feature awarding the "J. Edgar Hoover Law and Order Memorial Award" to Paly's new Dean of Men, Don "Quack" Guidoux.—Ed. note

for organizing proletarian workers. That's happening right now in Vietnam, in Bolivia. It happened in Cuba.

OBSERVER: The USM believes external pressures will bring about the revolution in America?

PHIL: At this point the major contradiction in the world is not between the proletariat and the bourgeoisie but between the imperialist countries and the undeveloped countries. In the imperialist countries the contradictions are going to increase—the economy is going to collapse. At some point there will be another depression. Much can be learned from the Chinese revolution. You have to realize we are not all good, and everyone else isn't all bad. There are good communists and good people who aren't in the party. That's the whole concept of mass line—merging with the people and serving the people.

OBSERVER: How do you apply the philosophy of Mao Tse-tung?

PHIL: In the course of the USM we have learned a whole lot from Mao's written accounts of problems within the party and how to solve them. Criticism and self-criticism, the concept of where correct ideas come from, the whole idea of merging with the people and conducting mass line, these are things that we try to apply. For example, criticism and self-criticism—we've had several quarrels within the organization, our method was always to have criticism sessions.

JOHN: In the newspaper, for instance, we try to apply mass line, like having Lyndon Johnson on the cover was basically a mass line thing and so was the pig page, the Guidoux thing.

OBSERVER: What are the real needs of high school students?

JOHN: It's a very difficult situation, because we are not dealing with people who are going to make the revolution. We're dealing with kids who have no economic problems. There are very few ways you can relate them to oppression. Lytton Plaza was an extremely successful mass-line thing. The people needed a dance on Friday night. The real need of the people is a coffeeshop. Things like that are very successful mass line. We've had some unsuccessful experiences. And there are things which are not mass line, like putting out a leaflet telling people to go to Richmond to the oil strike—you get twenty or thirty.

OBSERVER: The people you want to work with, the proletariat, think socialists, and even reformist socialists, are crazy. How do you deal with that?

PHIL: The only way you can deal with that is through practice. As Mao says, you don't just sit back and write a book on "here's how we deal with the working class." You do it by working with the limited understanding you have, and in the course of your work you'll develop it.

JOHN: In the limited working-class experience we have, we found the working class is very revolutionary—I mean the oil strikers. We went there hoping the workers would accept us, would like us. And Jake Jacobs made a speech saying, "We see that the students are revolutionary, and we are willing to fight with you." That's a very important thing—the fact that students and workers were able to feel a sense of comradeship after the alienation and intellectual chauvinism that goes on among students. I think that Richmond was a historic thing, the first time that I know of that students and workers have gotten together in a common struggle.

RANDY: We need some whole new theories for America.

PHIL: They'll have to deal with how you build the revolution, that's the only important thing at this point. How you seize state power, how you get the people behind you in America.

OBSERVER: What are your expectations for yourselves?

JOHN: We'll probably get killed off in the unsuccessful insurrection.

PHIL: I think we'll see fascism before we see the revolution. I think it's inevitable.

JOHN: The best thing for this country as far as the ruling class is concerned would have been if Gene McCarthy and people of his sort maintained power. But they're not going to. Liberalism is the best way to smash revolution. People like Gene see that, but they are losing out to the reactionary elements, and they are going to continue losing out, because people aren't going to take any bullshit. People used to believe the liberals that students were really interested, all aroused. But they don't believe that anymore because they see students smashing windows day after day, creating destruction. Obviously it's a direct threat to them and they are going to try to smash students. The only logical thing for them to do now is to turn reactionary and authoritarian and smash dissent.

OBSERVER: What is going to happen to you?

RANDY: We'll probably look like we've lost, we'll probably be smashed. But we'll still be there, we'll build up an organization and eventually win.

PHIL: That's why we have to build a disciplined organization, so we can survive things like that. In the end either we win, or the world ends. Either we win, or there's an atomic war. I don't see any real alternative.

OBSERVER: What about popular-front tactics, uniting with liberals?

JOHN: You have to do two things—you have to put forward the correct line, but you can't be elitist. You can't put down everybody who's not a Marxist-Leninist. That's the most stupid thing you can do. If there's an issue that needs to be fought, you're willing to unite with the Midpeninsula Free University, for example. We did that last time, at Lytton Plaza. We'll do it again.

OBSERVER: What do you have to say to activists in other high schools?

JEAN: Beware of liberals.

RANDY: Essentially, the people you have to spend all your time with—arguing with, fighting with, hassling with, and organizing —are the students. Not the teachers, not the administration, not the school board, and not, goddamn it, your parents. That's the most important thing we learned in the Cubberley strike. We thought for a brief moment that our parents were our friends. Of course, in the end they were the worst enemies we had.

JOHN: That's not excusable, by the way. That's an error in the strike that should not have happened, because it had already happened in the Paly strike last year.

RANDY: It happened from this one meeting, when we were all suspended. One mass meeting was taken up entirely by the parents one by one getting up there and smashing the administration. We thought for a while, "God, our parents are good." But as the discussion came closer to the end, it became evident that our parents wanted us back at school that Wednesday—forget the strike, forget the issues, forget everything. The only reason they allowed us to get suspended was because we didn't ask them. If we'd asked them about the strike, or asked their opinion, or asked them anything, we'd have been sold out long before. So don't even hassle with them. Ignore them, go around them. And talk with students—that is where the time should be spent.

JEAN: About half the striking students are still saying, "Wow, our parents were really great."

PHIL: It's very important to beware of liberal teachers.

JOHN: And beware of wreckers in your organization. People who want to express moral indignation. Those people have to be lanced, like a boil, you know.

PHIL: You have to develop leaders in each school. You have to gather together the active element into a collective.

JOHN: One way is to hammer out a statement of principles.

PHIL: It's important for the active nucleus of people who are revolutionaries—or who are willing to become revolutionaries—to gather together. At the same time, it's equally important for those people to go out to the rest of the people.

JOHN: You have to avoid elitism. The people, the students, don't like it. We have a lot of opposition to the USM in the schools because the students have a picture of what we were last year— essentially about five or six people who *were* the USM.

PHIL: One goes with the other. If you don't bring together the leadership, and have a collective and practice criticism and self-criticism, that engenders elitism. You think you are being non-elitist by practicing the SDS style of organization: the person who does the work makes the decision, or organization, just bullshit. In reality what happens then is that you have an unconscious leadership, a leadership that develops but isn't really conscious of itself. Doesn't really try to overcome the problems it has with leadership. Doesn't try to apply mass line. In reality that is more elitist than gathering people together in a closed collective so that you can analyze your experience and then go back to the people.

OBSERVER: And when the collective has been formed?

JOHN: You do what we are doing right now. You set yourself the task of siphoning off as many of the disenchanted students as possible. You form study groups, put out newspapers with a scientific analysis, organize activities during which you are constantly expounding the correct line. Gain people that way—people become interested during the struggle, come into the organization.

OBSERVER: What issues do you work on?

JOHN: It's hard to say, because we know that reformist issues are pointless, but it's necessary.

PHIL: You seize on any issue, basically. Rely on splits in the administration, like the thing at Paly. They threw out Ray Ruppel after the strike and got George Millar. If they had brought Ray Ruppel back, there would have been a big mass movement, because everybody hated the guy and wanted Millar. Exploit any split within the enemy, any issue.

RANDY: Make sure it's sound.

OBSERVER: How would you use that issue—the principals?

PHIL: That's united front with liberals. You have the demand for the liberal principal. You say: "We think Millar is bad, we think Ruppel is bad, but we think the *people* have a right to decide who the principal is going to be." So at the same time you put forward a concrete analysis and apply mass line.

JOHN: But it depends on the type of high school. You *know* when the issue comes—it just is there.

RANDY: The thing is to get on your feet as fast as you can at the beginning of the school year.

JOHN: Next year there will be a USM again. There are people coming in who will be interested.

18

We're Not Grinning Anymore * (*1969*)

Karen Butler, Naomi Carnes and Jackie Glover, seniors at Taft High School in the Bronx, New York, were interviewed by Julius Lester over Radio WBAI in New York (February, March, 1969).

LESTER: *What is it like at Taft High School?*

KAREN: Well first of all I'd like to say that there is no outward atmosphere of racial tension at Taft. It's all covered. Blacks and whites seem to get along. But I find that if we do get involved in very serious discussions—nothing so ridiculous as should whites hate blacks or blacks hate whites, but really deep down discussions about self-determination for black people—you will find large differences between the blacks and the whites.

LESTER: *Can you give me a specific example?*

NAOMI: Oh yes. I had a run-in with a teacher when he realized that I was in support of some black militant students who had published a black theology. He was very surprised that I was in support of them. He said: "I've never felt any animosity from you. How can you back up what these fellows have to say?" I answered: "It's very simple. We're all black. We all have the same situation. We all have the same goals. We might not all be

* Reprinted by permission of *Leviathan* (June, 1969).

following the same route, but we intend on getting to the same place. So we must present a united front."

I found the same attitude in many of the teachers after the UFT strike. They are constantly trying to cut me off from the rest of the black students by telling me: "Naomi, you're an intelligent student, and you want to go to college." I say: "This is very true. And I'm also a black student; what does that have to do with it?" There's always this kind of undertone, you know. You always feel like you're being plucked—like a petal from a flower. And that's what's happening.

JACKIE: Everything was fine before the strike. But once they were on the picket line, we could see what was going on. We saw hatred in the teachers' eyes. We saw, we heard the threats that they gave to teachers who were not on that picket line. Like we had 10 teachers who came into the school and helped us open it. They told us they had been threatened; their time cards were destroyed; very malicious comments were made from the picket line. Now while I was out there I saw all this, so when I came back I had a different attitude altogether. When I came back the teacher said: "You don't smile any more." Now here I was out of school for 10 weeks because of the teachers' strike, and they want me to smile! There was nothing funny to me. And then they said: "Well, Jackie, your attitude has changed. You used to be a nice, sweet girl." I'm not sweet any more because I saw for the first time what was really going on in that school.

During the strike we set up classes; there were at least 200 kids. It was decided that we would set up our own library because the one upstairs was locked. Our whole thing was black awareness. We wrote a notice saying we would like to start this black library and students could borrow books. We urged all the kids to give books, stating that no black library would exist in Taft without the support of the students. (Now this was during the strike, mind you.) After the strike, the very next day, a teacher Xeroxed copies of this notice and put them into the teachers' mailboxes. She said there were black books in the library upstairs and we didn't need a special library. We said that wasn't the point.

KAREN: According to this teacher, the statement in our library notice charged that there was no black library now or that the

library would be destroyed. Later we met with librarians and
they didn't object to a black library. But one librarian did not
feel Leroi Jones was acceptable to a high school because he was
profane. This was ridiculous.

JACKIE: *Catcher in the Rye,* that's the most profane book out and
they have 32 copies in Taft's library. We said, all right, you
don't want Leroi Jones in your library—fine. That's why we
want our own library.

KAREN: The incidents after the strike went on and on. We'd like
to talk about one important one which has led to the expulsion
of one of our brothers, Ron Dix. According to the administration, it was for distributing "unauthorized literature." You could
say, well, why not get it authorized? But that is like being a
slave, going to the owner and saying, "Will you authorize this
leaflet calling for a rebellion tomorrow night?"

NAOMI: There were three students involved, Ron Dix, Jerry Hud-
son and Ronald Smith; they were specifically trying to promote
black awareness with their literature, contrary to whatever else
many students may have heard. Before Ron Dix was expelled
and before the three brothers resorted to printing their own literature, we held three meetings with the faculty and the principal to resolve the problem of "unauthorized literature." The
administration claims that literature unsigned by any teacher in
the school is "unauthorized." Yet you can walk down the halls
any day and have someone shove something into your hand
about a new discotheque, a dance, a track meet, about anything
at all. But as soon as the word *black* appears—boom—"unauthorized literature."

JACKIE: When the brothers passed out this flyer called "Dig It,"
about the extra 45 minutes of school, things really began rolling.
After it was brought up, the brothers admitted the flyer was
worded badly. The school wouldn't let it drop at that, claiming
it was anti-Semitic. The school sent them down to the B'nai
B'rith and the man there couldn't find anything anti-Semitic
about the literature. But the teachers insisted it was anti-Semitic.
All right. The brothers produced another leaflet. This one was
beautifully worded. It was given out. (As soon as we who are
considered militants start passing out anything, white students
run over faster than black students; they don't wait for you to

hand it to them.) So they started grabbing the leaflet and I watched one white fellow flip through it, see the word "Jew," and stop. He began reading a quote from the *New York Times* that said Jews control the New York City school system. That's all he read. It was after this leaflet that the trials began.

LESTER: *Who held the trials?*

NAOMI: The principal, administrative assistant—they had UFT teachers there—our Afro-American club adviser, and the guidance counselors and teachers who had had the three brothers in their classes. It really was a kangaroo trial. They started by saying the three brothers should be thrown out of school because of anti-Semitic literature, etc.

JACKIE: Now Ron, Jerry and Ronald had written the literature together, but they were going to be tried individually. The brothers said they wouldn't go in separately.

The main purpose of the trials was to scare them. They did it to another brother last year, brought him to trial. I don't know what they told him but he was scared enough to cut his hair and beard. But they couldn't scare Ron, Jerry and Ronald, so they threatened them with suspension. The brothers said, go ahead if you want to. But the school didn't, just then, they were afraid the community would go into an uproar if three brothers were suspended. What did happen was that the school called all types of students to a meeting: militants, the Student Organization, hippie groups. At the meeting one of the teachers said "We want to establish peaceful coexistence." Others started throwing words around like justice, equality and democracy. You can't tell a black man about justice and you don't tell him about equality—there are no such things. So we laughed at those terms. They said we weren't serious, etc. and the meeting was adjourned.

LESTER: *When they got the brother and told him he was suspended, what reasons did they give?*

JACKIE: The major thing was the supposed rule he had broken by distributing "unauthorized literature." But he didn't distribute it except on request. It turns out that one teacher specifically asked him for a copy of the leaflet. This teacher then turned him in and he was told to leave the school. Ron said he wasn't leaving unless his parents were called. A policeman was called to remove him. The policeman manhandled Ron who is a minor.

Aside from this and the fact that police are constantly in the school, it was some time before Ron's parents were called. This was hardly due process.

NAOMI: I'd like to go into this suspension because there is a process stated in the Rules of the Board of Education whereby a student and his parents must be at three hearings which are entitled, I believe, suspension hearings. It seems that the meetings we held during December (1968) are now being titled "pre-suspension hearings." Now none of our parents were present; none of them were notified. This means they weren't suspension hearings at all. This was the due process that was *lacking* in Ron's suspension.

LESTER: *The teachers, of course, have the power to keep you from graduating or kick you out of school, and they get rid of the bad niggers and use them as an example; the rest keep cool after that. All three of you are seniors. Have they moved against you at all yet?*

KAREN: Today I was called down to the administration office for not standing to say the pledge. Now, I've not been standing to say the pledge because it was against me personally to say it. If I did stand to say it, I would be out and out lying. Now, according to this school official, I was breaking a school law. I said that I was not aware that any such law existed, and if I didn't know of its existence, I could not very well break it. I asked to see it in writing; it was not produced. Then he started saying that I was such a good Negro student, and didn't I think I had gained anything from this country? I said that as Karen Butler I had personally gained a lot from the school system, but as Karen Butler the black person, I had gained nothing. "Well, why don't we speak about you as Karen Butler," he said. Oh no. We speak about me as Karen Butler, part of a black mass in this country that is oppressed. There's no singling me out. I can gain a lot from singling out, but I am part of a mass.

JACKIE: The whole thing is this system has scared these people. These brothers and sisters in Taft are scared. You ask them will you sign this? "Oh no! I'm not going to touch it because I might get into trouble." Or: "Am I going to get into trouble if I sign it?" We say what kind of trouble? "I may get sent to the dean.

Oh no, I'm not going to sign it." This is how the system has worked on them. It's scared a whole lot of students. It's got them too scared to move.

For example, one day I got a pink card [disciplinary referral to the dean] just for reading a notice on a UFT bulletin board which was telling chapter members not to come to any more meetings with students. Now this teacher who gave me the pink card ran to my Leaders Club adviser and told her about it. (Leaders Club is for the outstanding girl athletes of the school. You're supposed to have leadership qualities and set an example. You help the gym teachers do practically everything in the gym: you help conduct classes, and do clerical work, etc.) So my adviser told me that my leader's white gym suit would have to be taken away because I was setting a bad example.

Now, they weren't worried about that pink card. The thing was that I was too black to be in that white gym suit. I was really speaking my mind, and they said: "Your attitude has changed." I said of course it has. I have seen what is going on in this school. So of course my attitude has changed. You don't expect a drowning man to be grinning? I find nothing to grin about. So she said: "It's your attitudes, your activities." I said what do you mean, my activities? "You belong to the Taft Afro-American Cultural Society, don't you? Well, I think you got into the wrong company, Jackie; you're really a nice girl." So what it came down to was that I asked how long my gym suit would be taken away. She said: "Until we see a 100 percent change in attitude and until you change your activities." I said in other words, drop out of the Taft Afro-American Society and forget my black brothers and sisters to get this white gym suit. She said: "I don't think you have to go so far as to drop out, but quiet down so everybody doesn't focus on you." So I figure, if I can't be black in a white gym suit, what's the sense?

NAOMI: The administration tried for a long time to talk me into being a good house nigger too. When they found that wouldn't work, I was threatened indirectly. I found myself frequently down at the dean's office for minor things, such as being a few minutes late to one classroom. Realize: lateness can get you suspended. I was called down and told by one of the deans of girls that if I didn't quiet my activities in the school (which she never did define to me) I would have to go before the character committee and . . .

LESTER: *Wait, wait. Stop! The character committee?*

NAOMI: That's what you have to go through to graduate from Taft high school. They decide whether or not your character is acceptable. I didn't find out about it until recently; many students never hear of it until their senior year. If they find your character unacceptable, your diploma will be withheld.

KAREN: Right. Just as a point of information, the character committee happens to be composed of white people, so being black obviously puts me in a rather precarious position. It was mentioned to me today about my not saying the pledge that if I continued to refuse to stand, I would be brought before the character committee.

JACKIE: A lot of the kids in the school are going to be shocked and a lot of the Negro kids are going to say "Oh no . . . Taft's not like that." But, I'm telling them now, you listen to what's going on. A lot of Negro students don't listen, they let everything slip by them. This is why we are having a big problem in our black history class where we have a white teacher. Every day we confront him and he gets upset and defensive because he's white. He came to us and said "Naomi and Jackie, you can't challenge everything I say or else we're not going to get anywhere this year." I said, I don't care if we don't get past Africa. We've got to learn the truth. He holds up John Hope Franklin's book and says, "Well, he's black, he wrote this." I said he didn't write history he only copied down what was written by the man before him who was white. So you're not teaching me black history, only what the white man put down on that page at that time which no black person has had a chance to rebut.

KAREN: A lot of Taft students ought to get hip. I was really a good Negro for three years in that school. I was in the honor school, and I was a perfect Negro. But with the strike, everything changed.

"Karen, you're an intelligent student" and "Karen, I don't understand." What they were really coming out and saying was that I was being influenced. Of course I'm being influenced; a lot of things came to me and made a lot of sense. I can get a lot of places by acting quite well and capitalizing on my honor school, but at the same time I realize it was only by accident that I happened to be in honor school. Most black kids are not.

They have a couple of shop classes down in the basement. Who fills those shop classes? Blacks and Puerto Ricans. I don't think truthfully I've ever seen one white person in that shop class. One day the shop teacher came over to me and said "Look at the great lamps they're making." I said what are they going to do with this when they get out of high school? And he said "Well, it's made out of finer wood than any company makes." I said fine, but the company's got the business. I don't care if they're making it out of paper, the company's got the business. I said that's fine for a hobby, but what are they going to do when they get out of school?

JACKIE: With the guidance counselors it's the same thing. When a black student fails two subjects: "Wouldn't you like to take a commercial course?" Next thing is "Wouldn't you like to take a general course?" And they shuffle you off with "You can't make it in academic."

When I was in the 10th grade, I had two years of Spanish already. I had biology already and was taking chemistry and geometry. Then I was approached and asked to take a pre-tech course, guaranteed to get me into a two-year college to study business. I said What? And give up my academic? "Because your average may not be high enough to get into college." As many colleges as want black students today to prove that they're not prejudiced? I mean, go on: I got no problem to get into college. Schools are writing to me like this: "You are an outstanding black student and you were recommended by so-and-so and please come to our college." And they're telling black students now that they can't go to college? Boy, they would take a black student with a 60 average just to prove that they're not prejudiced. The brothers and sisters have to get hip to that. Don't let these people tell you you can't go to college. You put your mind to it and you can do anything.

19

Jeff Jones and Doug Norberg

Mission Rebellion * (*1969*)

Not long after the strike at [San Francisco] State began, organizers in the Mission district sought to develop support for the strike in the Mission district, especially from students at Mission High School. Several rallies were held after school hours in Mission Dolores Park, across from the school. While the attendance at the rallies was not large, those students who did attend were inspired by the strike at State, especially by the Third World Liberation Front. Realizing that students at Mission were more concerned with their own survival than with the strike at State, they began to look into the scene at Mission High.

The Students

Mission High School has about 2050 students: 450 blacks, 680 whites, 750 latinos, and 75 Chinese. Its students came from families with the lowest incomes in the city, averaging $5300 per family. The latinos are the poorest of the ethnic groups, averaging some $3500 per family. The unemployment rate for male Spanish-speaking residents of the Mission dictrict is as high as 18 percent; half

* Reprinted from *The Movement* (March, 1969, issue). At the time this was written, Jeff Jones and Doug Norberg were students at San Francisco State College.

of those lucky enough to find jobs are found in three miminal employment categories: operatives, service workers and laborers.

Thirty-nine percent of the students at Mission are bilingual; that is, they have learned, or are now learning, English as a second language. There are no programs at Mission to help these students, outside of standard remedial language instruction. The channeling system in the schools, based as it is upon the results of intelligence tests, biased for those of bourgeois and petty-bourgeois white training, leaves little hope to the average student at Mission. The teaching staff, poorly trained and poorly paid in comparison with the whiter schools in the district, offers little encouragement to the student. Those teachers who have sought to develop bilingual programs and programs of ethnic studies have been met with cynicism by other faculty members and indifference from the administration.

Big Biz & Cops

Increasingly, the schools of San Francisco, particularly the working-class high schools, are balanced by the control of the police on one hand, and the influence of major corporations on the other. The corporate control comes by way of the San Francisco Industrial Education Council, a branch of the National Alliance for Businessmen, locally coordinating the educational interests of Pacific Telephone and Telegraph, Pacific Gas & Electric, Southern Pacific, and Lockheed, among others. Functionally it works like this: PT&T helps develop the vocational program at Mission; it "loans" engineers to do demonstrations in electronic classes; it gives presentations on the world of work and how ethnic groups can advance (showing examples: a black lineman, a black long distance supervisor, etc.)

PT&T helps the administration of the school directly, as well. On occasion, they loan their public relations staff to the school during times of crisis; when the school administration needs new desks and filing cabinets, they have found PT&T much more effective in filling the order than the Board of Education downtown. In return for all this, the school administration sets up a job placement center to deliver the goods—cheap manpower—to PT&T.

The police work in and around the school to keep the colony tame. There is a counselor at every high school in the city, who acts in liaison with the Police Narcotics Bureau. The Police Communuity Relations Bureau develops programs for the recruitment of cops, thereby maintaining a presence on campus for the supervision of "dissident elements." The old hall monitor system, civil service jobs, has been found inadequate to the needs of security in the school, so the Board of Education has allocated and is now training "security guards" to police the schools in a more effective manner. All of which does little to inspire educational zeal among the students. The number of students at Mission has declined by 200 every year for the past three years, as the dropout rate has exceeded ⅓ of all the students enrolled. Out of the 2050 students, between 450 and 600 are absent daily. The average student at Mission is absent 82 days out of the school year.

The Strike

The tension and the frustration of the students has often expressed itself in fighting among students—black against brown, black and brown against white. The current strike at Mission grew out of a fight between the black and latino students January 22–24.

When the police Tactical Squad was called in, the students rallied under the leadership of the BSU in fighting the cops, demanding that they be pulled off campus. The BSU called a strike for Monday, January 27. The latinos circulated a leaflet, saying: "We got ourselves together last week fighting the blacks. Now it's time to fight the *real enemy.*"

The administration reacted to this show of unity among the students in two ways. First, they called separate convocations for white, black, and brown students, to supervise the drawing up of demands and requests. The immediate result of this was that the black and latino students showed, in their demands, their unity around a set of political demands. They obviously had their shit together. The white students, on the other hand, reflected their fragmentation and intimidation by coming up with nothing.

Secondly, the administration sought to isolate the radical leadership from the student body by bringing in the police and launching a series of suspensions. While this did take the leadership out of action—it's harder than hell to get out of the Youth Guidance Center if your parents are not behind you—the administration had misgauged the new militancy of even the most apolitical students when faced with a line of cops. The police action politicized a whole lot of students and involved many white students who had been only peripherally involved. Rallies and demonstrations were held the next two days, involving greater numbers of students every day. The four-day weekend between semesters gave the latino and black leadership the opportunity to pull their demands together into a more cohesive whole.

The Demands

The new semester began with the arrest of three latino community organizers for leafletting. The following day, 200 students, a few parents and a group of community people presented 17 demands to the Board of Education, giving the Board a 10-day period to deal with them. The demands included black and ethnic studies courses, abolition of laminated ID cards, election of hallway monitors, more Third World teachers and counselors, expulsion of undercover and uniformed cops and improvements to the cafeteria and other facilities and services. Of special significance is a demand for abolition of IQ tests which contain cultural and class bias and are used to disqualify and discourage minority group students.

The Board responded with an incredibly complex committee structure for discussion of the demands, leaving the students pissed and calling for another strike beginning 4th period Wednesday, the next day.

Wednesday morning the police busted 24 students on truancy and a variety of other charges. Following a noon rally in Dolores Park, the strikers decided to reenter the building for maneuvers; the police returned and busted seven nonstudents (community organizers, newsmen, people just passing by) and three students. The students were charged with truancy; the nonstudents, with trespassing and participating in a riot.

The remainder of the week was occupied with low-keyed discussion of the demands among students—constantly interrupted by arrests and suspensions (75 students were arrested during this week alone)—and with the building of parents' and teachers' groups around support of the demands. While community people decided to demonstrate in the Mission High administrative offices on Monday in protest to the use of the police on and around the school, the initiative was seized by various Tio Tacos (Uncle Toms), leaders of the Mission Coalition (a mix of left and liberal latino community organizations).

These leaders led the group to the Board of Education building, instead, where they were given promises that 1) the administration would print and distribute copies of the 17 demands to students on Tuesday; and 2) that students would be "given" their home room hours Thursday for discussion of the demands. It appears at this writing that the administration will try to show that these discussions prove the lack of student interest in the demands, and wash their hands. They'll be washing their hands in glue.

Problems

A sustained fight in the high schools is a difficult task. Materialist hang-ups (cars, clothes, etc.) are all ways that students are co-opted away from uniting and fighting against their oppressors. Pig repression is swift and effective. [On] Wednesday (Feb. 5) 27 students were busted for truancy as part of an effort by the pigs to scare off any confrontation as a part of the strike. Most kids assume that if you are truant and caught, then you are guilty. There is no concept of self-defense.

We must challenge this acceptance of the system, and offer an alternative. Through a program of juvenile self-defense, we hope to launch an attack on the courts and police, as well as expand political consciousness. Many of the white kids, who are hostile to the TWLF because they don't want to be forced to study black and brown history, etc., are sympathetic to the demands that have to do with cops on or near the campus.

Some say that organizing H.S. students is not the most important work to be done. We say the fight against racism is the major fight at this stage, and the presence of 20 to 30 percent of the white students at Mission High on a picket line supporting the TWLF will contribute greatly to the expanding awareness of the existence of racism in the society, and the forcing of people to chose between supporting it and fighting it, as has been caused by the strike at State. Even more than college students, high school students bring it closer to home.

20

The Value Orientation of Community Organization and Social Work (*1966*)

This statement was prepared by a group of Community Organization students at the University of Michigan School of Social Work (Spring, 1966).

"I regard as my primary interest the welfare of the individual or group served, which includes action for improving social conditions." The practical and relevant implementation of this statement from the NASW (National Association of Social Workers) Code of Ethics serves as a basic value orientation for a vigorous community organization program.

The first principle of this value orientation is a strong and viable commitment to a policy of providing equal opportunity for the development of each person's potential abilities. This principle lies at the root of our democratic society and is reflected again in the NASW Code of Ethics: "Social work is based on humanitarian democratic ideals . . . professional social workers are dedicated to service for the welfare of mankind and to the marshaling of community resources to promote the well-being of all without discrimination . . . social work practice is a public trust that requires of its practitioners belief in the dignity and worth of human beings. . . ."

While lip service has been paid to the provisions of the NASW
Code we have quoted, social work professionals have been negli-
gent in applying them to situations which involve a confrontation
with the established structure of government or other social services. From rent strikes in Harlem to national voter registration
laws, social workers have failed to develop a professional rationale
for encouraging and supporting movements of social change and
protest.

Since our present society obviously does not live up to its democratic ideals in all situations, a commitment to a policy of equal
opportunity for the development of each person's abilities inevitably
leads to involvement in a broad variety of strategies for social
change—everything from protest demonstrations in the streets to
committee meetings in the marbled halls of federal departments.
Necessarily, this concept of social change embraces theories of both
contention and cooperation.

Community organization students and practitioners who consider a strong commitment to democracy, social change, and the
integration of cooperation and contention techniques as inappro-
priate for a professional social worker must realize that failure to
come out on the side of broad-ranging social change implies a commitment to the status quo as a policy and to stagnation as a practice theory.

While the NASW Code of Ethics is compatible with and indeed
encourages the development of a "Welfare State," nowhere in the
Code are there expressed guidelines for the development of a
"Participant Democracy." It is incorrect to equate the "Welfare
State" with the "Democratic State," since the former may be realized by various forms of anti-democratic politics. We think it in-
cumbent upon a profession claiming a commitment to "democracy"
to guard against the confusion of means and ends. If social workers
are serious about democracy, a commitment to the "welfare of the
individual or group served" is not sufficient. A democracy which
does not provide maximum opportunity for the individual to participate in those decisions which affect his life is no democracy at
all.

Flowing from the implementation of participant democracy is
a firm belief in the self-determination of all clients. Applying this
belief in self-determination to the various community groups which

furnish the contexts of community organization practice, it is clear that the practitioner's "bag of tricks" must include theories and techniques enabling him to bring his expertise to bear on a broad spectrum of community concerns, motivations and activities.

Community organization programs, therefore, should ideally be designed to prepare practitioners who are able to analyze and improve upon all programs of social change whether they emphasize contention or cooperation and wherever they occur. . . .

Many students entering schools of social work are experienced in social protest: some have worked in the civil rights movement. This group is looking for advanced *techniques* and a *context* in which to continue that kind of work. The problems of urbanization, minority groups and the poor and the nature of social movements are of vital interest to this group and should indeed be studied by all social work students. A more central place should be assigned to the theory and practice of conflict strategies. . . . We feel that the curriculum at present vastly underplays the role of conflict. As we have all learned from the civil rights movement, deliberate lawbreaking, protests, boycotts, and sit-ins have often paved the way to negotiation by creating a crisis that demands immediate resolution, leading to gains on the part of the "weaker" side. As the relevance and immediacy of the civil rights movement affects more and more students, we feel that there will be an increase in the number of these students, who may be somewhat at odds with the traditional aims of "generic" social work. These students may not be committed to the profession of social work, especially as it is often weakly led by the NASW, and may feel they have little in common with the professional social workers whom they encounter. About 10 percent of the graduating class at the University of Michigan in 1964 volunteered for the Peace Corps: these are the people who want to do "social work" and would probably find the c.o. curriculum more congenial than any other form of graduate training. By its insulation from practical political considerations and lack of accommodation to such new sources of motivation, the school risks failing to hold this rich potential source of recruits, even if its publicity attracts them to enroll.

This feeling that c.o. is something special within social work can be reflected by many students' feelings that they would never have entered social work if it weren't for c.o. Many of these students may not work in traditional social work agencies upon graduation, and in present circumstances find their own agency's goals conflicting with those of established social agencies which form the vanguard of NASW. . . .

What do the students want in the way of curriculum? The answer is in one word: Diversity. We believe in the right of self-determination: that every student be able to shape his graduate career as much as possible. We, therefore, recommend that there be a reduction in the number of required courses and that we be able to make use of professors outside the school. Students should be able to choose from among courses in the Social Services, Human Growth and Behavior, and Group Processes sequences those he feels will be most useful to him. These sequences should be organized with a more realistic acknowledgment that every student should not have to study such a wide range of material at the expense of his own special interests. We also appreciate the opportunity for directed readings and alternative assignments within courses, and would like to see this method employed more widely. . . .

Community organization is moving into new spheres of activity, as evidenced by the latest issue of *Personnel Information,* which carried an advertisement placed by "Action for Appalachian Youth," an organization interested in recruiting community organization practitioners. This is a far cry from practice in the realm of welfare councils and fund-raising activities. Necessary though such activities are, it would seem that students entering the school are more and more choosing a community organization sequence with this sort of "action and service in the interest of social justice" in mind. (The phrase quoted is from the above-mentioned advertisement.)

If we are to be trained to undertake such action, field placement must give us the opportunity to practice our developing skills. It must provide supervision consistent with this aim and it must be flexible enough for us: 1) to become acquainted with the communities in which we are working and allow the people of those communities to become effectively acquainted with us, and 2) to take courses not presently offered by the School of Social Work which relate to economic and political situations about which we must know in order to practice in fields of social action. . . .

The difference between two and three days of field work in many agencies is the difference between 40 and 60 percent participation, the difference perhaps between being a burden or a part-time spectator and being a positive contributor to the agency's programs. The very essence of social work education is the practice, under guidance, of principles learned in class. Without this, class material is empty verbiage; interesting, but empty. Whatever "it" is which transforms us into social workers in two years, "it" is in the field. While we are aware of special exigencies, we cannot understand the logic behind this change and cannot express strongly enough our desire that three-day placements be reconsidered for second-year students.

It would seem that our criticisms can be summarized as follows: While community organization curricula have traditionally trained workers for practice in the chest and council field, changes which call for corresponding change in curricula and field placements are taking place; there is a need for flexibility and for increased communication on several levels; finally, now is certainly not the time for regressive steps, for if community organization is to continue to play its traditional role adequately, as well as recruit needed personnel for new programs and fields of practice, the needs of potential practitioners must be met. To turn out quantities of people who can sign M.S.W. after their names makes not one bit of sense if the training such people have received is of such poor quality as to raise the question (as it is being raised now) about the adequacy of social work practice in many fields.

21

Radical Education Project * (*1966*)

RADICAL EDUCATION PROJECT: an independent educational, research and publication program initiated by Students for a Democratic Society, dedicated to the cause of a democratic radicalism,
and aspiring to the creation of a New Left in America.

Democratic radicalism is renewing itself around the basically
moral proposition: People should have the opportunity to participate in shaping the decisions and the conditions of economic, political and cultural existence which affect their lives and destinies.

This theme is not new. Indeed, it is deeply rooted in the tradi-
tions of utopian and scientific socialism, popular democracy and
humanism. But it has acquired a new urgency and concreteness in
the radical action movements of the last six years. It has become the
unifying point of moral reference in the opposition to the corporate
state, in the anti-war movement, in the critique of authoritarianism
and paternalism in the university, and in the freedom struggles of
Negroes in particular and the American under class in general.

The Purpose of REP

TOWARD A NEW LEFT IN AMERICA. The vitality and the idealism
of the new movements are related in part to the directness of this

* Reprinted by permission of the Radical Education Project. The Radical
Education Project staff prepared this statement of purpose.

relatively nonideological moral position. But a left movement requires more than idealism and passion: Intellectually, it must have knowledge; it must have understanding and analysis; and it must have a social program and prescription which translate radical vision into concrete realities. Organizationally, it must expand its appeal and its participation beyond the populations of students and economically exploited. These groups may form the militant base of the movement, but the problems of the "affluent" in America—union members, professionals, the broad middle class, the intelligentsia, etc.—are in some ways even more pressing and serious than those of the under class and outsiders. Not only do more people experience them, but they are newer, less clearly understood and less subject to simple institutional or economic remedy.

The task of the movement, now, is not only to seek immediate political objectives—locally and nationally. It must begin a longer-term job: to create, or coalesce anew, a generation of democrats—people, not only youth, who can maintain a radical value commitment and identity and who will extend the movement into new areas. The commitment is to radical democracy, both as an end and as a means. We are concerned not merely with the evident moral failures and abuses of American society. Our job is to lay bare the social roots of those abuses. Our goal is not simply to facilitate a remedy to individual problems as they become so great as to be intolerable; it is to transform the institutions and thinking which produce and multiply abuses. Our attack must be both on narrow issues and on the ideology and institutions which keep issues narrow. On this basis, it may be possible to create a politically relevant, undisguised radical program for America.

BROAD OBJECTIVES. The intent of the project is to make explicit the meaning of radical democracy for America: it must in the course of its activities make clear what institutions and conditions are to be changed and the nature of their replacements as well as those aspects of contemporary life that are important to preserve and strengthen.

The project does not start with a "political line": its intent is to develop an analysis which is adequate for our times.

The unifying thread in its work will be the insistence that conclusions stem either from experience or research (or both) and not simply be extrapolated from a dogmatic framework. Too much of what has passed for education is simply the ritualistic repetition of slogans. The work of the project will not be bound to follow in the "masters' footsteps," although it shall head for the same goal. The project is not a substitute for political action or organization. It seeks to complement the action thrust of the movement by insuring that the necessary intellectual and educational resources are available. The project does not envision being a central bureaucratic headquarters for coordinating all educational work on the left. It attempts to visualize and stimulate a "movement turn toward education" which includes many independent strands of activity. The project will hope to add to that activity by the creating of "task forces" and study groups and performing other educational tasks.

ORGANIZATION OF STUDY GROUPS AND TASK FORCES. The project is obviously a major and ambitious intellectual enterprise. What is outlined in this paper might be considered a "Five Year Plan." We will begin with two basic organization forms: the Task Force, whose major functions will be original scholarly research, and the presentation of educational programs to people in the movement; and the Study Group, which is seen primarily as an instrument of self education on the local level, although it certainly might make original contributions of scholarship. These groups (especially task forces) might be organized nationally, with interested people from around the country (and abroad) being in touch with one another by correspondence and occasional conferences. Or they might be organized locally, around a core of people in a particular SDS chapter, university, city or region. In many cases there might be a number of local groups functioning on a particular problem as well as a national task force of which they would be a part.

Potential Agents of Change

America is a highly organized society. Radicals must function within this organized context. It is clear that social change is a product of a coalition of forces. At the base of any such coalition, if it is to produce radical change, must be independent insurgencies, insurgencies committed to the idea of the people taking into their own hands the forces shaping their lives and futures.

A difficult problem concerns the relation between these insurgencies, which we are working to build, and the more established or organized "agents of change." In understanding and being able to influence this relationship, rests the key to successful political strategy.

The prerequisite for this understanding is a detailed knowledge of "liberal" and "progressive" organizational structures. In general we need to know a great deal about the organization structure, the character of leadership and any internal factions, its links with the larger society, the processes of decision-making, the positions on salient issues, the nature and recruitment of membership, its press, and the major issues of internal controversy, the freedom of left opposition internally and the historical development of current rigidities in the institution. If it is an ideological organization, we need to know its ideology or its debates on ideology: its highest strategic priorities, its view of democracy and civil liberties, its view of the process of world change and domestic politics, its view of the nature of the "American state," its view of the Soviet state and of Cold War politics, imperialism, etc.

Policy

The movement exists to solve problems. Besides identifying strategic issues the movement must have proposals as solutions (or as steps toward the solutions) of those problems. These proposals constitute its policy.

The movement organizes on the basis of discontents. At many points in the society, discontents are being manifested in ongoing struggle and conflict—in universities over educational policy; in ghettos over slum housing and poverty; in unions about wages, working conditions and job security; in rural areas between small farmers, farm workers and corporate agriculture; in the political system over numerous issues of social reform; in many places about the war in Vietnam and civil rights, etc.

Power is not a value in its own right, but for what it makes possible. These struggles in which the movement participates have radical potential, for the issues they raise touch on the contradictions within the American ideology and between myth and reality. They are the struggles to which the establishment relates, seeking to prevent their extension to radical consciousness. It may employ a palliative rhetoric, or ameliorative concessions or police power, but its aim is the same: to disrupt or exhaust or co-opt discontent, to keep issues narrow, and to prevent unrest from consolidating into generalized opposition.

Radicals have an important place as activists in these struggles. But often we have been ineffective because we have not had a concrete program which makes sense to the people in motion and carries their thinking beyond the reforms or rhetoric which the system is willing to offer.

Programs Toward New Constituencies

Research and education are, in many situations, a basis for organization and a form of action. Where possible, REP will attempt to develop special programs to increase the potential of its educational activity to expand the scope of the movement. Thus, the study of cultural institutions will involve a self-conscious effort to establish contact with radical artists. Similarly, the research on agents of change will involve making contact with radical democrats in the various "mainstream" organizations, attempting to develop regular forms of communication among these people and between them and other groupings in the movement. The task force on the university would have as part of its aim to develop an association of university-based radicals. A similar function would hold for the task force on intellectual centers.

There are four special programs now envisioned:

REFORM OF THE ACADEMIC DISCIPLINES
RADICALS IN THE PROFESSIONS
INTERNATIONAL INTELLIGENCE NETWORK
THE ARTS

As the project develops, it is hoped that other programs will be formulated to help relate the movement to workers and trade unionists, to liberal religious groups and to anti-poverty and community organization programs.

REFORM OF THE ACADEMIC DISCIPLINES. It is well recognized that "higher education," even in our best universities, often approaches indoctrination. Universities are organized and subsidized to produce graduates who will keep America rolling. Students are molded to the values, theories, and patterns of thought which subtly and cumulatively bestow legitimacy and inevitability on the status quo. History looks often only at the mainstream; the dialectic of tension and conflict within man, his works and his society is neglected. The type of objectivity canonized in social science methodology tends often to separate knowledge from values, and thereby from public relevance. In teaching and textbooks, the insights, analyses, alternatives, and unanswered questions of the "Left" are generally dismissed, distorted or ignored. In the study of literature and the arts, formalistic analysis saps man's creative products of their social meaning and thereby, often, of their spiritual impact.

Yet, the dissatisfaction felt by many students and teachers has not expressed itself in a self-conscious criticism of the method and content of the established academic disciplines. It is not enough for intellectuals to support radical action movements; they must turn their minds to a systematic reconstruction of the tools and products of their own work.

This section of the project will attempt, through the formation of task forces in a few important areas, to begin this reconstruction of intellectual theory and teaching. The initial task of each group will be to develop radical educational materials for students in introductory liberal arts courses.

These materials may be: "a thinking man's guide"—a radical critique and reformulation of the discipline geared to the introductory textbooks that students are required to use (e.g. Samuelson's text in economics); supplementary reading material and annotated bibliography; guides for the organization of "counter courses"; question and answer sequences—"scenarios"—to force the instructor and class to deal with relevant issues and to expose the value biases of the "accepted truth." These materials would be made available to SDS and other students through the local chapter and sympathetic faculty, and, hopefully, also through sale at the local bookstores as a supplement to the required texts.

Initial groups will be organized in Economics, Sociology, Political Science and History. The economics group, for instance, will prepare a radicals' guide to Samuelson's Economics I text. It might develop a guide for students in labor relations and international economics. The history group might prepare a guide to introductory American History courses and Modern World History, keyed to several standard texts. Effort will be made to organize similar groups in Philosophy, Anthropology, Psychology, Literary Criticism and other areas as interest is expressed. All of these groups could, of course, develop material geared to other than introductory courses.

The suggested material deals with the major problem areas and deficiencies in introductory undergraduate education. Their preparation and use, besides contributing to the intellectual development of students coming into the "movement," should make more coherent the intellectual substance of democratic radicalism and should make the classroom situation more exciting and dynamic for all concerned. . . .

There is no presumption here that the answers are in hand and the only job is to spread the truth that a few "radicals" already possess. Nor is there a view that "knowledge" should be adjusted to the needs of ideology. Quite the contrary, the problem is that the development and teaching of knowledge and philosophy have been adjusted to fit the society. Responsible intellectuals must seek ways and means to change society to the dictates of knowledge and philosophy. The implications and imperatives of that ideal—that knowledge should have public relevance—are little known; but they should be the concern of radicals in the universities.

RADICALS IN THE PROFESSIONS. The left is well aware that the professions not only give poor service to those who need it the most, but that they also enshrine conservative values and function as institutional bulwarks to the status quo. Too often, it seems that the idea of profession as a means to social status and mobility has replaced the ideal of a profession as a means of public service.

Yet many, if not most of the present campus radicals will, in a few years, themselves hold positions in the professions. The environment of the profession combined with the content of professional education or training will tend to make, increasingly, the individual's radical value commitment less and less relevant to his daily work.

Two lines of program are needed to counterbalance this natural tendency—the tendency of the society to isolate and transform the individual before he can organize and transform the society. First, there must be an intervention in the process of professional education. The value issues in the profession must be made specific and concrete. The ways and opportunities for the radical to act in the profession consistent with his value commitment must become part of professional education. And second, there need to be professional associations or "fraternities" committed to radical social involvement which can reinforce and serve as a reference group for the radical in the profession.

The REP project on the professions is directed to both of these objectives. It will attempt to organize groups of radicals in, or preparing for, professions. It will assist these groups in preparing and disseminating educational materials dealing with: the structure of the profession; the dominant values of the profession; its links with and relation to the status quo; the treatment of dissidents in the profession; the range and limits of freedom; the nature and a critique of the nature of the professional education; a manifesto of values and professional responsibility; a program describing the institutional and technique changes needed in the profession; and a guide to opportunities and ways of operating in the profession which contribute to the social change ideals of democratic radicalism.

INTERNATIONAL INTELLIGENCE NETWORK. The task force group working on the "nations series" pamphlets will try to build a resource group of left-wing scholars on each important national area and it will seek to establish and maintain frequent correspondence with radicals active in left movements abroad. These contacts will provide a basis for building an international intelligence network for the peace movement. There is now a need to formalize connection with a group of people closely tuned to international events, particularly in the Third World, who can serve as quick sources of intelligence as issues come up. This would involve monitoring the foreign press and official records, collecting "gossip" about the internal workings of the foreign policy apparatus, making available analyses of international events that appear in American and foreign journals, etc. We should devise ways to make contact with the increasing number of Americans who venture overseas in various capacities and come back sharing our alienation from present United States foreign policy and its assumptions.

THE ARTS. An important part of the REP program is the encouragement of criticism and creative work in the arts. In addition, the project will attempt to build organizational forms of benefit to those radical artists and critics who wish to maintain a relationship with one another and with the movement. Concretely, these forms might involve:

a) a magazine of the "radical sensibility" which would include poems, stories, visual arts, criticism, and so forth. The magazine would serve as a forum for communication among radical artists and critics, and as an external organ for making public ongoing creative work. The aim would be to develop an identity among artists and critics in terms of the sensibility underlying their artistic struggle, rather than the particular medium in which it is expressed.

b) a young writers series that would publish in book or pamphlet form the work of artists and students of the arts and would seek for these publications widespread distribution and consideration within the movement and without.

c) distribution of the various small magazines of literature and the arts, criticism and social analysis. Many of these magazines are being put out, often publishing exciting and important work, but they have small circulation and are little known to the movement or public at large. REP will attempt to promote the best of these journals.

PART V

REVOLUTION: *MAKING IT*

AND WAITING FOR IT

I<small>F</small> the *Port Huron Statement* was a Declaration of Independence for the student movement of the 1960's, then its spirit
is likely to endure through much of the 1970's, a spirit of individual
freedom and fulfillment, equality of opportunity and a new measure of social justice. It can be argued that in the last decade much
has been achieved. Public facilities have been permanently deseg-
regated in most of the South and millions have been added to the
voting rolls. Students (and in many cases, faculties) have gained
a larger role in university decision-making. The antiquated notion
of *in loco parentis* is finally giving way to a treatment of students
as adults—whose extracurricular lives are none of the universities'
business. The attitude of the nation toward the war in Vietnam has
been turned around and Lyndon Johnson's "retirement" forced.
A whole range of black studies programs and special supports for
black (and other "minority") students have been established. Perhaps most important—as we have suggested and illustrated earlier
—widely dispersed cadres of young, articulate radicals have
emerged in the secondary schools, the colleges and universities,

and indeed, throughout virtually every phase of American institutional life.

But the war goes on, racism and racial segregation are, according to most indices, increasing. The cities approach financial bankruptcy, and growing concentrations of the inner cities' disenfranchised poor are locked in mortal combat with the affluent suburbs. There has been a great deal more argument than action in the democratization and modernization of the universities. The beginning of the end of poverty is not yet in sight.

With the unwillingness and inability of America to make significant strides forward in social progress, the mood, rhetoric and action styles of the student movement have sharply changed. The heroic nonviolence of the early sixties is increasingly giving way to a defiant, antagonistic neo-Marxist militance that sees violence as the only real means to rapid and significant change.

From the most liberal to most revolutionary tendencies, the spirit of dissent continues to grow. As Newfield points out:

In my visits to college campuses I have noticed many students, probably a numerical majority on the large, urban campuses, who are alienated and dissatisfied, and willing to act on certain vague/liberal/radical notions: immediate, unconditional withdrawal from Vietnam; less repressive laws concerning drugs, sex, and abortion; less bureaucracy; abolition of the draft; more relevant college curricula and more student influence in the running of the university; a passion to eliminate hunger and racism; fury at the programmed, hollow man in the White House.*

In the final analysis, the young radicals see our system itself as deeply flawed. The needed change cannot take place within our current governmental structure. Like a giant cookie mold, it has built into itself the shape of permanent social inequities, class conflict, materialistic greed, militarism and low tolerance for conflicting ideologies. It is thus a system which can only reproduce itself. New molds must be created. Current heroes of the Left—like Che Guevara, Castro, Ho Chi Minh and Mao Tse-tung—are conceived of as having participated in the initiation of new life-styles.

Although we can trace two distinct, although scarcely separate,

* Jack Newfield, "SDS: From Port Huron to La Chinoise," *Evergreen Review,* December, 1969, p. 59.

thrusts toward the development of a counterculture and the heightening of the conditions under which a revolution might take place, there are some areas of clear agreement. An alteration in present power arrangements must take place in which new participatory models of governance and decision-making can be established. Both trends may be seen as anti-fascist, in the sense that they express a restoration of belief in the ability of the masses of men to initiate what is in their—and humanity's—best interest. An openness and imprecision must be maintained. A new society is emerging (or will be forced to emerge), and the developing social structure must be kept pliable—available to personal and societal improvement, reform and innovation.

As we have tried to illustrate, the dissenters have come to their radicalism by many routes. But most seem to have been influenced by a desire to keep faith with the liberal, humanistic values and beliefs of their parents and of the American radical tradition.

What is in store for the next decade? Predictions for the student movement are hazardous at best, but perhaps some tentative projections may be in order. With intensified repression of youthful protest, we anticipate a bipolar response. The politicized revolutionaries will turn in the direction of guerrilla tactics—terrorism, bombing, sniping, looting, "trashing" (relatively minor property destruction) and the like. International analogues will be increasingly sought to revolutionary movements around the world. More generally, the level of violence will increase, along with more secretive organizations and organizational style. Dissent tactics are likely to be more of a "hit-and-run" variety, than the "siege" efforts of the recent past. Those engaged in building parallel institutions and a counterculture will expand their efforts and fields of recruitment—younger students, young workers, young professionals. A broader variety of communal living arrangements will be established; new forms of interpersonal relations will be explored. More simplified life-styles which emphasize sharing rather than competition are likely to emerge.

This all presupposes a general climate of repression, with law and order rather than peace and justice as a first priority. It is not an optimistic view. People will be killed and injured. Property will be destroyed. Polarization of white and black, young and old is likely to increase. There will be more dropouts from the educational system and establishment life-styles. Traditional roles, values and institutions—already under enormous pressure—will erode further in the public confidence. A set of credibility gaps, on an order unknown in the American experience, are emerging. The technology of a post-modern era is upon us; social machinery to match it moves further from our grasp almost daily. Certainly there are other possibilities. But the signs at present suggest that our society and our rulers are unwilling to seriously consider them.

The articles in this section are a very modest attempt to capture some of the crosscurrents noted above. As earlier pieces in this volume suggested, a faction within SDS was moving toward the "masses" by considering the possibilities for alliance with the working class. Fred Gordon's paper develops this idea as a basic policy. The selections by the Women's Liberation group and the demands put forward by the "United Black Population" of the University of Michigan illustrate other factional interests and their particular relationship to institutional change. The documents concerning the split within SDS of RYM II (Revolutionary Youth Movement) and Weatherman (RYM I) serve to poignantly depict analyses of the need for (and means for achieving) revolutionary change.

The final set of articles describes actions which movement people might take while awaiting more fundamental social change, or to support meaningful change efforts occurring elsewhere. Eric Prokosch offers some imaginative suggestions for challenging usual classroom procedures. "The Americana Game" is a role-playing device for radicalizing students by having them participate in a game. Michael Locker discusses how one may draw a bead on the relationship between the university and the military-industrial complex. Finally, the Wisconsin Draft Resistance Union suggests one of a broad range of innovative approaches to creating socially relevant guerrilla theater. Perhaps it is more a celebration of new possibilities than lonely whimperings of despair.

22

Fred Gordon

Build the Campus Worker-Student Alliance * (*1969*)

Several articles in this issue discuss an idea that's new in SDS—allying with campus workers. Around the country, SDSers will be getting jobs on campus, getting to know campus workers, and discussing our politics, supporting their struggles against exploitation and racism, and, where campus workers are not yet themselves making demands on the administration, exposing and fighting to end some of the extreme abuses to which these workers are subjected.

What's the reasoning behind this strategy?

During the past few years, many SDSers have seen that a mass-based student movement that can fight imperialism and racism must ally with working people. Thus we developed the idea of worker-student alliance. Students (and the mental workers most become) *need* in fact to ally with working people. Both groups are oppressed by the same class, which owns the industries in which workers are fiercely exploited, and which controls the schools as well. In order to make a worker-student alliance possible, we've tried to develop a pro-working-class student movement. Thus we've

* Reprinted from *New Left Notes* (September 20, 1969, issue). Fred Gordon was a student at the University of California.

backed strikes, from telephone to transit to United Parcel, trying to involve many other students, raising our politics with the workers. We've supported welfare and other community struggles, fought the racist attitudes dividing white and black workers. On campus, we've fought anti-working-class ideas among our fellow students, tried to organize struggles in an explicitly pro-working-class way. For example, we've come to see that students should fight ROTC because it trains officers for wars like Vietnam and for putting down black rebellions and strikes in the U.S.—that is, ROTC attacks working people. Other ways of fighting ROTC, aimed at "purifying the university," really build the students' anti-worker attitudes, and must be rejected.

The idea of a pro-working-class student movement has been the key in drastically changing SDS. Last fall, the old national leadership was able openly to write off workers as "reactionary, bought off," etc. These ideas are still around, but many SDSers have rejected them. We have seen that just building a student movement—*any* student movement—is not enough, that we need a mass student movement *that serves the people,* that serves working people here and all over the world. This understanding is no small gain.

But it's not enough. The purpose of a pro-working-class student movement is to win students and mental workers to ally with other workers. But this strategy can't succeed unless, in practice, that alliance gets built. After a certain point, either you reach your goal or you stop running. It is impossible to build a pro-working-class student movement indefinitely without more and more building actual alliances with workers.

This has been discussed a good deal over the summer, especially by roughly a thousand people involved in the SDS Work-In. How should we develop the alliance—what steps do we have to take?

A Real Alliance

The conclusion of many is that the best way to begin the transformation of SDS from an increasingly *pro-working-class* movement to one in fact *allied with workers,* is to begin on campus. In a sense, the fact that we didn't realize this earlier is a serious criticism. In some places where this strategy was discussed, people thought there weren't any campus workers at their schools . . . it turned out there were "only" a few thousand. Supposedly trying to build a pro-working-class movement, nevertheless our anti-working-class atti-tudes led us to miss the exploitation going on on "our" own cam-puses!

The University as Boss

The universities are bosses, plain and simple, employing hundreds of thousands of workers. These people are terribly exploited—lousy pay and working conditions, no job security, student part-timers used to cut down the full-timers' pay, racist pay differentials and employment practices. Many have been fighting school admin-istrations harder—and a lot longer—than SDS. Allying with these workers is very possible—and absolutely necessary, if we are seri-ous about serving the people. ("I want to serve the people if they're miles away and it's all very abstract, but getting a regular, unglo-rious job at school, getting to know the workers, and fighting along-side them, and organizing struggles around their interests among many students is beneath me"—this is not a very good approach.) For most of us, campus worker-student alliance means a much more serious approach. It's one thing to have a big demonstration against ROTC. Of course, we should keep on doing that, but it's a lot harder for many of us to develop real roots among campus workers, getting to know them as well as the more working-class students who often are not attracted to SDS. So campus worker-student alliance means upping the ante for us! But as the rich and their government tighten the screw on the people, we *have* to up the ante—on our own commitment and on how much we accomplish. Otherwise we'll turn into a bunch of fancy-talking "radical" phon-ies on a self-serving ego trip. Who needs us?

Tactics

Space prevents a much fuller discussion of the thinking behind this strategy. A pamphlet on the question should be out soon. Here are some tactical ideas on how we can proceed.

1. We should get jobs, now, in school cafeterias, libraries, hos-pitals, offices, print shops, as janitors, gardeners—everywhere. Find out the real situation from the workers. (Our limited experi-

ence shows that it's usually pretty horrendous and getting worse.) A related step is for those of us who've moved off campus to go back to the dorms. Being "radical" doesn't mean keeping away from the people. This means taking other students' problems more seriously and linking the struggles of campus workers to our fight against anti-working-class and racist ideas among students. This will help us get to know dorm workers also.

2. As soon as possible, issue a pamphlet and/or leaflets exposing your particular school as a boss. Find out the history of your school as a boss and let people know that, as well as exposing the current situation.

3. Where workers are already engaged in organized struggle against the administration, we should organize mass support. Where they're not, chapters should study the situation and launch struggles against particular abuses.

4. Get to know the workers, discuss politics with them. Bringing the issue to students in a mass way (as discussed in point 3) will help show the full-time workers we're serious. Our attitude should be humble, but not opportunist. That is, racist ideas, mistaken notions about the war, etc., should *always* be argued against. At the same time, we should remember that campus workers have been hurt a lot more by these things than we have. They understand the situation, in many ways, far better than we do. If you want to serve the people you have to learn from them.

Two things should be kept in mind in general. One is that fighting around a campus worker-student alliance is often an excellent way to fight racism. Many campus workers are black—often they have the most difficult jobs. Racist hiring, pay, and employment practices are used to squeeze more out of nonwhite workers as well as to build racism among whites. Fighting the superexploitation of nonwhite campus workers hits at the very roots of racism and helps expose the racist nature of the university as well as challenging the racist attitudes of white students and workers. (Our previous failure to organize such struggles in most places reflects our own racism!) Some of the biggest campus struggles of the last year grew out of campus worker-student alliances—for instance, at Duke and the University of North Carolina.

Second is that we can start *right now*. While many fights—for union recognition, overall changes in conditions, and wage raises—

usually require the mass participation of campus workers, we can raise certain demands immediately, even if the workers aren't themselves already fighting openly around these questions. Doing this is only possible if, by working side by side with full-timers, we learn examples of flagrant abuses. Initiating struggles around these grievances will help us develop really close ties with campus workers and begin to raise the issue of campus worker-student alliance in a mass way on campus.

23

Ellen Cantarow, Elizabeth Diggs,
Katherine Ellis, Janet Marx,
Lillian Robinson and
Muriel Schien

I Am Furious (Female)* (*1969*)

The ultimate goal of a radical women's movement must be revolution. This is because the condition of female oppression does not "depend on," is not "the product of," is not "integral to" the structure of society; it *is* that structure. The oppression of women, though similar to that of blacks, differs from it in that it depends not on class division but rather on a division of labor premised on private property and resulting in the family as primary unit for the functioning of the economy. "The modern family," says Marx, "contains in embryo not only slavery . . . but serfdom also, since from the very beginning it is connected with agricultural services. It contains within itself in miniature all the antagonisms which later develop on a wide scale within society and its state. . . ."

The conditions of female servitude prevail today, and remain, in miniature, the basis for, if not the exact embodiment of, the contradictions that divide all of us in order to preserve the smooth functioning of the system. IBM, General Motors, and our corporate universities depend on a highly mobile and docile labor force for their perpetuation and furthering. They own men—that is, they set down rules regulating men's labor and thereby the structure of

* Reprinted by permission of the Radical Education Project. The authors were Harvard and Columbia members of the Women's Caucus of the New University Conference.

their lives. In turn the structure of men's lives determines what women's lives will be. A women, once married, goes where her husband goes. Whether or nor she herself holds a job, it is understood that her real and legitimate vocation is child-rearing. The mythology that society has constructed to make female subjection a positive good is massive and profoundly rooted. In America, this has been carried to the point of cultural hyperbole; for the first time in human history motherhood has become a full-time, 12 to 14 hour a day occupation. This development is in fact extremely recent, having occurred only since the Second World War. . . .

Revolution will not take place until women reject and redefine their position in a society that must keep them under control by directing their search for fulfillment into the inexhaustible realm of consumption. Nothing could be more beneficial to a profit-based economy than a large population whose sole measure of its own worth lies in internalizing the concept of "marketable goods." It pays to keep the little woman alone at home with her children, visiting and being visited by other women against whom she can measure her "progress" by the yardstick of accumulation. What keeps her here is the sense of power she derives from her position in the family, the sense that it is she and she alone who teaches the children to brush after every meal, she and she alone whose market preferences determine what is on the supermarket shelf, she and she alone who feeds them their portion of "culture," she and she alone who can have babies. And for this she is exalted above the God who makes a tree. Who could ask for anything more?

Not she, that's for sure. Not when everything she associated with "becoming a woman" fills her with gratitude toward her oppressors. What has she done to deserve all these things? Her husband even washes the dishes for her sometimes, and takes the kids to the park on Saturdays so that she can do her hair and her nails in peace. What will it take to turn her against those who exploit her by offering, for no money down, all the things through which she has been taught to find her fulfillment? What is it that a liberated, post-revolutionary society must offer in their stead? Our goal must be to rediscover our real needs now, if in fact we have ever known what they are, and make these the basis of actions that would serve as a model for the movement as a whole.

*   *   *

The prevalence of psychotherapy in American life is another force working to stabilize oppression by reconciling women to their condition. (And the clientele of psychiatry *is* largely female.) All of us—women in particular—are encouraged to believe that our individual "hang-ups," although they are the results of objective social conditions, are to be treated as isolated, idiosyncratic cases. Liberation is defined as freedom from these "hang-ups," but all too often is interpreted as adjustment to the status quo. Freedom from guilt about sexual activity reverses the mystique of female chastity, but equates erotic pleasure with human self-realization. What the "Sexual Revolution" has actually done is to establish a new bartering system, on the premise that one kind of freedom can only be won at the sacrifice of another; fulfillment "as a woman" (orgasm, childbearing, motherhood) is made from fulfillment as a person. . . .

The objective locus of our oppression having been made our very bodies, our movement must necessarily differ from the American radical movement to date. The reason that Women's Liberation can serve as a model (indeed, as the basis) for a revolutionary movement is that we have no choice *but* to consider the most basic fact of the most elemental oppression of all: our bodies, whose enslavement depends on the mystification built up around them. As long as women's bodies are not theirs to control, such myths will be used to perpetuate the servitude.

We may say that the single most important goal for a women's movement is the control by women of their own bodies. This does not mean free fucking, for free fucking is simply a more enlightened form of the old snare: it is Freudian pseudo-liberation. The phrase "to control one's own body" is most largely symbolic, and means control over all areas of our lives, since all the conditions of our servitude proceed from the false physical premise. What we are saying is that at such time as we control our physical destinies, we also will be able to enjoy a full work identity as well. . . .

The transformation of society which women's liberation movements are seeking is more far-reaching than merely overthrowing capitalism and establishing socialism in its place. Before capitalism existed, oppression of slaves and women formed the economic basis for society. Slavery has been expanded to de facto apartheid and imperialism by capitalist societies. Women have been systematically made empty, commercial products whose sole human function is to flatter, feed and fuck the imperialist white male. Not only must the distribution of wealth be made just, but also distribution of labor: property-based relationships between the sexes result in the oppression of women. If female oppression is incorporated into the "revolutionary" state, fundamental abuses of capitalism reassert themselves. Any revolution based on male chauvinism is doomed to failure, as is any revolution based on racism. The untapped revolutionary potential of this country (the untapped hatred for the white men who run the society) resides in women.

Obviously, women's liberation movements do not cite the male per se as the enemy. For "to treat comrades like enemies is to go over to the side of the enemy" (Mao). A tendency among some women's liberation groups is to treat all men in the movement as enemies, or to advocate "making it" professionally—a concept conceived of and dictated by men. This tendency works against women's liberation in the long run because it means certain co-optation. But Mao's dictum works the other way round: for men to treat women in women's liberation as enemies is to go over to the side of the system. Male "supremacy" is in many ways the basis of capitalism, and it is as important to the cause of revolution in this country to root out this as it is to root out racism. Just as blacks are the initiators of the anti-racist movement, having known its oppression in their daily lives, so women must instigate the struggle against male chauvinism, since they experience daily its oppressive power. Women must realize that their own, real interest lies not only with individual "success," but with transforming and finally overthrowing the oppressive regime. Only when struggle comes out of conscious political self-interest can it succeed.

Many "radical" men, affirming the priority to our struggle of the fight against racism, are annoyed when we draw an analogy between racial and sexual oppression. No one with a sense of proportion claims that the two evils are identical, and no one is attempting to drain the sympathy generated by one form of suffering into another form. What we do maintain is that the differences are in degree, not in kind, and that male chauvinism is just as incompatible with revolutionary principles as racism.

Socialists recognize the economic basis of both black and female oppression. Not only is racial and sexual oppression coetaneous with private property, but both groups have historically *been* property themselves. Under capitalism both groups constitute a "marginal" source of cheap labor on which the system feeds. When capitalism becomes strained, both groups swell the ranks of the unemployed and the allegedly unemployable. Both are channeled into alienated labor service jobs with no intrinsic meaning and little material gain. Exploitation of both women and blacks is necessary to support the contradictions of the capitalist system, which cannot produce both profits and full employment, let alone provide meaningful work for all members of society.

The psychic consequences of economic conditions are also similar for members of both groups. For most of us, our race and our sex are unequivocal, objective facts, immediately recognizable to new acquaintances. Thus, an immediate reaction occurs, as whatever stereotypes one has about either group go into operation mechanically, without regard to whether an individual conforms to the stereotype. Self-hatred in both groups derives not from anything intrinsically inferior about us, but from the treatment we are accustomed to. For middle-class white women, that treatment takes a less ugly form—at least there are material comforts along with the degradation—but that doesn't increase respect for oneself. The self-images of both groups are defined and manipulated by the cultural media, and both are made the victims of the consumer mentality, so that capitalism exploits us at both ends of the productive process.

Women and blacks have been alienated from their own culture; they have no historical sense of themselves because study of their condition has been suppressed. We understand that our historical function has been that of pawns, but we are given no basis on which to construct any other view of what people like us have done, no tools with which to destroy the existing mythologies about ourselves. Both women and blacks are expected by our economy to function as service workers. Thus members of both groups have been taught to be passive and to please white male masters in order to get what we want.

Unusually gifted members of an oppressed race or sex are treated as exceptional and made to feel their "superiority" to the group of which they must remain an inalienable part by virtue of an objective fact. The group is thus deprived of some of its natural leadership. Similarly, we all recognize that racial conflict between black and white workers redounds chiefly to the benefit of those who exploit labor. A racist white worker is substituting his "white skin privileges" and the sense of superiority they entail for real power. Similarly, the male chauvinism that is most blatant in the working class provides the exploiter with an immediate and permanent division in that class. Oppressed groups are thus cut off from their natural allies, as well.

Perhaps the greatest irony in the situation is that so many black men—including workers in the black liberation movement—are hostile to women's liberation. They have looked at the matriarchal history of American Negro society and blamed black women for destroying their manhood, rather than their true castrator, the white man. They have thus attempted to replace black women in their "natural," that is, oppressed, condition. But both they and the white men who reject the race-sex analogy seem to forget that more than half the black race is female and that you cannot liberate a people by keeping half of it in bondage. Black male chauvinism, supposed by many to be more tolerable on political grounds than white, is counterrevolutionary. While ignoring the potential strength of black women, it also maintains the myth of "the white man's women" as most desirable. This caters to white supremacist conceptions of the black while damaging the political power of the black movement. Even Eldridge Cleaver, who is responsible for the male chauvinist phrase "pussy power," arrives at this conclusion in *Soul on Ice*. White women are oppressed because of their sex; those who are workers are oppressed because of class and sex. Black women are oppressed because of race, sex and class. We cannot struggle for the liberation of society by tolerating, much less encouraging, the greatest injustices of the existing order.

Too much movement activity has been based on organizing about other people's needs. For instance, ERAP failed because it was founded on if not false, at least misdirected consciousness. Although correctly recognizing and assessing the effects of an exploitative society on poor people, it incorrectly assumed that outsiders not of the same class could organize them. In many places in the country SDS is now up against the same fact. In order to build a strong and profound movement, it is the task of all of us to begin to consider the difficult realities of our own circumstances.

The revolution we seek is very far off, but we can begin to act on our ideas in our own lives, *now*. We must begin now, because we must raise consciousness in all men and women of the objective conditions of their oppression. We have formulated immediate and specific goals related to our roles as college and university students and teachers, but we must realize and remember that these "goals" are only tools, a means to the ultimate goal of real liberation for all people. The immediate aims are means of survival which will give us time and space for immediate ends. Radicals have often been confused on this point. We are so afraid of being co-opted by satisfaction of demands that *can* be met that we refuse to tempt our purity by articulating immediate goals at all. But if we trust our own ideology, we must realize that the capitalist system cannot provide justice for all.

24

Black Student Demands (*1970*)

These demands were presented by "The United Black Population" of the University of Michigan (February, 1970).

The Black students of the University of Michigan, fully aware that the countless problems of our communities require the attention of college trained brothers and sisters who have access to a concerned and relevant university type structure, issue the following demands to this university.

Recruitment

It is our understanding that one of the basic steps that the University must take toward the desired attitudes of relevance and genuine concern is the substantial increase in the number of Black students and faculty. Ergo the following: in order to increase *graduate student* enrollment of Blacks, we demand the hiring of several full-time recruiters. These men and women need not hold Ph.D. degrees in their respective fields. They shall represent clusters of disciplines in the professional schools as well as Rackham. They shall be selected by a committee comprised of Black students, faculty (of the given cluster) and administrators. They shall be hired

for periods of three to five years and shall be reviewed by the afore-
mentioned committee at the end of their terms. The committee
shall at that time make recommendations as to their rehiring or
dismissal.

These recruiters shall have as their primary interest recruiting
and shall not take an academic appointment except as it shall not
interfere with their duties. The discretion of the recruiter shall be
the sole determinant in this matter. The recruiters shall all be active
members of the admissions boards of their respective clusters, and
shall have the right to make guaranteed financial commitments to
prospective students. These truthful statements shall include all
stipulations attached to the acceptance of the grant.

Student involvement is to be encouraged by these recruiters and
where a student has both the time and the desire to do so, his ex-
penses shall be paid for any recruiting he might do. Any student
who recruits should be aware of the activities of the total recruiting
effort just as each recruiter must have a similar awareness.

Undergraduate recruitment poses certain problems which require the hiring, by a similar committee, of at least nine additional
full-time recruiters. These men/women, who shall be hired for the
same three to five year period and subject to the same stipulations
as those earlier mentioned, shall serve specific districts. The districts are as follows: Detroit and suburbs (three recruiters), Ann
Arbor-Ypsilanti, Muskegon-Grand Rapids, Saginaw-Bay City,
Flint-Pontiac, Kalamazoo-Benton Harbor-Battle Creek, and Lan-
sing-Jackson. There shall be one area designated as "Out-state,"
encompassing all other areas in Michigan where a substantial minority population is located, or where interest is high. The remain-
ing recruiter shall serve as coordinator of the program. All of the
recruiters shall be on the admissions board and shall be able to make
the same binding financial commitments as their graduate counterparts.

A concerted effort is to be made to recruit out-of-state students
and this shall be the co-ordinator and the "Out-state" recruiter.
They shall establish a nationwide communications network with
Black population centers. Toward this end (recruitment of out-of-
state Blacks), there shall be available funds for students from those
areas to recruit if they so desire. These students shall have access
to all visual aids and information that the other recruiters have.

The same type of relationship, of volunteer student recruiters, shall be sought in state areas;

. . . Except in the School of Education which has presented a valid demand for a twenty percent population figure in the academic years ahead, we set as our minimal Black population in Ann Arbor by 1973–74 ten percent of the total population. This shall increase yearly until the overall population of Blacks shall approach, if not exceed, the proportion of Blacks in the state. More specifically, we demand that in the academic year 1971–72, there shall be an incoming class which includes at least 450 Black freshmen and 150 transfer students, as well as 300 new Black graduate students.

There must be a concerted effort at recruiting more Black faculty, especially in the School of Education which has demanded that twenty percent of their total faculty be Black. These faculty persons are not to be stolen from our brothers and sisters at Black universities and colleges.

Supportive Services

We know that for numerous reasons Black students have difficulty in dealing with this environment, i.e., the standard white system. For this reason, an intensive supportive services program must be instituted to serve the new Black student population. J. Frank Yates presented such a proposal last year. It has not been acted upon. We take this brother's proposal as our own and require immediate action upon the same.

Financial Aids

Obviously, one of the reasons that there are not more Black students here is money. The University has enough of that resource to substantially increase the amount going toward *Financial Aid for Minority Students*. Further:

The Parents Confidential Statement creates a ludicrous living-cost figure and needs to be revamped. It must allow for the hidden costs in an individual's budget.

A University-wide Appeal Board of students, faculty and administrators must be set up to deal with all student appeals on grants.

Tuition waivers are within the jurisdiction of the Regents of the University. We demand that such waivers be granted to in-state minority students who are admitted under the special programs which can be evolved with the joint efforts of Black students and faculty.

Martin Luther King Fund—There must be a reopening of the active solicitations of the business community. The University must revitalize its efforts to gain donations from Michigan industries to guarantee the solvency of the fund. New literature must be published under the policy advisement of the MLK student committee. Further, a student referendum shall go before the student body in this March's S.G.C. election which shall request that each student assess himself $3.00 for the academic year 1970–71 for the undesignated account of the fund.

Black Studies

We consider Black Studies to be an integral part of both the recruitment and the supportive services of this University. But more importantly, the concept of Black Studies is one which brings to a culmination the concept of relevancy in the community of the University. The student community (Black) shall have an active part in the shaping of this area.

However, we realize that we are not fully cognizant of even how to approach one area that the Center shall encompass, i.e., Service. In order that we may have the maximum input of all individuals who have an interest, we desire that a sum be set aside for (1) the salary of an acting director of this service section, and (2) for a staff of at least ten persons who shall work with him on a full-time basis to determine the direction that department will take.

Further, until what we consider and state to be an adequate forum of community and university is established to decide a definite direction of the Center, there shall be no permanent executive commitments made on behalf of the Center.

House

The University must establish a Black Student Center in our community. The East University site, though it may be accepted on a temporary basis, can never adequately serve as the desired link between community and university.

In all University publications and classrooms we shall be called Black and not Negro. There is no such thing as a Negro student population here, and we shall not answer to such an offensive term.

Lastly, we desire to express our support of our brown brothers and sisters, the Chicanos, in their more than reasonable demands for one recruiter and fifty Chicano students on campus this Fall.

We do not expect the University to procrastinate on or effectively table these demands in subcommittees; they are for immediate and positive action.

25

Toward a Revolutionary Youth Movement * (*1968*)

This is a resolution passed at the December 1968 National Council meeting of the Students for a Democratic Society.

At this point in history, SDS is faced with its most crucial ideological decision, that of determining its direction with regards to the working class. At this time there must be a realization on the part of many in our movement that students alone cannot and will not be able to bring about the downfall of capitalism, the system which is at the root of man's oppression. Many of us are going to have to go through important changes, personally. As students, we have been indoctrinated with many racist and anti-working-class notions that in turn have produced racism and class-chauvinism in SDS and were responsible largely for the student-power focus which our movement has had for many years. Student power at this stage of our movement has to be seen as economism: that is, organizing people around a narrow definition of self-interest as opposed to class-interest. We are moving beyond this now, but that movement must be planned carefully and understood by all.

The fact that we saw ourselves as students as well as radicals,

* Reprinted by permission of Radical Education Project.

and accepted that classification of ourselves and many of the false privileges that went along with it (2-S deferment, promise of the "good life" upon graduation, etc.) was primarily responsible for the reactionary tendencies in SDS.

Main Task

The main task now is to begin moving beyond the limitations of struggle placed upon a student movement. We must realize our potential to reach out to new constituencies both on and off campus and build SDS into a youth movement that is revolutionary.

The notion that we must remain simply "an anti-imperialist student organization" is no longer viable. The nature of our struggle is such that it necessitates an organization that is made up of youth and not just students, and that these youth become class-conscious. This means that our struggles must be integrated into the struggles of working people.

One thing should be clear. This perspective doesn't see youth as a class or say that youth will make the revolution by itself. Neither does it say that youth are necessarily more oppressed than older people, simply that they are oppressed in different ways. There are contradictions that touch youth specifically. To understand why there is a need for a youth movement, first we must come to see how youth are oppressed.

Oppression of Youth

Youth around the world have the potential to become a critical force. A youth movement raises the issues about a society in which it will be forced to live. It takes issues to the working class. They do this because, in America, there exists an enormous contradiction around the integration of youth into the system. The period of pre-employment has been greatly extended due to the affluence of this highly industrialized society and the lack of jobs.

Institutions like the schools, the military, the courts and the police all act to oppress youth in specific ways, as does the work place. The propaganda and socialization processes focused at youth act to channel young people into desired areas of the labor market as well as to socialize them to accept without rebellion the miserable quality of life in America both on and off the job.

The ruling class recognizes the critical potential of young people. This is why they developed so many organizational forms to contain them. Many young people have rejected the integration process that the schools are supposed to serve and have broken with and begun to struggle against the "establishment." This phenomenon has taken many forms, ranging from youth dropping out as a response to a dying capitalist culture, to young workers being forced out by industry that no longer has any room for the untrained, unskilled, and unorganized. Both the dropout and the forced-out youth face the repressive nature of America's police, courts, and military, which act to physically and materially oppress them. The response from various strata of youth has been rebellion, from the buildings at Columbia to the movement in the streets of Chicago to Haight-Ashbury to the Watts uprising.

Revolutionary Youth

We must also understand what role a youth movement would have in the context of building a revolution. An organized class-conscious youth movement would serve basically four functions in building revolutionary struggle:

1) An organized revolutionary youth movement is itself a powerful force for revolutionary struggle. In other words, our struggle is the class struggle, as is the Vietnamese and the black liberation struggle. To call youth or even the student movement a section of the bourgeoisie which must simply support any struggle fought by working people is economism. The struggle of youth is as much a part of the class struggle as a union strike. We ally with workers by waging struggle against a common enemy, not by subjugating our movement patronizingly to every trade union battle. We also ally with the liberation struggle of those fighting against imperialism, recognizing that this is the true expression of the working class at its most conscious level.

2) Youth is a critical force which—through struggle—can expose war, racism, the exploitation of labor and the oppression of youth. We do this by putting forth our class analysis of capitalist institutions via propaganda and sharp actions. Exemplary actions

of the youth movement lead to higher consciousness and struggle among other people.

3) Because we can organize—as a student movement—around those contradictions which affect youth specifically, we can organize young working people into our class-conscious anti-capitalist movement. These young workers will (a) strengthen the anti-capitalist movement among the work force, (b) provide an organic link between the student movement and the movement of working people, and (c) add to the effect that we will have as a critical force on older working people today.

4) The expansion of the base of the youth movement to include young working people changes the character of our movement importantly: because it fights the tendency of our student movement to define itself in terms of "student interest" rather than class interest.

Because we see a revolutionary youth movement as an important part of building a full revolutionary working-class movement we must shape our own strategy self-consciously now with a view to that youth movement. This means that, in addition to expanding our base to include more young working people, we must insure the class-consciousness of our movement now, and we must attack the class nature of the schools we are organizing against.

Racism

Building a class-conscious youth movement means fighting racism. SDS must see this fight as a primary task. Racism is a central contradiction in American society, since racism is an inherent part of capitalism and a primary tool used to exploit all working people. In order to fight racism, we must recognize that there is a struggle being fought right now for black liberation in America with which we must ally. This fight for black liberation is at once an anti-colonial struggle against racism and the racist imperialist power structure, as well as being part of the class struggle because black workers are among the most oppresed. It is through racism and its development into colonial oppression that black people are maintained as the most oppressed sector of the working class. Racism (white supremacy) ties white people to the state by splitting them from the most aggressive class struggle.

We must also fight racism within our own movement and among youth in general and make our loyalty to the black liberation struggle more solid. While recognizing that "black capitalism" is not a solution to the problem of racism, we must be careful not to dismiss the anti-colonial nature of the black liberation struggle by simply calling it bourgeois nationalism.

Implementation

The implementation part of this proposal should not be seen as a national program of action but rather as some suggested actions as well as some necessary actions to be taken if such a youth movement is to be built.

1. BUILD CLASS-CONSCIOUSNESS IN THE STUDENT MOVEMENT IN THE DEVELOPMENT TOWARD A REVOLUTIONARY YOUTH MOVEMENT.

a. SDS organizers should direct the focus of their energies to organizing on campuses of working-class colleges, community schools, trade schools and technical schools as well as high schools and junior colleges.

b. Attacks should also focus on the *university as an arm of the corporations* that exploit and oppress workers. Corporations that exploit workers should be fought on campus. (Aside from producing napalm, Dow Chemical Co. has plants in 27 countries of the Third World and is among the largest international corporations.)

c. SDS should move toward the building of alliances with non-academic employees on the campus based on struggle against the common enemy, the university. SDS should view the university as a corporation that directly oppresses the working class.

d. SDS should move to "destudentize" other students by attacking the false privileges of the university—e.g. the 2-S deferment should be attacked on that basis.

e. Some of us should move into factories and shops as well as into working-class communities, to better understand the material oppression of industrial workers, as well as to eradicate prejudices against workers.

f. We should move into the liberation struggle now being fought inside the armed forces and take an active part. Up until now, we have paid only lip service to that struggle of mostly working-class youth.

g. Youth should be made to see their own struggle and the struggle of the Vietnamese against imperialism as the same struggle. The war must continue to be an important focus for SDS organizing.

h. We must join the fight against the class and racist nature of the public school system.

i. Dropout and forced-out youth both should be encouraged to join our movement.

2. ATTACK ON INSTITUTIONAL RACISM. We must view the university as a racist and imperialist institution which acts to oppress the working class and is the brain center of repression against the liberation struggles at home and around the world. Programs should be developed which aggressively attack it as such and attempt to stop it from functioning in that manner. Targets should include:

a. Police institutes on the campus.

b. The real estate establishment.

c. Centers for counterinsurgency (both domestic and foreign) including research and planning centers and sociology and education schools which teach people racism so that they can help defeat the struggles of the blacks.

d. Racism in the classroom, especially in high schools where students are forced by law to sit and listen to racist and class-prejudiced distortions of history.

e. A fight should be waged for the admission of black students and brown students to help wage the fight against racism on the campus. Blacks are carrying on the most militant fights both on and off the campus, and more black admissions means a more militant campus movement. We must also expose the racist and class nature of admissions systems and the high school track system and demand that the schools be opened up to the community so that they too can struggle to stop its oppression.

26

Mike Klonsky, Noel Ignatin,
Marilyn Katz, Sue Eanet
and Les Coleman

Revolutionary Youth Movement II
(RYM II) (*1969*)

. . . Six months have passed since we came together around the idea of transforming SDS into a revolutionary youth movement. The practice which has taken place within our movement has now made it possible to reevaluate the RYM and reestablish the principles of unity for our movement. The tremendous growth of SDS, the repression that has come down on the whole movement and the heightening contradictions throughout the whole society have made our job much more serious. . . .

How is it possible that there can be a Revolutionary Youth Movement such as is coming into existence today?

All societies, at all times, face the contradiction between the new and the old, between what is growing and what is dying out. The youth movement in America is, in the first place, an expression of this contradiction. The young tend to be the most open, innovative, and self-sacrificing. They are invariably the first to rebel. Mao says that while the future belongs to all of us, in the last analysis it belongs to youth.

Our society is dying out. Not only here but on a world scale, in a historic sense. Imperialism, the monopoly phase of capitalism, is nearing its closing hours. Our epoch is the epoch of the final collapse of imperialism and the final worldwide victory of socialism. Imperialism, fully moribund, manifests its decay everywhere. It pollutes all that is fresh, alive, vital, and growing. The young in general, but particularly among the oppressed classes and strata, are among the hardest hit by decaying imperialism. Hardest hit and most willing to fight back—that is the youth movement.

The ruling class would like to portray youthful rebellion as simply a generational or biological phenomenon. In fact, it stems from the particularities of American imperialist development. The youth movement has developed in proportion to the increasingly pronounced decay of this system. The fifties witnessed the temporary stabilization of U.S. rule. The American century lasted about 10 years. From a relatively isolated imperialist power, World War II has enabled the U.S. monopolists to dominate most of the world. But by 1960 the consequences of that insane scheme were becoming apparent. The short-lived empire began to crumble. Young people were victimized on every hand.

The draft forced the military burden of fighting and dying in an unjust war onto the young. The increasing exclusiveness and discrimination within trade unions affected young workers, particularly black and brown workers. Automation contributed to the general capitalist trend toward greater unemployment which affected job seekers with little experience severely. The decay of bourgeois ideology made the schools into jails—either of force or boredom—which taught through repetition and answered through irrelevance. The decay of bourgeois culture, inevitable in a climate of imperialist war and injustice, precipitated a cultural rebellion among those who were only just establishing their life-style. The domestic militarization, particularly of the schools, made rebellion against all forms of bourgeois authoritarianism, from the principal on down, a matter of pride to the most advanced among the youth. The upsurge of national liberation struggles at home and abroad provided heroic examples of other possibilities. Cuba, Vietnam, and African struggles as well as the revolutionary spirit of the Chinese provided inspiration and models. Finally, the sharpness of the contrast with those who came to adulthood in the fifties and whose outlook reflected that earlier phase—all this contributed to making the youth movement central to the U.S. revolutionary movement.

It is insofar as SDS has spoken to this condition of youth that our organization has grown and been able to play its part in the struggle to defeat U.S. imperialism and build world socialism. . . .

The youth movement today—composed of black, brown, and white youth from different class backgrounds—is not something that has the task only of "lighting the match" and then flickering out. This youth movement must build and last if the struggle is to be successful. Youth must be in the front ranks of all phases of the struggle, just as now they are in the leading role in raising the fight against the main enemy—U.S. imperialism—throughout the whole society. . . .

There are five main ways in which the youth movement relates to the anti-imperialist struggle as a whole. These are its principles of unity and its strategy for action.

1) The youth movement must build itself into a unified fighting force against the imperialists. Given the particular oppression of youth under imperialism, it's possible and correct to unite youth from all classes into the struggles against imperialism. With the escalation of correct anti-imperialist struggles, the RYM must bring more and more working-class youth into its ranks. . . .

2) The revolutionary youth movement can be one of the main ways of bringing the anti-imperialist movement to the proletariat as a whole. Especially today when the white sectors of the proletariat are dominated by the bourgeois ideologies of white national chauvinism, male chauvinism, anti-communism, the anti-imperialism movement must greatly intensify its efforts to win the proletariat. . . .

3) A key aspect of the youth in foment is its struggles against white supremacy. Struggles against the white supremacist practices of the schools this year have fundamentally challenged the basis of this decadent, oppressive society. We must carry this fight into all aspects of our work. . . .

4) Further division and control of the proletariat has been effected through the ideology and practice of male supremacy. Male supremacy has arisen out of the relation of women to the means of production in society: that of unpaid necessary social labor in the maintenance and reproduction of the labor force as a reserve army of labor used to keep down wages in general. Thus women are all degraded as sexual objects and are superexploited: paid lower wages and denied access to the skills and trades for men.

The youth movement must fight against the male supremacist structure of this decadent society and the manifestations of this in the superstructure. . . .

5) The youth movement can play a role in the development of a party by fighting anti-communism, developing communist ideology, and taking communist ideology to the mass of the people.

Program of the RYM

1. ANTI-IMPERIALIST PROGRAM IN THE SCHOOLS
   A. 1. End to tracking
      2. No flunkouts or disciplinary expulsions
      3. Open admissions for all black and brown students
      4. The teaching of the true history and social conditions of this decadent, imperialist society
      5. A real understanding of communism and of movements of national liberation
      6. End to male supremacy in the teaching of classes, the content of courses, and the "tracking" of women into secondary roles and employment
      7. A guarantee of decent employment for youth who are not given the chance of higher education
   B. 1. We support employees in their struggles to extract a better life in return for their work in the schools.
      2. We join in the struggles to make the schools provide day care centers, low-income housing, cultural youth centers, etc. for the surrounding community.
      3. We will attack the existence of military training and research programs, police institutes, etc. in the schools and stop their functioning by any means necessary.
      4. We will attack the imperialist functions of the university for its programs of university expansion, etc.
   C. We will give special support for black and brown student demands, because their demands challenge the key feature in imperialist institutions today: the oppression of black and brown peoples and the attempt to win white people to the support of that oppression through the offering of white-skin privileges. We support the 10-point program of the Black Panther Party on the campuses. . . .

2. ROADS TO THE WORKING CLASS. Serving the people means giving material support to the many militant strikes and wildcats. In doing this we must attack the employer—the corporation or company—on an anti-imperialist basis whenever possible. . . .

We must take our movement to the youth in the military by going into the armed services and contributing our support to the anti-imperialist movement which already exists among the GIs. . . .

To pull back from our work with the masses would be exactly the result desired by the bourgeoisie. They have escalated their attack on the movement, and the only way to beat that attack is to carry through a strategy for winning the war against the bourgeoisie, and ultimately defeating imperialism.

Therefore our essential program to fight repression is to carry through the program of the Revolutionary Youth Movement to reach out to the masses, particularly the proletariat, and to serve the needs of the people. . . .

While courts are still available to us as a means of defense, we should use them to the fullest extent, using the opportunity each time we appear in court to make clear the political nature of the police, courts, and attacks on individuals.

In addition we must be prepared to defend ourselves by whatever means necessary when the courts can't serve even the minimal protection they now provide. We must become skilled in the use of weapons and be prepared to use them to defend ourselves if attacked. We must also prepare ourselves by securing our offices and homes to prevent them from confiscating important files and materials.

As the armed might of the state comes down on the people and the movement as it has done recently in Greensboro, Berkeley, and hundreds of other places in the black and brown communities, we must respond by preparing the people for armed self-defense and eventually for armed struggle.

Armed attacks by the state must be used by the movement to explain to the people the necessity of arming for self-defense and the nature of the state. We must take every opportunity to explain that the state cannot be challenged except through revolutionary violence. This is its nature. . . .

We must take seriously the job of helping to build the communist party. There is no such communist party which exists today, no party which both repesents the interests of the proletariat and has any mass base among the proletariat. There are things which we can do to help prepare for it.

27

Karin Ashley, Bill Ayers,
Bernardine Dohrn, John Jacobs,
Jeff Jones, Gerry Long,
Howie Machtinger, Jim Mellan,
Terry Robbins, Mark Rudd
and Steve Tappis

"You Don't Need a Weatherman to Know Which Way the Wind Blows" * (*1969*)

People ask, what is the nature of the revolution that we talk about? Who will it be made by, and for, and what are its goals and strategy?

The overriding consideration in answering these questions is that the main struggle going on in the world today is between U.S. imperialism and the national liberation struggles against it. . . .

So the very first question people in this country must ask in considering the question of revolution is where they stand in relation to the United States as an oppressor nation, and where they stand in relation to the masses of people throughout the world whom U.S. imperialism is oppressing.

The primary task of revolutionary struggle is to solve this principal contradiction on the side of the people of the world. It is the oppressed peoples of the world who have created the wealth of this empire and it is to them that it belongs; the goal of the revolutionary struggle must be the control and use of this wealth in the interests of the oppressed peoples of the world. . . .

The goal is the destruction of U.S. imperialism and the achieve-

* Reprinted by permission of Radical Education Project.

ment of a classless world: world communism. Winning state power in the U.S. will occur as a result of the military forces of the U.S. overextending themselves around the world and being defeated piecemeal; struggle within the U.S. will be a vital part of this process, but when the revolution triumphs in the U.S. it will have been made by the people of the whole world. . . .

The struggle of black people—as a colony—is for self-determination, freedom, and liberation from U.S. imperialism. Because blacks have been oppressed and held in an inferior social position as a people, they have a right to decide, organize and act on their common destiny as a people apart from white interference. Black self-determination does not simply apply to determination of their collective political destiny at some future time. It is directly tied to the fact that because all blacks experience oppression in a form that no whites do, no whites are in a position to fully understand and test from their own practice the real situation black people face and the necessary response to it. This is why it is necessary for black people to organize separately and determine their actions separately at each stage of the struggle.

It is necessary to defeat both racist tendencies: (1) that blacks shouldn't go ahead with making the revolution, and (2) that blacks should go ahead alone with making it. The only third path is to build a white movement which will support the blacks in moving as fast as they have to and are able to, and still itself keep up with that black movement enough so that white revolutionaries share the cost and the blacks don't have to do the whole thing alone. Any white who does not follow this third path is objectively following one of the other two (or both) and is objectively racist.

. . . The vanguard (that is, the section of the people who are in the forefront of the struggle and whose class interests and needs define the terms and tasks of the revolution) of the "American Revolution" is the workers and oppressed peoples of the colonies of Asia, Africa and Latin America. Because of the level of special oppression of black people as a colony they reflect the interests of the oppressed people of the world from within the borders of the United States; they are part of the Third World and part of the international revolutionary vanguard. . . .

We have pointed to the vanguard nature of the black struggle in this country as part of the international struggle against American imperialism, and the impossibility of anything but an international strategy for winning. Any attempt to put forth a strategy which, despite internationalist rhetoric, assumes a purely internal development to the class struggle in this country, is incorrect. The Vietnamese (and the Uruguayans and the Rhodesians) and the blacks and Third World peoples in this country will continue to set the terms for class struggle in America.

Why a Revolutionary Youth Movement?

In general, young people have less stake in a society (no family, fewer debts, etc.), are more open to new ideas (they have not been brainwashed for so long or so well), and are therefore more able and willing to move in a revolutionary direction. Specifically in America, young people have grown up experiencing the crises in imperialism. They have grown up along with a developing black liberation movement, with the liberation of Cuba, the fights for independence in Africa, and the war in Vietnam. Older people grew up during the fight against Fascism, during the cold war, the smashing of the trade unions, McCarthy, and a period during which real wages consistently rose—since 1965 disposable real income has decreased slightly, particularly in urban areas where inflation and increased taxation have bitten heavily into wages. This crisis in imperialism affects all parts of the society. America has had to militarize to protect and expand its empire; hence the high draft calls and the creation of a standing army of three and a half million, an army which still has been unable to win in Vietnam. Further, the huge defense expenditures—required for the defense of the empire and at the same time a way of making increasing profits for the defense industries—have gone hand in hand with the urban crisis around welfare, the hospitals, the schools, housing, air, and water pollution. The state cannot provide the services it has been forced to assume responsibility for, and needs to increase taxes and to pay its growing debts while it cuts services and uses the pigs to repress protest.

In all of this, it is not that life in America is toughest for youth or that they are the most oppressed. Rather, it is that young people are hurt directly—and severely—by imperialism. And, in being less tightly tied to the system, they are more "pushed" to join the black liberation struggle against U.S. imperialism. Among young people there is less of a material base for racism—they have no seniority, have not spent 20 years securing a skilled job (the white monopoly of which is increasingly challenged by the black liberation movement), and aren't just about to pay off a 25-year mortgage on a house which is valuable because it's located in a white neighborhood. . . .

. . . Agitational demands for impossible, but reasonable, reforms are a good way to make a revolutionary point. The demand for open admissions by asserting the alternative to the present (school) system exposes its fundamental nature—that it is racist, class-based, and closed—pointing to the only possible solution to the present situation: "Shut it down!" The impossibility of real open admissions—all black and brown people admitted, no flunk-out, full scholarship—under present conditions is the best reason (that the schools show no possibility for real reform) to shut the schools down. . . .

One way to make clear the nature of the system and our tasks working off of separate struggles is to tie them together with each other: to show that we're one "multi-issue" movement, not an alliance of high school and college students, or students and GI's, or youth and workers, or students and the black community. The way to do this is to build organic regional or subregional and city-wide movements, by regularly bringing people in one institution or area to fights going on on other fronts.

This works on two levels. Within a neighborhood, by bringing kids to different fights, and relating these fights to each other— high school stuff, colleges, housing, welfare, shops—we begin to build one neighborhood-based multi-issue movement off of them. Besides actions and demonstrations, we also pull different people together in day-to-day film showings, rallies, for speakers and study groups, etc. On a second level, we combine neighborhood "bases" into a city-wide or region-wide movement by doing the same kind of thing; concentrating our forces at whatever important struggles are going on and building more ongoing interrelationships off of that. . . .

Three principles underlie this multi-issue, "cross-institutional" movement, on the neighborhood and city-wide levels, as to why it creates greater revolutionary consciousness and active participation in the revolution:

(1) Mixing different issues, struggles and groups demonstrates our analysis to people in a material way. We claim there is one system and so all these different problems have the same solution, revolution. If they are the same struggle in the end, we should make that clear from the beginning. On this basis we must aggressively smash the notion that there can be outside agitators on a question pertaining to the imperialists.

(2) "Relating to Motion": the struggle activity, the action, of the movement demonstrates our existence and strength to people in a material way. Seeing it happen, people give it more weight in their thinking. For the participants, involvement in struggle is the best education about the movement, the enemy and the class struggle. In a neighborhood or whole city the existence of some struggle is a catalyst for other struggles—it pushes people to see the movement as more important and urgent, and as an example and precedent makes it easier for them to follow. If the participants in a struggle are based in different institutions or parts of the city, these effects are multiplied. Varied participation helps the movement be seen as political (wholly subversive) rather than as separate grievance fights. As people in one section of the movement fight beside and identify closer with other sections, the mutual catalytic effect of their struggles will be greater.

(3) We must build a movement oriented toward power. Revolution is a power struggle, and we must develop that understanding among people from the beginning. Pooling our resources area-wide and city-wide really does increase our power in particular fights, as well as push a mutual-aid-in-struggle consciousness.

The RYM and the Pigs

A major focus in our neighborhood and city-wide work is the pigs, because they tie together the various struggles around the state as the enemy, and thus point to the need for a movement oriented toward power to defeat it. . . .

Thus the pigs are ultimately the glue—the necessity—that holds the neighborhood-based and city-wide movement together; all of our concrete needs lead to pushing the pigs to the fore as a political focus:

(1) Making institutionally oriented reform struggles deal with state power, by pushing our struggle till either winning or getting pigged.

(2) Using the city-wide interrelation of fights to raise the level of struggle and further large-scale anti-pig movement-power consciousness.

(3) Developing spontaneous anti-pig consciousness in our neighborhoods to an understanding of imperialism, class struggle and the state.

(4) And using the city-wide movement as a platform for reinforcing and extending this politicization work, like by talking about getting together a city-wide neighborhood-based mutual-aid anti-pig self-defense network.

All of this can be done through city-wide agitation and propaganda and picking certain issues—to have as the central regional focus for the whole movement.

Repression and Revolution

As institutional fights and anti-pig self-defense off of them intensify, so will the ruling class's repression. Their escalation of repression will inevitably continue according to how threatening the movement is to their power. Our task is not to avoid or end repression; that can always be done by pulling back, so we're not dangerous enough to require crushing. Sometimes it is correct to do that as a tactical retreat, to survive to fight again.

The Need for a Revolutionary Party

The RYM must also lead to the effective organization needed to survive and to create another battlefield of the revolution. A revolution is a war; when the movement in this country can defend itself militarily against total repression it will be part of the revolutionary war.

This will require a cadre organization, effective secrecy, self-reliance among the cadres, and an integrated relationship with the active mass-based movement. To win a war with an enemy as highly organized and centralized as the imperialists will require a (clandestine) organization of revolutionaries, having also a·unified "general staff"; that is, combined at some point with discipline under one centralized leadership. Because war is political, political tasks—the international communist revolution—must guide it.

There are two kinds of tasks for us.

One is the organization of revolutionary collectives within the movement. Our theory must come from practice, but it can't be developed in isolation. Only a collective pooling of our experiences can develop a thorough understanding of the complex conditions in this country.

The most important task for us toward making the revolution, and the work our collectives should engage in, is the creation of a mass revolutionary movement, without which a clandestine revolutionary party will be impossible.

28

Eric Prokosch

Bored in Class . . . ? Guerrilla Tactics in Anthropology Classes * (1967)

Anthropology: a fascinating, exotic subject; a glimpse into the minds of strange peoples; a chance to expand your consciousness by learning about other ways of life.

Or so it should be. But sad to say, if you take an anthropology course you will probably spend your time memorizing dull details: "The Kwakiutl practice the potlatch," or "Pressure-flaked tools were characteristic of the Upper Paleolithic." There is little chance to relate what you learn to your own experience; in fact, you may very well be encouraged *not* to think in terms of your own experience (because this would be "cultural bias"). And what about your instructor? You would expect him to be the most broad-minded person around, but in fact he will probably turn out to be like other instructors—unimaginative, dresses conservatively, makes you take silly exams, and all the rest of it.

Well, when you are suffering through an anthropology course, just think: thousands of other college students are probably suffering too. There is little you can do by yourself to bring the whole

* Reprinted from *New Left Notes* (May 15, 1967, issue). At the time this was written, Eric Prokosch was a student at Stanford (California).

silly structure crashing down. So why not try a tactic of guerrilla warfare? Strike where the enemy is weakest!

Here are a few suggestions:

(1) Through historical accident, anthropology in the United States (unlike other countries) consists of three pretty much unrelated subfields: physical anthropology, archaeology, and a third which deals with human societies and cultures. You may enjoy one subfield, but it is unlikely you will enjoy all three. Probably your instructor also hated one of the subfields; but he had to learn it, and you will too, because that's the way things are. So figure out which subfield your instructor is weakest in; keep asking more and more detailed questions till he admits he doesn't know; and then you can innocently say: "Well, if you don't know it, why do *we* have to learn it?"

Another tactic is to keep asking how each new fact you learn is related to the ones you learned before. Since the pattern of marriage among the Eskimos has very little to do with the shape of the human foot, for instance, sooner or later the standard answer "All these facts broaden your knowledge of man" will give way to "I don't know, but *you'd* better."

(2) Sooner or later everything in American anthropology comes back to this fundamental assertion: "Values (or "cultures") are relative." (In other words, what's wrong for some people is right for others.) When your instructor comes out with this pearl of wisdom, ask him: "What about Nazi Germans, gassing the Jews and putting Slavs to forced labor? Wasn't that part of their 'cultural heritage' of Nordic superiority?"

This will be a hard question to answer because, in effect, the doctrine of "cultural relativity" works as an excuse for avoiding moral questions. (This may be one reason why anthropology has become so popular lately.)

(3) Anthropologists "study" people. Perhaps it is humiliating and unpleasant for the people, but anthropologists are willing to be insensitive on this point, in the interests of "science." Just remember—if anthropologists can study other people, it is also fair game for you to study the anthropologists. Observe your instructor. Notice his way of speech, his deference to superiors, the car he drives, the clothes he wears, as indications of his social position or "culture." Confront him with your findings and see if you can get him

to say: "We do that to 'primitive' peoples, but you'd better not try it on us."

(4) When your instructor is boring you with details of the settlement pattern or kinship terminology of some tribe, be brave and ask him about something you would really *like* to know—like "How do they feel about sex?" or "Don't they hate all these white people who moved in and started telling them what to do?" If he answers "That is not of scientific interest," then you will know that anthropology is just as "culture-bound" as the people it tries to study.

These suggestions are offered in a spirit of fun—not spite. It's not all your instructor's fault. He didn't invent the field. But he's the guy with the power, and besides, there are probably lots of other bored students in your class who would welcome an opportunity to think about something new and unexpected.

29

Karen Wald

The Americana Game * (*1968*)

The Americana Game is a new type of political propaganda that
requires total "audience participation." The game was played at
San Francisco State during the "Ten Days." Many who would
never attend a speech or a rally stopped to view this new political
media on the lawn. Almost all of the Commons lawn was staked
out in a maze of lines with cards bearing descriptions of some facet
of American life, picture collages representing the same thing,
forks where the player must take a choice, and cards of "chance"
at which the player's next step was determined by the card he drew.

The starting point for the game began with a series of picket signs
introducing the player to the socialization process in America.
Cards bore such inscriptions as "25%: Your parents read Spock—
you have Pacifist tendencies"; "30%: Your parents read Reston &
Lippman—a typical liberal, wishy-washy upbringing. You realize
the problems of society but can rationalize anything."

After early socialization comes high school, and the first choice.
The player must decide to follow the path of continuing high school
(after cards give him a good idea of what *that's* like) or to drop

* Reprinted from *The Movement* (July, 1968, issue). The "action" was
organized by SDS on the San Francisco State College campus. Karen Wald
was a student at Berkeley.

out. If he continues, his next choice isn't until he graduates. If he drops out he is immediately faced with the draft. This is a common barrier represented by a chance card at a great many forks in the road. If the player is drafted, he is sent over to the induction center. There he goes through basic training, where cards inform him, "Your sergeant has an IQ of 56. He makes you stand at attention for 2 hours because you looked at him funny" and "Do 50 push-ups for not knowing that the spirit of the bayonet is 'to kill.' " After basic training, a chance card sends him into the U.S. Striking Force around the world (Guatemala, Detroit, Laos) or to Vietnam. If sent to Vietnam, a chance card either lands him in the VA hospital for life, or dead.

The Dropout

But if the high school student chose to drop out, he may have been one of the lucky few who didn't get drafted this time. He is now a member of that great minority group (poor white or black) of "high school dropouts." Rows of cards depict what his life is like, the difficulty of getting a job, the condescension, and finally, get-ting laid off when the company "suffers" a 1% drop in intake. The player is now back in the slum he was born in, and must make a choice. If he hasn't gone off to become a junkie, the choice card tells him, "As you have seen, whenever you have begun to improve your life, something has happened to knock you back down again. You now see that under our social system it is very hard for a per-son like you to better yourself. You have 2 choices. If you want to fight the system and try to overthrow it, if you want to risk going to jail, risk losing what little you have, risk getting killed, then take the path to your right."

If he decides not to risk it, the player becomes a lackey of the system, and ends up secure and well off, but at the price of the oppression of others. If he decides to "fight oppression" he goes along a path that has signs describing JOIN, SCEF, the Panther's Ten-Point Program and the beginning of repression. A sign soon greets him: "The COPS are looking to arrest YOU and kill YOU be-cause you are fighting to end racism and control your life and your community" and points out that the Panthers are only one such group facing this.

Along this path, a chance card may inform the player, "You have been arrested as a result of your struggle against the system. You are held on $40,000 bail until your trial (6 mos.). A white, middle-class jury (who already knew you were guilty because they read the papers) convicts you in 23 minutes. You are sentenced to 20 years. Go to jail near the start of the game" (the jail is a frequent chance card, and is to be described later). Or, if the player is lucky, he may get away, and continue to organize and struggle. Or he may be dead, "accidentally" shot in a riot. If he continues to the end of the line of struggle the final card recites the Declaration of Independence.

And after High School?

But what if the high school student continues instead of dropping out? At graduation, he must choose whether to go to work or to college, or whether to take a side trip and become a hippy (a path he may also get to from some stage of his college or worker career). If he becomes a worker (assuming he has overcome the inevitable barrier of the draft) his life is described as he trudges along the path. A card bearing a string of beads directs him "This is your assembly line. Please move the beads to the right, then back." But as a worker he comes to a choice fork as other workers form a union and decide to strike for decent wages and working conditions. He must decide whether to go on strike with them with all the hardships that entails being described for him or to scab. Cards make it clear the cops and the news media are all on the side of the boss.

The scab ends at a dead end. But the path isn't easy for the strikers, either. Overcoming the hardships of the strike, he is faced with a sell-out on the part of the AFL-CIO leadership who have been pressured by the government, and enter into a sweetheart contract with the boss. Another fork appears for the player-worker to choose—the path of the AFL-CIO, with its security and benefits, but also the human cost—or independent union activity? If he continues as an independent union organizer he ends up on the path labeled "revolt," and fights the system as the radical high school dropout did, with this path too ending with the Declaration of Independence.

The College Kid

And now back to the college student. If he avoids the draft (and his chances of this are good) the cards and pictures give him a good dose of what college life is like—classes of 1500 students, taught by televisions; dormitory rules, etc.—and then the choice, to continue or drop out. The path to the left is dropping out, and (after the draft barrier) sets him on the path where he chooses, as did the high school graduate, to become a worker or a hippy. If he continues, he has two choices. He can go to the right, acquiescing in college life even though he's seen what it's like. He ends up after graduation in private business or government service. In either case he has material success, but again not without cost. As a government worker he's told he can't organize or demand higher wages—it's unpatriotic. Private enterprise bears pictures of "You at 40" and concludes "Your children have run away. Why?"

But the college student may decide to continue as a student activist. The activist is shown, through pictures and photographs most of us are now familiar with, the trials and problems and repression he will face. After a while of this he is given a choice, to go back and acquiesce, and a long line returns him to the path leading to graduation, business or government service. If he chooses not to do this, he will be suspended. Once suspended, he becomes a full-time organizer—once again, if his drawing from the chance cards doesn't send him into the army as his punishment for not acquiescing.

The Organizer

The organizer follows a line of cards describing the hardships he will endure—the problems with his family, the lack of income, the need to relearn all of his old concepts. There are no immediate rewards, but instead jail and beatings, all again revealed through too-familiar newspaper clippings. And again, he is given the choice of going back into the system. If he fails to give in this time, he becomes a full-scale militant with increasing police attacks against him. But in the end, he too concludes with the Declaration of Independence.

A verbal description of this game cannot come close to actually walking through the maze, reading the cards, seeing the pictures, making the choices and taking the chances. You also lose the flavor of hearing the comments and seeing the looks all around you.

The coed, who clearly would not have been at a political debate, greeted by a fraternity-type walking by, "Are you reading all these cards?" "Oh, no," she replied, embarrassed. "I was just walking by" and she continued along the path with him. But she had been reading the cards.

Inside the jail—a roped-off area separate from the rest of the game-maze, where a card instructed you to stay for ten minutes then reenter where you left—a "prisoner" sent there by a chance card asked me, in a very lifelike manner, "Are you a reporter describing jail conditions, or were you a demonstrator?" and another mumbled sincerely, "Gee, I hope I don't get any more cards that send me in here!" as he fidgeted away his ten minutes.

Propaganda!

In the most candid and simple description of the huge life-game, one coed exclaimed in surprise, "Why this is *propaganda!*" "You're damn right it is," smiled one of the SDS organizers of the game. And for those organizers wondering how to end their radical isolation from a liberal campus with visual media, without losing the political content of what they are trying to do, the Americana Game proved a highly effective and successful piece of propaganda.

30

Michael Locker

Campus Reconnaissance * (*1968*)

Throughout Asia, Africa, and Latin America a power struggle of monumental proportions is being waged between revolutionaries and U.S. technology. The well-tested strategy of Washington is clear; technological intervention has been refined to service a complete system of social controls. The strategy and the system is three-pronged: nationalist liberation forces opposing U.S. domination must be (1) isolated, splintered, and contained through infiltration, manipulation and co-optation; (2) failing at this, the United States must provide the local military with the training and equipment needed to uncover, isolate and destroy armed insurgency *before* a popular base is established; and (3) failing at this, the U.S. military must take over and directly confront and defeat popular armed struggle by offsetting its numerical superiority with sophisticated search-kill technology.

On all counterrevolutionary fronts—infiltration, manipulation, indirect and direct armed confrontation—universities have provided essential resources for waging more effective battles. Without the "scholarly" efforts of political scientists, sociologists, economists, psychologists, and anthropologists, isolating the rebels and

* Reprinted from the North American Congress on Latin America. Michael Locker was a student at the University of Michigan.

"managing social change" in a "backward" society would be impossible. Without the brainpower of engineers, physicists, chemists, biologists and computer experts, sophisticated military hardware for detecting and destroying insurgent movements would not be available. Aside from training and channeling such skilled personnel for the "national interest," the university provides a relatively "neutral" and relaxed setting for conducting government and corporate research or operations. As any industrial psychologist would say, academics are far more imaginative, productive and happy when they identify with their product. Behind the guise of an academic discipline and claims of "objective" research, a well-paid and essentially self-supervised professor can safely develop the latest nerve gas without ruffling his sensibilities. The university setting is an attractive cover that eliminates conscience and maintains high productivity. The military-industrial complex is relying heavily on the innovative abilities of the academic world for de-

COMMONLY USED ABBREVIATIONS

ACC	Army Chemical Center	CBR	Chemical, Biological, Radiological
ACDA	Arms Control and Disarmament Agency (DoS)	CFSTI	Clearinghouse for Federal Scientific and Technical Information
AEC	Atomic Energy Commission		
AFOSR	Air Force Office of Scientific Research	CI	Counterinsurgency
		CIA	Central Intelligence Agency
AID	Agency for International Development (DoS)	D.Ag.	Department of Agriculture
ARO	Army Research Office	DASA	Defense Atomic Support Agency (DoD)
ARPA	Advanced Research Projects Agency (DoD)	DoD	Department of Defense
ASTIA	Armed Services Technical Information Agency (DoD)	DoDIAC	Department of Defense Information Analysis Centers
		DoS	Department of State
CBW	Chemical and Biological Warfare	FCRC	Federal Contract Research Centers

COMMONLY USED ABBREVIATIONS (*cont'd*)

FY	Fiscal Year		tional Security Affairs
GPO	Government Printing Office	ODDRE	Office, Director of Defense Research and Engineering
HEW	Department of Health, Education and Welfare	ONR	Office of Naval Research
INP	Independent, nonprofit	PHS	Public Health Service
IP	Independent, profitmaking	R&D	Research and Development
MAP	Military Assistance Program	RDT&E	Research, Development, Test and Evaluation
NASA	National Aeronautics and Space Administration	U	University
NIH	National Institutes of Health	USA	U.S. Army
NSA	National Security Agency	USAF	U.S. Air Force
		USMC	U.S. Marine Corps
NSF	National Science Foundation	USN	U.S. Navy
OASD, ISA	Office of the Assistant Secretary of Defense, International	USNOTS	U.S. Navy Ordinance Test Station
		WSEG	Weapons Systems Evaluation Grant

feating revolutionary solutions to the increasing exploitation and misery of the Third World.

Given such a situation, radicals and revolutionaries who want to crystallize the real issues involved in government-sponsored projects must zero in on the direct role such "academic work" plays in wars against national liberation. Most liberals and some radicals, confining their analysis to a narrow and outdated definition of the university, demand greater campus "autonomy" to insure "objectivity." This is not the real issue. By restricting its analysis to purely local and domestic concerns, this line of dissent becomes vulnerable to attack on civil-libertarian grounds if it increases its militancy. But by broadening the analysis to confront the reality of how the government uses scholarly research for counterrevolutionary purposes, the real issues are brought into focus. And in order to focus and fix attention on the real issues involved, it is absolutely necessary to secure detailed information on the academic project's potential and actual utilization. Undoubtedly the substantive nature of the project and the depth of involvement will largely determine the limits of discussion, the lines of division, and ultimately the type of demands and the form of struggle that can develop. But without detailed knowledge of the practical application of scholarly research, it is almost impossible to break through liberal obfuscation in the rarefied university atmosphere. As long as civil libertarian abstractions are allowed to preempt the overriding realities of human conflict, a politics of confrontation will seem illegitimate and self-defeating. This of course is exactly what the administration is aiming for; if the radicals escalate their demands and tactics before shifting debate away from liberal abstractions, they can be isolated and defeated. Only the widespread dissemination of detailed information of the political (as opposed to the scholarly) objectives of a project can prevent this from occurring.

How then does one gather those details about a project that best reveal its actual function? There are certainly no foolproof formulas; yet experience has demonstrated that specialized sources and an investigatory technique can be helpful. Precision with regard to details and the ability to follow up seemingly insignificant leads are crucial in entering any strange culture. The specialized jargon of government research and operations is especially difficult to master. Strange euphemisms creep into the language of project titles (e.g., "The Defeat of a Target Through Thermal Heat," "A State-of-the-Art Study on the Impairment of Voluntary Nervous Systems"). The acquisition of specialized information and the aid of a friendly expert in the field will uncover what is behind such titles.

Investigating Government-Sponsored Operations

Most all government-sponsored operations are handled through a contract or grant. Each government department funds its own contracts and/or grants and makes public in various forms information about unclassified agreements. Unfortunately, since there is no single public list of all government contracts and grants, the investigator is obliged to work with fragmentary and diverse sources. By shifting back and forth between various sources and utilizing various techniques, however, he will usually be able to accumulate enough detail to determine the political content of the project.

DEPARTMENT OF DEFENSE UNIVERSITY CONTRACTS

UNIVERSITY	AMOUNT	UNIVERSITY	AMOUNT
Johns Hopkins University	$50,394,000	Stevens Inst. of Tech.	$1,271,000
Mass. Inst. of Technology	$47,308,000	Georgia Tech. Research Inst.	$1,269,000
Stanford Research Inst.	$30,693,000	University of Colorado	$1,264,000
University of Michigan	$19,492,000	Washington University	$1,194,000
Stanford University	$18,569,000	University of New Mexico	$1,143,000
Columbia University	$16,203,000	Syracuse University	$1,119,000
University of California	$16,149,000	University of Cincinnati	$1,109,000
Cornell Aeronautical Lab.	$14,961,000	Univ. of Southern Calif.	$1,058,000
I.I.T. Research Inst.	$13,952,000	University of Rochester	$1,056,000
Penn. State University	$11,830,000	Purdue University	$1,046,000
University of Illinois	$10,875,000	University of North Carolina	$964,000
Franklin Institute	$9,117,000	University of Arizona	$950,000
University of Washington	$6,434,000	Yale University	$907,000
University of Pennsylvania	$5,932,000	Oregon State Univ.	$883,000
Cornell University	$5,452,000	University of Virginia	$865,000
Syracuse Univ. Research		New Mexico School of Mines	$845,000
Corp.	$5,343,000	University of Hawaii	$787,000
George Washington Univ.	$5,229,000	Univ. of Rhode Island	$770,000
University of Denver	$5,074,000	Iowa State University	$762,000
Harvard University	$4,286,000	Tufts University	$759,000
University of Texas	$4,073,000	Rensselaer Polytech Inst.	$724,000
New York University	$3,929,000	University of Florida	$490,000
University of Dayton	$3,670,000	Texas Western College	$679,000
Cal. Inst. of Technology	$3,584,000	Catholic Univ. of America	$663,000
Princeton University	$3,568,000	State Univ. of New York	$656,000
University of Chicago	$3,444,000	Case Inst. of Technology	$603,000
Ohio State Univ. Research		State Univ. of Louisiana	$597,000
Fdn.	$3,416,000	Utah State University	$563,000
Brown University	$3,011,000	Indiana University	$491,000
Northwestern Univ.	$2,742,000	Rutgers University	$483,000
Duke University	$2,631,000	University of Tennessee	$471,000
American University	$2,594,000	Boston College	$449,000
Brooklyn Polytech. Inst.	$2,468,000	Georgia Inst. Technology	$410,000
University of Maryland	$2,314,000	Emmanuel College	$407,000
University of Miami	$2,139,000	Temple University	$403,000
Carnegie Inst. of Tech.	$2,077,000	Notre Dame University	$400,000
University of Minnesota	$2,061,000	Western Reserve University	$398,000
University of Wisconsin	$1,928,000	Dartmouth College	$381,000
Northeastern University	$1,914,000	Rice University	$379,000
University of Pittsburgh	$1,780,000	Ohio State University	$378,000
New Mexico State Univ.	$1,663,000	Brandeis University	$376,000
Purdue Research Fdn.	$1,629,000	University of Alabama	$366,000
University of Alaska	$1,598,000	Oklahoma State University	$359,000
Texas A&M Research Fdn.	$1,397,000	Lehigh University	$339,000
University of Utah	$1,367,000	University of Missouri	$339,000
Illinois Inst. of Tech.	$1,305,000		

U.S. Department of Defense: *500 Contractors Listed According to Net Value of Military Prime Contract Awards for Research, Development, Test and Evaluation Work, Fiscal Year 1966.*

The investigating job involves four basic procedures: (1) searching printed sources produced off-campus, (2) searching printed sources produced on-campus, (3) searching other printed sources for details on the project's subject content, personnel and facility, and (4) field work to acquire details not readily available in printed sources.

Searching Printed Sources Produced Off Campus

Most government-sponsored university operations are unclassified and some departments' contracts or grants are listed in public documents.* The problem is not so much secrecy as obscurity; most people do not know the sources exist or where they can be located.

I. U.S. Department of Defense, *100 Companies and Their Subsidiary Corporations Listed According to Net Value of Military Prime Contract Awards.* Washington, D.C. Free from the Department of Defense. Annual.

II. U.S. Department of Defense, *500 Contractors Listed According to Net Value of Military Prime Contract Awards for Research Development, Test and Evaluation.* Washington, D.C. Free from the Department of Defense. Annual.

III. a. U.S. Department of Commerce, Clearinghouse for Federal Scientific and Technical Information, *U.S. Government Research and Development Reports.* Springfield, Virginia. Semi-monthly.

III. b. U.S. Department of Defense, Defense Documentation Center, *Technical Abstract Bulletin.* Alexandria, Virginia. Semi-monthly.

III. c. U.S. Department of Defense, Defense Documentation Center, *Technical Abstract Bulletin* (classified "Confidential"). Alexandria, Virginia. Semi-monthly.

* Throughout this section "government-sponsored operations or projects" refers to all endeavors financed and/or run directly or indirectly by any part of the U.S. Government for any service, product, idea, advice, etc. Any individual connected to such operations or projects in any capacity, financial, advisory or otherwise, will be considered part of that operation. In a contract the project's subject and operations are set by the government department and sold to the recipient (sometimes on a competitive basis), while in a grant the recipient first submits a proposal which the government can award funds for on a nonprofit basis.

IV. U.S. Department of Army, Office of the Chief of Research
and Development, *Army Research Task Summary: Fiscal
Year 1961.* Washington, D.C.

Government Printing Office.
  Eight volumes:
    Vol. I—*Life Sciences, Psychology and Social Sciences*
    Vol. II—*Chemistry*
    Vol. III—*Physics*
    Vol. IV—*Engineering Sciences and Earth Sciences*
    Vol. V—*Materials*
    Vol. VI—*Electronics, Mathematics, Operations Research, Planning and Systems Research, and Interdisciplinary Research*
    Vol. VII—*Index*
    Vol. VIII—*Recapitulation of Funds* (Classified).
V. *Aerospace and Defense Research Contracts Roster. Fiscal
Year 1965.* Compiled by Frost and Sullivan, Inc., Washington,
D.C. Bowker Associates, Inc., 1966. Annual.
VI. U.S. Department of State, Bureau of Intelligence and Research, *Government-Sponsored Research: Europe and the
Soviet Union; Asia and the Middle East; Africa; Latin America;* and *International Affairs.* Washington, D.C.
VII. U.S. Department of State, Agency for International Development, *AID-Financed University Contracts.* Washington,
D.C. Annual.
VIII. U.S. Department of State, Agency for International Development, *Current Technical Service Contracts.* Washington,
D.C. Annual.
IX. National Science Foundation, *Grants and Awards for Fiscal
Year Ended June 30, 1966.* Annual. Washington, D.C. Government Printing Office.
X. U.S. Department of Health, Education and Welfare, Public
Health Service, *Public Health Service Grants and Awards.*
Washington, D.C. Government Printing Office. Annual.
  Five parts: Part I—*Research*
            Part II—*Training*
            Part III—*Construction*

Part IV—*Health Service*

Part V—*Summary.*

XI. National Aeronautics and Space Administration, Office of Grants and Research Contracts, *Grants and Research Contracts.* Washington, D.C. Annual. Available from NASA.

XII. Atomic Energy Commission, *Financial Report.* Washington, D.C. Annual. Available from AEC. Lists total value of contracts by institution.

XIII. U.S. Department of Commerce, *Commerce Business Daily.* Washington, D.C. Government Printing Office. Daily on business days.

XIV. The Smithsonian Institution maintains a national registry of research in progress called "Science Information Exchange." This is not a printed document but rather a service that will, upon request, send an investigator all the "Notice of Research Project" documents on file for a given subject. The project descriptions are excellent and the coverage is vast. But only "Research investigators associated with recognized research institutions" may request information, giving this excellent source a "restricted" classification. The full address is: Science Information Exchange, 300 Madison National Bank Building, 1730 M Street, N.W., Washington, D.C. 20036.

The "Restricted" (R) classifications of sources III b and XIV are administrative, *not* security designations. Therefore, it is perfectly legal to ask a "qualified" person to search these sources and turn over the results.

While relatively complete information is available in the above sources on most contracts and grants funded by the AID, NSF, NASA, and PHS, other departments (the DOD, DOS, ACDA, CIA, and AEC) are not fully covered by unclassified listings. The latter departments are also more crucial when it comes to foreign policy and military operations. Except for the CIA, however, a large number of projects can be uncovered through these sources.

Searching Printed Sources Produced On Campus

To rationalize the management and flow of information on campus research, the administrations of large universities have set up special offices for handling all aspects of contracts and grants. These offices prepare regular reports listing all the current contracts and grants on campus. Though this type of document is sometimes restricted (at the University of Michigan it is classified "Administrative Confidential"), it is often possible for the campus newspaper to acquire a copy. The same research office usually puts out a regular newsletter and/or journal distributed to all the faculty with a list of new contracts and grants rendered to individuals and institutions on campus. The school's annual report as well as those of departments and research centers and institutes will always contain contract-grant data. Minutes of department or trustees' meetings make interesting reading at times, as do alumni publications. And if all this fails, the investigator should find out where the school maintains its list of technical abstracts of written material produced by faculty members.

At any large university, the list of contracts and grants an investigator will compile from the above sources will rapidly become unmanageable. Those projects funded by government departments deeply enmeshed in military and overseas activity should take priority. On the other hand, an investigation of a small, private liberal arts college will probably not turn up any military projects outside the behavioral sciences, though this situation may be changing as a result of Pentagon policy to hook such schools into the military-industrial network (e.g., Project Themis). Projects from more domestically oriented departments (e.g., NSF, PHS) and "peace-loving" sections of our government (e.g., Peace Corps training, AID student and cultural exchanges) will predominate; they should not be overlooked.

Whatever the number and type of projects uncovered, the crucial job of demonstrating their contribution to counterrevolutionary efforts still remains. To surface your findings immediately is to invite "confrontation" within the liberal context. The basic information collected on project contracts and grants will have to be analyzed and persuasively interpreted from a political viewpoint before its disclosure can achieve its disruptive, radicalizing, and action-generating potential.

Searching The Project's Subject Matter, Personnel And Facility

After the existence of military-related contract/grants on a particular campus has been determined, the investigator's work has just begun. He should then collect information on a project's subject matter, personnel and facilities. The printed sources for these subjects follow:

A. SEARCHING THE LITERATURE ON PROJECT SUBJECT MATTER. There are ten source categories for finding out more about the project subject matter and utilization:

(1) *Signed Contract or Grant and Project Reports:* Acquisition of the actual agreement signed between the sponsoring government department and the receiving body will provide background information on and possible application of the project. The agreements are classified when the project is so designated by the government (whether federal or state public information access laws apply to unclassified projects is not clear to the author). The AID permits inspection of their unclassified contracts.

In-progress and final project reports written for the sponsoring government department can be very helpful but are difficult to acquire. Sources IIIa, IIIb and IIIc above would be the most help in locating such reports.

(2) *University, Department, or Institute Reports.* As mentioned above, these readily available sources often contain detailed descriptions of the project's subject matter.

(3) *Abstracts.* Abstracts enable the investigator to (a) quickly locate the essential facts of a written document, (b) locate the complete document and (c) survey the whole subject field within which a particular document is found. The U.S. Commerce Department's publication, *U.S. Government Research and Development Reports,* and the old and new (classified) Defense Documentation Center, DOD, *Technical Abstract Bulletin* announce availability and publish abstracts of R & D reports issued primarily from work being sponsored by the DOD, AEC, and NASA.

Abstracts of articles published in scholarly journals can be found in *Abstracts of Computer Literature, Peace Research Abstracts, Sociological Abstracts, Psychological Abstracts,*

Chemical Abstracts, Historical Abstracts, Economic Abstracts, Biological Abstracts, Educational Recap, Indicus Medicus, International Political Science Abstracts, Social Science Abstracts, and *Dissertation Abstracts.* Research institutions also maintain and sometimes publish their own abstracts of work done by employees (e.g., *Selected Rand Abstracts*).

(4) *Annotated Bibliographies.* Divided along subject lines, annotated bibliographies serve the same general functions for books that abstracts serve for articles. The *Bibliographic Index* (New York, H. W. Wilson Co., semi-annual) is an invaluable tool for locating bibliographies and keeping track of new additions.

(5) *Indexes.* For cross-referencing, indexes like the following, for example, should be checked: *Applied Science and Technology Index* (New York, H. W. Wilson, monthly), *New York Times Index, Science Citation Index* (Philadelphia, Institute for Scientific Information, quarterly), *Essay and General Literature Index* (New York, H. W. Wilson and Co., monthly), and *Cumulative Book Index* (New York, H. W. Wilson and Co., monthly and cumulative).

(6) *Proceedings of Professional Associations.* Professional conferences, conventions and meetings often have sessions related to government-sponsored activity. The papers and discussions in such a setting are often (a) far more advanced than the published material in the field, and (b) often attended by government representatives who publicly and frankly state the assumptions behind "academic" research. Papers and transcripts are available directly from the association, and are announced in their respective journals or *Directory of Conventions.*

(7) *Scholarly Publications.* Divided along discipline and subject lines, the professional journals often have articles demonstrating how government-sponsored activities are utilized. The *Standard Periodical Directory* (New York, Oxbridge Publishing Co., annual) has a comprehensive list of these journals indexed by subject and title. Also see the Library of Congress, *A Directory of Information Resources in the United States: Physical Sciences, Biological Sciences and Engineering* (Washington, D.C., Government Printing Office) and *A Directory of Information Resources in the United States: Social Sciences* (Washington, D.C., Government Printing Office).

(8) *U.S. Government Congressional and Executive Publications.
The U.S. Government Publications Monthly Catalogue* (Washington, Government Printing Office, monthly with cumulative index) has a subject index and incorporates most federal material. Congressional hearings and reports, especially those of the House and Senate Appropriations, Armed Services, Education, and Government Operations Committees and their subcommittees contain lengthy descriptions of all government-sponsored activity, testimony from administrators and statistical data. See especially the bibliography prepared by the Senate Committee on Government Operations, Subcommittee on Government Research, *An Inventory of Congressional Concern with Research and Development* (Washington, D.C., 89th Congress, 2nd Session, U.S. Senate, 1966); House Committee on Government Operations, *Conflicts Between the Federal Research Programs and the Nation's Goals for Higher Education, Report* and *Hearings,* four volumes (Washington, D.C., 89th Congress, 1st Session, U.S. House of Representatives, 1965); U.S. House of Representatives, House Appropriations Committee, Armed Services Subcommittee, *Hearings on 1967 Defense Appropriations,* three volumes (Washington, D.C., 90th Congress, 1st Session, U.S. House of Representatives, 1967), see especially volume 3. In addition, each government department sponsoring research has its own periodical(s) and reports that should be consulted.

(9) *Industry Trade Journals and Newsletters.* University research is put into hardware production and operation by private corporations. To utilize the findings of "academic" research, industry keeps close watch on its development and discusses the implications in a vast number of trade publications geared to the defense market. Unusually frank, these publications make a habit of indicating how research projects fit into the total picture of a weapons system or military strategy. *Technology Week, Ordnance, Aviation Week and Space Technology, Munitions, Missiles and Rockets,* and *Electronics* are just some of the many items available to the public. Many others are produced by defense contractors as in-house organs and get less circulation. The *Standard Periodical Directory* lists hundreds of trade publications according to subject.

(10) *Military Publications.* The number and diversity of publica-

tions totally devoted to promoting military operations is stagger-
ing (see *Standard Periodical Directory's* "Military" section).
Even more frank than the industry trade publications, they offer
very concrete examples of how research is put into good use in
the field. For a start you might look at *Army, Army Research
and Development, Naval Research Reviews, Review of the Air
Force Materials Research and Development Program, Military
Review, Army Information Digest, Air University Quarterly Review, Marine Corps Gazette. The Air University Library Index
to Military Periodicals* (Maxwell Air Force Base, Alabama,
quarterly) is a subject index to over sixty military publications
not found in other indexing services.

B. SEARCHING ACTIVITIES AND ASSOCIATIONS OF PROJECT PERSON-
NEL. Any individual found to be connected to a government-sponsored project should be investigated in terms of past and present
activities and associations. Information of this type can throw additional light on the real purposes and motivations behind a project.
Look at the individual's *employment history* (i.e., name of his
previous employers, period of employment, title or rank, location),
and indications of an unusual skill, competence or prestige in a
specialized field (e.g., degrees, awards, professional associations,
positions on committees, consultant status, the subject of his written work and where it was published or presented). Any connections with the government, industrial defense contractors or defense
research centers (see sources I and II above for a list) indicates
the person deserves more investigation. Repeated circulation from
one organization to another, holding more than one position simultaneously, shifting rank or field suddenly—these are all patterns of
behavior that suggest relationships of possible importance in shaping decisions and controlling research.

Such information for faculty members of a university or college
is relatively easy to come by in biographical resources published by
professional associations or societies, the government or private
corporations (i.e., *American Men of Science*). The university or
research institution certainly maintains such information, but it is
not readily accessible (except possibly to newspaper reporters).
Hardly any profession today is without a published directory that
contains some biographical information. A good list of the primary

sources can be found in Bernard Klein (editor), *Guide to American Directories* (New York, McGraw Hill, Sixth Edition, 1965) and more secondary sources are listed in *Biographical Information: Where to Find It* (Detroit, Gale Research Co.). The *Biography Index* (New York, H. W. Wilson Co., monthly and cumulative) might also prove helpful.

Sources listed under Section A above indicate how to uncover works authored by a known individual (abstracts, bibliographies, and indexes).

C. SEARCHING INFORMATION ON RESEARCH FACILITIES. The environment in which a project is enmeshed can be an indication of its ultimate utilization. Interlocking relationships through financial and personnel connections give some hint of the politics behind an organization's activities. Such information also brings into play individual motivations and rewards which can go a long way in puncturing liberal abstractions.

The best public source is usually descriptive and promotional literature produced by the research institution. *The Research Centers Directory* (Detroit, Gale Research Co., Second Edition, 1966) and its periodic supplement, *New Research Centers* (Detroit, Gale Research Co., quarterly) gives basic information i.e., location, activities, fields of interest, source of funds, administrative personnel) on university-related and independent nonprofit research units. For data on industrial nonprofit and profit research units see William W. Buchanan (editor), *Industrial Research Laboratories of the United States* (Washington, D.C., Bowker Associates, Inc., 1965), and numerous directories of scientific resources in a geographical location that are listed in Bernard Klein (editor), *Guide to American Directories,* cited above.

While many industries research facilities are not officially part of the university, many are located near the campus and relate to faculty members through employment, contracts or grants, and consulting. A person in this position should be investigated and if his work contributes to counterrevolutionary efforts, vigorously challenged. The artificial division between "on" and "off" campus work should not be allowed to blur the substantive issues involved in such research.

Other directories of research centers that might be helpful for just basic facts are: Office of Naval Research, Department of the Navy, *Directory of Department of Defense Information Analysis Centers* (Washington, D.C., Government Printing Office, 1965); Department of State, External Research Staff, *Research Centers in Developing Areas* (Washington, D.C., Department of State, 1964) and *Language and Area Study Programs in American Universities* (Washington, D.C., Department of State, 1964).

As always, a search of the periodical literature and the local press should uncover articles on the research facility.

Field Work

No matter how good or thoroughly researched, material uncovered in printed sources should be supplemented by interviews, observations and inside information. High and low level personnel connected with the project or in the same department or research facility should be interviewed in private, on or off the record. Space the interviews carefully, order the questions beforehand, and use details collected from printed sources to frame your inquiries. The order can bring out contradictions while concrete questions inform the interviewee that you have a working knowledge of the project and have entered his "reality." Ask the subject for copies of his printed work and if he wants to keep things "off the record" assure him that you will not attribute that information. You may feel more confident with two people asking the questions when the subject is an important figure. Most of all, an interview is *not* a debate; if it unintentionally turns into an argument you can easily nullify its information-gathering purpose and prematurely close off some excellent sources.

It is essential to observe the research facility and such events as department meetings, conferences, seminars, training sessions, special courses or any other gathering connected to the project. Often these events are attended by civilian or military representatives of the government. Get to know "the other side of campus"—the institutes and laboratories—in order to familiarize yourself with their size, layout and operations.

At times interviews and observation cannot be directly undertaken without creating a role that legitimatizes their necessity. Covers can be easily erected by getting a friendly faculty member to authorize the research through a course or enlisting the aid of a campus newspaper reporter. In some situations where security is tight inside informers will be the only way to secure vital information. Personal contact with friends or political associates who have positions providing access to the information (i.e., secretaries, research assistants) can prove quite helpful. If necessary someone may have to take a job on the project or in the research facility to gain access to such information. Persons in positions of public authority such as federal or state congressmen, senators, executive officials and their assistants, can easily acquire restricted (but not necessarily classified) information and forward it to you. Their desire to do so is usually proportional to the effect it might have on their own political well-being. Whatever the method, the problem of getting inside information (no matter its classification) essentially involves finding a person with legitimacy in the authority's eyes who has access to the material and can transmit the data either secretly or without the threat of reprisal. Obviously such a person should be handled with discretion and the smaller the number of persons who know about it the better your chances of success.

The university's role in the struggle against national liberation forces is a product of this society's drive for economic, social and military domination of the Third World. The academic community has been carefully enlisted in the struggle and the number of points where the university intersects with the counterrevolutionary effort has markedly increased over the last twenty years. Government-sponsored research is simply one crucial point of intersection; recruitment, training, industrial contracting, interlocking directors, endowment investment in foreign-oriented or defense firms, foundation grants and student exchanges are some other vital university activities that lend valuable assistance to private and public attempts to penetrate and control other societies. In short, the university's role in building and maintaining our overseas empire takes several forms and must be opposed on many fronts. By making public the real functions of the university's technological contribution to that empire, we are making a crucial beginning.

31

Wisconsin Draft
Resistance Union

What Is Guerrilla Theater, Anyway? * (*1968*)

Prologue

The idea for the Guerrilla Theater Caravan started in bare skel-
etal form. We knew of no place in the country where guerrilla theater had been used as an integral part of a long-term organizing
project. Thus, we had no precise model to follow. Since none of us
on the original WDRU staff had any previous involvement with
guerrilla theater in the past, we had to thoroughly hash out and develop the ways the Caravan could meet our organizing needs
around the state.

A caravan was originally conceived by the staff as being a valuable way to expand and promote the purposes and goals of the
Summer Offensive. It was seen to be a dynamic and dramatic way
to communicate our political perspective to as many people around
the state of Wisconsin as possible. Further, and most importantly,
we saw guerrilla theater as a catalyst which, at its best, could spark
people to join the movement for radical social change. The radical
organizing potential in guerrilla theater was clearly visible. The
task of defining exactly how that potential could be realized was

* Reprinted by permission of Radical Education Project. The Wisconsin
Draft Resistance Union was composed of students from the University of
Wisconsin at Madison.

left to those who would eventually comprise the Caravan. The problems that were crucial at first were: What kind of people does the Caravan need? How do you effect a balance between the political and theatrical aspects of guerrilla theater? How does the specific organizing function of the Caravan make it different from usual guerrilla theater?

It was evident that the people on the Caravan had to have a nearly homogeneous political perspective. This meant that the members had to be radicals and had to understand, if not feel, the different ways American society oppresses all of us. This proved to be not much of a problem since everyone who was interested in joining the group possessed these attributes to one extent or another. The staff institute which was held at the beginning of the summer was designed explicitly for the purpose of developing every staff member's political perspective to a level of common sophistication. Although there were political squabbles among the members of the Caravan over tactics, the important thing was that we all agreed with the long-range or strategic goals of organizing. This is the first criterion for any guerrilla theater group which sees itself as part of a state or local organizing project.

The second problem, that of reaching a balance between the theatrical and political aspects of the Caravan, plagued us all summer long. The need to develop certain theatrical skills was not readily accepted by those members of the troupe who saw themselves first and foremost as political organizers. The others among the troupe whose experience was not from the movement but from radical theater on the U.W. campus were inclined to see the Caravan's needs in terms of developing a repertoire, practicing movement, improvisation, and physical and vocal liberation. The first few weeks we spent developing those theatrical skills, much to the displeasure of many members of the Caravan. When we began to get out on the road and travel around to different towns we realized how our performances were enhanced precisely because we had those skills. The theatrically oriented members of the troupe, on the other hand, increasingly saw the need to develop the skills of political organizing. Thus the two points of view reached a natural balance as the summer progressed.

The political needs of the Caravan were seen as the factor that differentiated us from other guerrilla theater troupes that we were familiar with, i.e., the San Francisco Mime Troupe, the Bread and Puppet Theater, etc. The Caravan was responsible to the Wisconsin Draft Resistance Union. It was an integral part—and perhaps the most exciting part—of a whole program of intensive constituency organizing. Everything that it did as a unit, everywhere it went had to be determined not by individual inclinations but rather by the political needs of the DRU. We had one unfortunate experience of going into a town to which we had not been invited. The circumstances were such that it was politically inexpedient for us to be there. We learned from that experience that we should only go to towns where there was a potential for the start or growth of a political movement, or where we were invited by an organizer for a specific event.

Each of the members of the troupe was different from a guerrilla theater actor in that each was also an organizer. Besides presenting our criticisms of America in our plays, it was essential that we be able to offer people programmatic ways of taking action to make America a better place. In order to be able to do this we had to be briefed on every town we went into. We had to know what stage the movement was at there; if there was a movement at all; and what kinds of things people would be ready to do. Often we would make small changes in our plays so that they would be more relevant to a particular audience.

At the beginning of the summer we came to the realization that the constituency most accessible for the Caravan was high school and college age youth. Therefore, depending on the situation in a town, we developed program possibilities for people of this age. Our ideas for program were presented in the rap sessions which took place after each performance and which provided the most exciting and provocative experiences of the whole summer. Underground newspapers, teach-ins on the war and the draft (for very provincial towns), setting up coffeehouses, leafletting—all were means we used at various times to unite people who had the beginnings of a radical outlook.

The ability (1) to be sensitive to political needs of young people, and (2) to respond to those needs by offering programs is the most crucial difference between the WDRU Caravan and other guerrilla theater groups. It is this difference that makes the Caravan a valuable model for radical organizing projects all over the country.

ACT I, EARLY SKITS

Scene 1, Beloit

Late in the spring, while the Caravan was still being organized, we received a call from Beloit College, that they needed help to do guerrilla theater on their campus. A black draft-resister was on campus, and members of the black student group wanted to dramatize his presence and raise questions concerning students and the draft. Four strangers were needed to portray a group of Military Policemen, coming on campus to arrest the draft-resister. So four of us went to Beloit, and met with the organizer there who had provided a front by establishing the play as a sociology experiment and who supplied maps and a script along with army surplus uniforms. We then met with the resister and rehearsed the arrest which was to take place that night in the cafeteria, with no advance publicity and only a few people aware that this was not real. We marched in and arrested him on schedule, and got out of the building, where we confronted the students who had followed us out with a political discussion of the implications of what had just happened. Although there were no incidents, it was apparent that we were believed to be real, and that two of the black students had almost reached the point of stopping us, one of them with a loaded gun. All in all the response was good, we made a lot of contacts, and agreed to return later for a more formal program.

Scene 2, Madison at Graduation

Flushed with this success, interest was aroused for the inclusion of guerrilla theater at the anti-commencement rally, the following Sunday. For this purpose we developed a mime skit, The Trap, depicting the university as a trap to train and channel manpower for the military-industrial complex. The play included the military and businessmen as street hawkers, who fail to interest young people in their "wares," whereupon they seduce an administrator with money and grants, who accepts the strings attached and sets up the Great University. The bars of the university appear to be too bare, so he attaches flowers to them, using their appeal to lure in the young student. The faculty are then called in, but every time the student reaches for knowledge, he is slapped back with a blue book, finally falling to his knees under a deluge of blue books. Angry, the student attempts to get out of the cage, but the administrator gives birth to a policeman, who beats the student back down. Finally the faculty come in to pick the student up again, and ready him as an automaton for graduation, before he is rushed off to Vietnam.

Scene 3, Return to Beloit

In the week following graduation, the WDRU held an orientation and training institute for some forty full-time summer volunteers who would be working on a variety of projects. Here for the first time the Guerrilla Theater Caravan was officially constituted, and the members were assembled who would be working on the Caravan throughout the summer.

Since the first engagement, the return to Beloit, was scheduled soon after the institute, work was begun immediately on the development of material, under the direction of Johnny Lerner, who had come in from extensive guerrilla theater experience in New York to aid in establishing the project.

After several days of extensive work on theatrical techniques, a skit was developed based on a script written by the Madison High School Guerrilla Theater. The skit concerned a student, graduating from college, and subjected to the draft, who is bombarded by conflicting and confusing advice from his mother, his hippy draft-resister friend, and an Army recruiter and businessman, as the draft approaches closer and closer, until finally overcome by the weight of unclear and conflicting alternatives, the student sinks to his knees to be taken by the draft and sent off to Vietnam. Most of the action was graphic with minimum props and dialogue, and using the supporting cast as a chorus, highlighting the action.

The play was designed to reach the fairly well-to-do and complacent students at this small, liberal-arts college. The skit was performed in the auditorium of the union, at an anti-draft rally, and was supported by a rock band, which helped to draw a crowd but was later a distraction. A political discussion followed the performance, beginning with a talk by one of the cast, and then breaking up into small discussion groups in the adjacent cafeteria.

Some useful discussion and contacts came out of the production, but generally we were dissatisfied with many aspects of the situation, including the material which we used, the format for the presentation, the excessive numbers of people in the company which limited discussion, and the general nature of the response from an essentially insular group of students. We decided that some basic changes were needed in the organization of the Caravan.

ACT II, BONG BONG THE CONG

Scene 1, Manitowoc

Following the Beloit experience, the Caravan's membership was consolidated, with some of the dropouts setting up a Madison-based guerrilla troupe to assist in campus organizing and other people moving into other projects. The Caravan, now consisting of eight full-time people including a high school student, a high school teacher, a person with newspaper experience, several people with extensive theater experience, and several with organizing experience, settled down to redefine its goals and work up new material under the guidance of another guest director. The result was a series of vignettes dealing with authority, power, and brutality, which were loosely integrated into a format quixotically entitled *Bong Bong the Cong.*

The skit opens with a parade of the players, carrying ladders, guns, flags, and costumes, and playing whistles, kazoos, washboard, tambourine, and cymbal. Although several performances were in more or less formal settings in coffeehouses, many were also out-of-doors at dances, parks, and beaches, so that the opening march not only set the stage, but was frequently used to gather audiences. This was followed by introductory remarks, ending in an example of "What Makes America Tick," in which a cop and a military man rotate together on the stage, beating a circle of supplicants, to a clocklike rhythm. This is followed by the cast forming a chorus line and singing a revised and somewhat obscene version of "Join the Army." In the quiet following the song, the stage is cleared and an officer enters and stands at attention, while a Vietnamese woman is shoved screaming onto the stage and systematically kicked and beaten by another soldier. Finally just before she is to be shot, the officer intervenes and selects instead a member of the audience who is inducted and ordered to shoot the peasant. If the inductee refuses to shoot under the threats and shouts of the officer and soldier, he is court-martialed and led off to prison. If he does shoot he is warmly congratulated and presented with a whore, flown in from Saigon, as his reward. This then dissolves into a sentimental rendition of "Johnny, I Hardly Know You," which changes into a burlesque treatment of the song with the cast laughing and dancing on the stage.

The cast then forms a line across the stage, representing authority figures including a parent, a minister, a guidance counselor, a cop, and a politician. A high school girl then questions each in turn about pertinent issues such as dress codes, contraceptives, curfews, and the 18-year-old vote, only to receive more and more vague answers, which finally degenerate into a chorus of grunts by the cast. At a gong, the line freezes and the young girl, who has been avidly listening, dances off stage saying, "Thank you very much, I understand." The stage is then cleared except for two ladders, and from offstage two voices are heard, one singing Requiem Mass and the other delivering a stylized political speech on "Climbing the Ladder of Success." Onto the stage come a large, robust oppressor leading a smaller, weaker oppressed on a leash. The oppressor admires one ladder, and using the oppressed's back as a stool climbs to the top, triumphant. The oppressed then tries to climb the other ladder with the oppressor's encouragement only to be repeatedly jerked back to the ground by the leash. Then, in anger, the oppressed seizes the leash from the oppressor, and begins shaking the ladder. As the cast quotes from Marat/Sade, "We want our rights and we don't care how, we want a revolution, *now,*" the oppressor is tumbled from his ladder. The 1920's style finale consists of the girls singing the chorus from "Indian Lake," while the boys sing "This Is My Country," ending with the admonition from one of the cast, "And it's your country, too!"

A week was spent rehearsing the skit which lasts about fifteen minutes. That weekend the premiere performance was given at a Youth Festival in Manitowoc, Wisconsin. Although WDRU had no previous organization there, the Caravan generated great interest among high school and college students in the audience. Long discussions continued into the night and on the next day.

When the Caravan left an initial organization was forming which continued through the summer.

Scene 2, Whitewater and Sheboygan

By this time, certain tensions began to develop in the Caravan which were expressed as an antagonism between the desire to get back on the road and the desire to create new skits. Unable to develop material because of this tension, the Caravan made an over-hasty decision to take off for a week around the southeast corner of the state.

Our first stop was in Whitewater where an extension of the U.W. is located. We had been communicating with a budding SDS chapter which had invited us down. In addition to the summer students, we also knew of an "Upward Bound" program for disadvantaged high school students from Milwaukee. Preparing ahead of time, we developed a special short skit on the program. In the skit, an administrator is patronizingly describing the program to the young student, explaining all they are doing for him, including education, culture, athletics, and religion. As each subject is mentioned the administrator loads books, pictures, sports gear, ikons, etc. onto the student who is driven by their weight to his knees, then to his back. The administrator then tells the student to reach out for success and plants his foot squarely on the student's balls while urging him to rise up, to lift himself higher. Finally, in apparent disgust the administrator announces that he will have to help the student and, reaching down, he stands him on his head.

The following day we moved on to Lake Geneva which is a popular resort famous for its July 4th riots. The idea here was to present our skit in true guerrilla fashion without prior contacts, but we just couldn't get started. We spent the day just swimming and drifting around. That evening we went to Williams Bay where we had contacts, but unfortunately they were not ready for us. Indeed, the presence of a truckload of bearded, long-haired radicals immediately alerted the cops and we were the center of much attention, particularly unwanted by the local organizer. The local people got us out of town as soon as possible. We went on to another town where we heard that a dance was being held, but when we arrived, we found a tightly controlled area where the kids could not come outside without forfeiting their admission and we could not go in without paying $2 apiece.

This brought an abrupt end to our "grand tour" as we realized that with no contacts or knowledge of the area we were badly limited in our ability to function. We agreed, therefore, that we would not go out again without some more prior planning, and more clearly defined function.

Two days later a different situation presented itself with a preplanned invitation to appear in Sheboygan. The organizing effort in Sheboygan has been progressing for some time, primarily among high school students, and projects such as an underground newspaper had already been initiated. However, the politics of the situation were still at a very low level. The problem was in trying to unite a number of student groups around the job of establishing a coffeehouse. The Caravan was asked to perform at an organizational meeting of these different groups. The skit was followed by general discussion which lasted for several hours about the skit, the political situation, and the problems of the coffeehouse. The meeting appeared to be successful and definitely enhanced by our presence there.

Scene 3, Racine, Wauwatosa, Watertown

The next skit we worked up was called The Groovy Machine. It was designed to be performed at teen-age dances. We first formed a circle, each of us assuming a machinelike motion and sound. The Operator would then come to each one of us inserting an IBM card and cranking us up. We started with the machine sounds, then we were programmed to say hip slogans such as I'm Hip, Sock It to Me, Groovy, etc. Then a hippy floats by singing "Flower Power," and is sucked into the machine assuming a machinelike movement. They burst into the song "It's So Groovy Now That People Are Finally Getting Together" and return to their slogans going faster and faster. Finally, the Operator programs the machine to say "I'm free," as they turn and face the outside of the circle, shaking imaginary bars, and sinking to the ground. As they fall to the ground in a circle the Operator jumps into the center triumphantly declaring, "Happiness is a well-running machine."

We had our first chance to try out the skit at a dance in Racine. Racine has a draft information center but the organizers there have been unable to reach out and create a movement. At the dance, kids were drunk, uninterested, and noisy. When we performed we were met with heckling from the audience. Very few people could hear us, people were making jokes about our white-face. While we were able to perform without incident, this was one of the few occasions where we were not able to follow the play with a political rap. We made no new contacts but did manage to give some moral support to the organizers.

The next day a few of us left the main group and went to a large suburban shopping center, which was having a sidewalk sale. We established two characters, an officer in military uniform, and an enlisted man who carried a rifle. The enlisted man was tied with a rope and led around by the officer, who was also beating him with a bamboo whip, shouting incoherent commands. This pair moved along the sidewalks of the shopping center and into a large super-market. The officer stopped to admire merchandise, buying an apple which the soldier must carry but the officer gets to eat. Added was a peasant woman who attempts to steal bread from the officer's pocket only to be shot by the soldier at the officer's command, with the scrap of bread being retrieved from the dead body. This received much attention and a generally good response. Although the police were later called by some storekeeper, we had long since broken off and returned to the truck. Again, while there were no tangible results, many people seemed to have been affected, and there was a positive effect on the morale of the Racine organizers.

That evening we traveled to Wauwatosa, a prosperous and very conservative suburb of Milwaukee, where we had arranged to perform at a church-sponsored coffeehouse. We received a good reception from the student management, who had been attempting for some time to initiate political discussions among the patrons of the coffeehouse, who came by, frequently after drinking, to sit and play cards. Again we performed both the *Groovy Machine* and *Bong Bong,* and were well received. The discussion afterwards was most interesting in that people were very interested in the questions which we had raised and which they never seemed to have thought of before. Lively small-group discussions were initiated which continued until early in the morning. Many people commented that this was the most exciting and provocative evening they had experienced at the coffeehouse.

The next night we went to a coffeehouse in Watertown, where we had arranged earlier for a performance. This was in a much smaller town, where the students were much more liberal but very apathetic. Again we presented our skits and held a political discussion, but there was great difficulty in eliciting anything other than a social response from the small group of people in the audience. We were generally dissatisfied afterwards, particularly after our success in Wauwatosa. One member of the cast, however, did have an enthusiastic talk with some high school chicks who were very excited about the idea of "Women's Liberation"—a concept which seemed to strike at something deep. Unfortunately, this was never followed up.

ACT III, SOOPER COMMIE HUNTER

Scene 1, Waukegan

Upon returning to Madison, and beginning to discuss the need for new material, we were particularly impressed by some forms of red-baiting which had come up from hostile members of the audience in several of the towns. We decided that this was an important concept to be raised in our presentations since it underlay so many of the present responses to the left in this country. We were also aware that Wisconsin was the home state of Joe McCarthy, and that we intended to reach Appleton, his birthplace, some time in the summer, and that our next stop, Waukegan, Illinois, was also an ultraconservative town. The result was an attempt to burlesque red-baiting and superpatriotism.

The skit opens with a businessman, with suit coat, hat, briefcase, and newspaper, entering on a bare stage. He announces that while he may appear to be a "mild-mannered, conservative businessman," this is not so and that the present threat from "creeping international communism" demands a man with superhuman powers. He then rips off the suit to reveal the painted T-shirt and cape of Sooper Commie Hunter, who is assisted by his little pal Freedom Boy (played by a girl). As he leaves he announces that he will return if anyone ever whistles "Yankee Doodle Dandy." This is followed by three vignettes demonstrating communism at work.

In the first scene a student playing a harmonica is accosted by a tough cop who beats him unmercifully, until the student, broken on the ground, crawls over and sinks his teeth into the cop's ankle. The cop then calls for Sooper Commie Hunter, who captures the "dirty commie" who is biting his ankle. The cycle is repeated in the second scene when a young girl reading an underground newspaper is met by her teacher who has just finished reading *Playboy*. The teacher grabs the paper from the girl, calling it "trash," and ordering her to her knees, places her foot on the young girl's neck. Startled, the girl tries to get up, and teacher calls S.C.H. In the final scene a small girl enters jumping rope, and a little boy comes over and tries to take the jump rope away from her. As the girl sinks weeping to the ground, still holding fast to one end of the rope, the boy calls for S.C.H., who retrieves the rope for him.

In all of these scenes Sooper Commie Hunter comes rushing out to discover the latest instance of communist villainy, praises the oppressor, and curses the oppressed, announcing to the audience that he recognizes the "Red Menace," "Yellow Peril," and "Foreign Aggressor" (this was sometimes done by putting masks on the victims). He then takes the victims to the back of the stage where he sprays them respectively with "tear gas," "Mace," and the new secret weapon "Left Guard." Finally he asks if the audience will support him in his fight, and spotting one doubter in the audience, arrests him as a "communist sympathizer." He finishes by machine-gunning all the victims as an example of what happens to those who would trifle with our values such as "Liberty, Justice, and Equality," and exits shouting "Thus always to Tyrants."

Waukegan was the most exciting project of the summer, an industrial city run by a repressive and almost feudal power structure where two WDRU organizers—one a native of the town—had begun to build a movement primarily among tough working-class kids. From the beginning they faced constant legal and political harassment. Following one particular outrageous bust for leafletting at a local dance, we were invited down to perform at the dance, one week later, as a show of strength. We were prepared by various horror stories about the town and counseling by the WDRU legal staff on how to act after we were arrested. It was therefore with some reluctance, but a high sense of purpose that the Caravan traveled to Waukegan. We had no opportunity to perform until Sunday afternoon, when we paraded in full costume to the far end of the beach, attracting a large crowd. In spite of some hostility both during and after the skits, we were able to hold political discussions in small groups. Finally after about an hour the Park Rangers arrived in force and asked us to leave. At this time the main group broke up, but smaller groups continued throughout the afternoon.

That evening, we prepared for the confrontation. The liberals had been mobilized to be on hand at the dance as observers, cameras and bail money had been arranged and the lawyers were standing by. The kids in the Waukegan Movement were on hand as scouts and witnesses, the band was contacted and arranged for us to go on at intermission. Unfortunately, our schedule was off by several minutes and the crowd had already been distracted by the cops and led down to the far end of the beach. However, we were able to draw many of them back with our opening parade, and they came running from different parts of the area (expecting to see a fight!) to form a circle around the playing area. This crowd was actively hostile, and began shouting and cursing, moving onto the stage, and throwing things, but we were able to finish the skit before the police stepped in to clear the area. As we started to leave, the cops began hassling some of us about a permit, and sympathies immediately switched to us as against the cops. We were ordered to leave, having accomplished only a symbolic confrontation and having done little to help the Waukegan Movement.

Scene 2, Wisconsin Dells

The next week the Caravan traveled to Wisconsin Dells, another major resort area, where a church-oriented coffeehouse had been established as a place of recreation for students working in the area for the summer. We performed all three of our skits, but the reaction afterwards was noncommittal until we began to be harassed by a group of southern racist Army reservists, who had gathered in the doorway. The situation was tense for several minutes with an exchange back and forth, until one of the priests invited the group in to sit down, followed by an extensive political discussion. We were invited to return but the priests were uptight about our skits, saying that the coffeehouse could not be too associated with anti-war things, even though most of the kids were anti-war and anti-draft.

Scene 3, Milwaukee

In the middle of the week we went to Milwaukee to appear at the Avant-Garde coffeehouse, a dull and druggy place. We performed all of our skits and were well received, but the discussion was curtailed because of a scheduled performance by some folk singers. While they sang, a bunch of tough guys attacked some hippy-looking kids outside. Several kids saw this through the window but did nothing. The political point of *The Groovy Machine* began to make sense.

Scene 4, Madison

Back in Madison, a controversy was raging over the appropriation of some $8,000 for police riot control equipment, and the Caravan decided to appear at the City Council open hearing to make our feelings known. What we decided upon was a takeoff on the Sooper Commie Hunter theme, with the addition of other supercrime fighters. We went to the meeting with our costumes—painted T-shirts and capes—concealed under street clothes. Our spokesman registered as a witness in *favor* of the appropriation. When he was called he delivered an impassioned rap in support of more and bigger riot equipment. Finally stepping down from the podium he pledged his own assistance in the struggle and, pulling off shirt and jacket, revealed himself as Sooper Commie Hunter. This was followed by the rest of the cast uncovering as Sooper Kike Krasher, Sooper Black Basher, Sooper Morals Snooper, etc., and dancing and singing around the council room. We then exited amidst confused laughter and clapping by the council members. This was well covered by the press who mentioned that even the following day some of the council members were unsure of what side we had been on, although it was clear to the press and others. When the vote was taken, the appropriation did pass, a foregone conclusion—but the press coverage was important.

Scene 5, Appleton, The Terrace

On the following weekend, still flushed from our "victory" in the Council Chambers, we made it at last to our sort of inverse mecca, Appleton, the home of Joe McCarthy. They had had there an enthusiastic organizing project during the summer, and a large crowd was assembled that evening in another church-sponsored coffeehouse. This was our most enthusiastic audience outside of Madison, and after thoroughly enjoying our program, they presented a short skit of their own, based on a right-wing instructor in a "Problems of Democracy" class. The following discussion was extensive and many ideas and concepts were exchanged.

The following day we appeared again at a local beach, providing an opportunity for other members of the movement to see our play, but without much other tangible success, because of cool weather.

Our final appearance was back in Madison, on the Terrace of the University of Wisconsin Student Union. This is a traditional gathering place for student radicals, intellectuals, and hippies, and we had appeared several times earlier in the season always with an enthusiastic response and good monetary donations. Fearing the skit *Bong Bong the Cong,* which was the only play we hadn't presented earlier, was too elementary for such a sophisticated audience, we explained that it was intended primarily for high school students. One of our friends from an Appleton high school jumped up after the skit and "testified" how he had been a fascist before the Caravan changed his life. The response of the Terrace crowd was very enthusiastic, and we received over fifty dollars in contributions to support the Caravan and the WDRU. This was a particularly satisfying note as we finished the season, with the cast splitting up for a rest before starting school. But it also indicated the potential for the reconstitution of an expanded guerrilla theater program in the fall, as students return to high schools and universities.

Epilogue

The term guerrilla theater is one which is used much too loosely and, as far as the Caravan is concerned, it never—except for two important situations—engaged in what we had originally conceived of as guerrilla theater. Instead, the Caravan worked with a pretty fixed set of skits, and did not in general attempt to create new skits to focus on what was happening in specific localities. On the other hand, the Caravan was not, either in conception or action, a traveling repertory company doing "political" plays. Rather, the Caravan over the course of the summer came to see itself primarily as an organizing tool servicing the needs of a number of new and isolated movements around the state. To a lesser degree the Caravan hoped to create the beginnings of new organizations in places where we had contacts, but where there was no defined movement. We attempted to do this first by exciting and leading generalized political discussions after our performances, and secondly by helping kids in small Wisconsin towns to see that the various oppressions they felt were not peculiar to their town and that the movement was likewise a bigger thing than what was happening in their town. Unlike most other guerrilla/mime radical theater groups, the Caravan saw itself connected to an ongoing political organization, the Wisconsin Draft Resistance Union, and its members all saw themselves and acted to various degrees as political organizers.

This format came about partly through discussion and largely by default. We had originally talked of staging more spontaneous and mind-blowing/audacious skits in supermarkets, on beaches, at dances, and so forth, hitting people with such things as the war, the draft, consumption-commodity life, and creating spontaneous discussion and tensions which organizers in the various towns might be able to use. Our move away from this was a result first of our success in Manitowoc, and second of our conception of DRU's immediate political needs. The movement at this time centers around high school and college age youth, the natural oppression they feel in their schools, the delegitimation of tradition authority, the injustice of the draft, curfews, dress regulations, etc. As organizers, we tried to make this growing anti-authoritarianism take a political direction, to help the kids make connections between their own feelings of oppression and the oppression of other groups in American society. Therefore, the Caravan came to see itself as relating to these youthful constituencies, rather than to a generalized and fragmented public. This is why we did not emphasize hitting shopping centers and the like.

The other, and perhaps more serious reasons that we fell into the coffeehouse circuit routine are these: the problems and inner dynamics of the Caravan itself, communications between the Caravan and the Madison staff, and communications between the field projects and the organization as a whole. The latter two problems remained enormous throughout the summer, but are mainly relevant here insofar as they were aggravated by the problems within the Caravan itself. As is common in troupes of this kind, a split among political and personal lines soon developed, which, at times, threatened to paralyze the Caravan or to cause its dissolution. The split manifested itself in the formation of a political faction and an artistic faction. This division was basically a political one, but was aggravated by personality differences. For this reason, decent political discussions became nearly impossible and the notion of formalized internal education was totally abandoned.

Perhaps the problems of the Caravan could have been dealt with in a political manner, but no one in the group proved able to do this, with the result that the rift at times became vicious and personal. Largely because of this, the Caravan fell into the easiest mode of operation, i.e., the repetition of already developed skits followed by political discussion. It is true that at times tensions subsided enough to develop new material, but none of the material, once developed, was subjected to much critical evaluation or change, aside from slight changes in lines to suit different towns. Even as a skit theater we were unable to develop new material to specifically address the concerns of the various movements. The flexibility and spontaneity demanded by guerrilla theater, i.e., non-coffeehouse theater, became out of the question (and we even stopped thinking in those terms).

The Waukegan Movement felt disappointed that we were unable to relate to and dramatize their struggle, and though their criticism did not come until several weeks later, the Caravan was unable to perceive this. This brings up the question of communication on the staff. Although the Caravan was aware of what was happening in Waukegan, we were hardly conscious of how the Caravan could serve their needs. This is partly a fault of the Waukegan organizers who did not force us in a systematic way to confront what they needed, partly this was the fault of the Madison staff which was unable to deal with the Caravan as part of a strategic whole and relate its viewpoint to the Caravan. Mostly, the fault lay with the Caravan which had ceased to see itself in a dynamic and self-critical way, and thus could not relate to new needs which broke its established routine.

There was also one important objective factor which shaped the Caravan's style: the lack of concrete struggle and confrontation in most of the projects. With the organizing concentrating on kids outside of their schools in the summertime, the Caravan saw no particular struggle to relate to.

Other manifestations of the Caravan's internal problems were the lack of discipline in getting to meetings on time, exercising and rehearsing seriously, systematically working on unfinished skits and masks, and the lack of growth of real internal democracy. The Caravan began the summer with two guest directors. The need for a director was continually felt after they left, but we decided not to have another outside director, rather one member of the group would take over that function. Having a director acted as a brake on collective decision-making. Ideally, a politically homogeneous group should try to do without imposed directorship.

This discussion has so far emphasized the unsuccessful aspects of the Caravan, but the truth is that the Caravan, as viewed by its members and by the people who saw it, was very largely successful and helpful to the growth of a political movement in Wisconsin and the Midwest. First, in every place except Beloit College and the Avant-Garde in Milwaukee (both drug- and hippy-oriented) the Caravan's skits and political raps excited long and interesting political discussions and were useful in attracting people to the movement. Second, in places where new movements were coming into existence the Caravan members outside of their role as actors helped give the kids a spark by relating them to a larger movement and by talking programmatically and politically. In Waukegan, for instance, we helped revive internal discussion on racism (a real thing for these working-class kids) and the nature of their movement. These are tasks which an organizer could perhaps have done as well, but our being actors and representing a certain politics in our skits probably forced this discussion more. The Caravan also hoped to enable kids to start using guerrilla theater on their own, though we were less successful in this owing both to a lack of time and to the style of theater into which we had fallen.

The Caravan was an experiment, and its successes merit its continuation and extension during the school year. In many ways its importance will increase when kids are back in those oppressive institutions and when the struggles over student power, dress codes, Dow Chemical, university complicity and the like begin to take shape. Under these conditions the Caravan will both have many more explicit struggles to relate to and will be forced to develop more of a guerrilla style in order to increase the level of political consciousness around these struggles, show up and mock university administrations and the like, and give kids the feeling that they can move. During the school year the Caravan will not be in coffeehouses; it will be relating to real activity, and it will have to have real daring to match the audacity of students capturing an administration building or taking over in their classrooms. Further, within the community, the Caravan will have to be able to dramatize the students' struggles and relate them to the needs and struggles of other constituencies. Our activity at the City Council hearing on riot control was a case in point, and showed the WDRU able to be politically relevant for many constituencies, even though we cannot organize them yet. An effective Caravan is expected and needed around the state and in Madison.

Clap Rap

After every performance we introduced the audience to our way of clapping. It requires that you use your entire body, not just the palms of your hands. We introduce it this way:

There's a story about the time El Teatro Campesino went to a lawyers' convention in California. After their performance one member of the group got up to speak. He spoke for a while and when through the stiff, middle-class lawyers daintily and politely applauded. The speaker, incredulous, cried out, "Don't you know how to clap? Let's show them how our people clap," and turned to the other actors. They started clapping their way.

Then we demonstrate. Everyone gets involved clapping, pounding feet, banging tables, shouting, in slow rhythm at first, getting gradually faster and faster until you can't do it any faster and collapse in exhaustion.

That's how to clap!

AFTERMATH. DEBACLE:
CAMBODIA AND BEYOND

In rapid succession, three critical events in the spring of 1970—
the invasion of Cambodia, the killing of four young white students
at Kent State and the deaths of two blacks at Mississippi State—
gave great impetus to the growing radical student movement in the
United States. A deep sense of outrage and betrayal was displayed
as universities and colleges (along with high schools) across the
nation in unprecedented numbers were brought to a halt and students demonstrated in the streets.

During the month after President Nixon's announcement of his
decision to invade Cambodia, 11,000 young men turned in their
draft cards—almost double the total that had chosen this means of
dissent in the preceding two years. Many students abandoned their
liberalism for an uncharted journey toward participation in a radical movement, guided by humanism and encompassing a new life
style and counter-culture. In this context, Tom Hayden's words
take on special meaning:

Do not wish to be a student in contrast to being a man. Do not study
as a student, but as a man who is alive and who cares. Leave the isolated world of ideological fantasy, allow your ideas to become part of
your living and your living to become part of your ideas.

For others, committed radicals like Steve Nissen, it was a time of intense organizing activity and reassessment of how a revolutionary movement might be most effectively built. In the following essay, he presents an analysis of the Cambodian incident as it has brought another generation of young people to a new level of political and social awareness. At the same time, he speaks of his own firmer resolve, a resolve to dig in for the long revolutionary struggle ahead.

32

Steve Nissen *

We Will Win (*July 1970*)

When President Nixon announced on April 30, 1970 that U.S. troops were crossing the border into Cambodia, he triggered the most massive and violent wave of student protest in North American history. Within a matter of days, 436 college and university campuses were closed, either through direct militant action by dissident students and faculty, or by nervous administrators who feared what might happen if they defied the call for a national student strike.

Suddenly, thousands of students, many of whom had never before been involved in a militant protest, were cast headlong into an intense struggle which placed them on the front pages of the nation's newspapers, generating widespread national concern and debate. The semester's end left the campuses quiet, but the turmoil has had a yet undetermined effect on the students and schools that were touched by it. However, if the past few years of escalating student unrest are any indication, the coming year should be very interesting indeed.

Youth is taking itself seriously now, and in the wake of the Kent State massacre, we understand that we are involved in a struggle for survival. Although many students are still giving the system one

* At the time this was written, Steve Nissen was a student at the University of Michigan. His essay was especially prepared for this volume.

last try, an increasing number of us are identifying ourselves as revolutionaries and settling down for the long struggle. We are beginning to reach out now to our natural revolutionary allies— the working class and oppressed minorities—leaving behind the comfortable womb of the college campus. We are developing a counter-culture and a counter-life-style to demonstrate an alternative to the sterility of this society. We intend to make war upon the American government and we intend to win.

Judging from their size and breadth alone, the post-Cambodia demonstrations were a striking illustration of the extent of discontent throughout a broad cross-section of college youth. Even more important, they were an indication of the willingness of large segments of youth to take to the streets to express their rage, shunning more conventional means of protest.

The campus strikes marked a new high point in the effort to interject politics and social concern into the traditionally apathetic and complacent environment of American institutions of higher education. These universities, modelled after their European counterparts, during the 1950's and early 1960's had been exemplary of the "ivory tower" philosophy of education. Although some elements of the faculties and administrations of these institutions still assert the "political neutrality" of the university, Cambodia and its aftermath signalled a growing deterioration of that posture. Students are simply unwilling to accept that an institution which subsidizes an ROTC program, develops new weapons for the Defense Department, and oppresses the community around it, can in any sense be termed "neutral."

The signs of these attitudinal changes appeared soon after the May unrest. Several major universities are giving their students time off in the fall to assist political candidates in the November (1970) elections. An increasing number of college presidents are now publicly mouthing their opposition to American foreign policy, an act which would have been viewed as heresy five years ago.

Of course, the universities were never really politically neutral to begin with, but there had not been, in the past, sufficient political agitation to stimulate students to challenge that view. Thus, the Cambodia protests were indicative *not,* as the media have suggested, of the growing "politicization" of the campus, but a reflection of the students' increasing awareness of the university's actual role in the society. This is a phenomenon characteristic of student activism—that each time students begin to move in militant manner around pressing political and social issues, they expose the dormant problems and contradictions underlying their initial concerns.

Thus, when students demand an end to military research, as they did at many schools during the May unrest, and the university refuses to comply, the dissidents are often stimulated to consider who really controls the university or why it feels such a strong allegiance to the defense-related research. The results may not be apparent immediately, but thousands of students who participated in the Cambodia actions will return to the campus in the fall with an increased consciousness of the underlying problems of the society and the inability of our present economic and political system to alleviate them.

Each time we strike out at the university's involvement in the war or failure to serve the needs of the community, we are faced by blundering and inadequate responses from the university hierarchy. Our concerns and demands are consistently ignored, rejected, or more recently co-opted. In the process the hypocrisy of the university and its officials is often exposed. "If President Fleming's against the war," students at the University of Michigan chant, "then what the hell is ROTC here for?" The institutions cannot or will not respond, and this invariably increases both the alienation and the resolve of the campus activists. The university can no longer hide behind the cloak of "academic freedom," in order to justify its activities. Students just aren't buying that bullshit anymore.

The response of the government has not been any more conciliatory. In the two months following the Cambodia demonstrations, no less than 43 state legislatures have considered bills aimed at repressing campus political agitation. Laws designed to cut off financial aid to students who are convicted of disrupting normal university activities or make their expulsion mandatory have been approved in a number of states. In the coming years, these laws will undoubtedly be used against student movements; rather than preventing trouble they will encourage it. Repression will only increase our bitterness and determination.

The prospects for the radical movement in America are bright, but the apparent success of the post-Cambodia student strikes fosters an illusion of strength in the student movement which is not really accurate. For the preoccupation of the movement with the Vietnam (now Indochina) war and its location on the college campuses is a weakness as well as a strength for the long-term revolutionary struggle in America. This paradox was never more apparent than in the weeks following the Cambodia invasion.

On the one hand, the strength of the Vietnam issue was evidenced by the widespread dissent it was capable of generating. The fact that over 400 campuses could be closed down *simultaneously* is characteristic of the war's unifying effect. But the effectiveness of the movement has been seriously limited by the fact that it has operated from the college campuses. We have repeatedly failed to reach out into other segments of the community and make contacts and alliances with them. And in the few cases where students have attempted to work with the non-student population, they have almost invariably abandoned even the more moderately left-wing aspects of their analysis in favor of political expediency.

A typical example of this phenomenon is the "Movement for a New Congress," a group organized after the Cambodia protests to work for "peace candidates" in the coming elections. The group held several workshops and seminars on the University of Michigan campus to instruct its supporters on techniques for canvassing the community to raise support for political candidates. During the discussions, it was often difficult to ascertain whether the Movement for a New Congress was organizing a political campaign or trying to sell encyclopedias. Students were repeatedly advised how to trick and cajole potential supporters into voting for "peace" candidates while deliberately suppressing controversial concepts and ideas.

It is clear from the widespread student activity in support of liberal politicians that most of them are not yet ready to abandon the "system." But the effects of the increased political consciousness are evident nonetheless. For the students who are organizing to support liberal candidates have become far more demanding of their politicians than the hero-worshipping "Clean for Gene" kids of two years ago. And many of them seem more cynical about the possibility that it is going to make any difference who is elected.

Despite their skepticism, it seems obvious that the vast majority of college students, at the present time, are neither revolution-

aries nor even radicals. For while many students took to the streets
to express their outrage at the Cambodia invasion, their reasons
for doing so are open to question. Most of the students who went
out on strike in May do not necessarily identify with the struggle of
the National Liberation Front. Perhaps they are distraught at the
killing, concerned about inflation, tired of war, afraid of the draft,
or eager for diversion of the nation's resources to pressing domestic programs. Or maybe they simply believe the war cannot be
won?

Whatever their reasons, the important thing is that they are
moving and thinking. Most significantly these students who have
chosen to remain within the system will be watching closely to
see if the liberals mean what they say. They will watching us, too,
to see what alternatives we present. This ideological war will continue for a long time and it is clear that the radicalizing effect of
actions such as the Cambodia demonstration clearly favor our side.

Many of the doves will lose outright. Those who win will undoubtedly disappoint some of their increasingly demanding supporters, and as happened in 1968 another large body of students
will be driven from liberalism to radicalism to revolution. In 1972,
if an Edmund Muskie or a John Lindsay becomes president and
poverty, racism, economic disparity, and militarism continue un-
abated it will become clear to even the more moderate activists
that liberals are incapable of solving the society's problems. Thus
time, and history, are on our side.

Meanwhile, despite its apparent tactical militancy, the student
anti-war movement has rarely presented an explicitly anti-capitalist
perspective on the war. It seems, for the most part, dominated by
concerned young people who share a common aversion to killing
and a neo-isolationist view toward Third World liberation struggles. The war is a "tragic mistake," they are told by the liberals,
and if you students just help us get rid of nasty Richard Nixon,
then everything will be all right. This analysis has been largely unsuccessful in co-opting students and other young people.

The electoral "peace" effort has a short-term appeal for activists
who are groping to find something constructive to do with their
energy. But the contradictions of this society are too blatant to be
ignored for long. The liberal politicians are not about to stop the
Standard Oil Co. from exploiting the people of Venezuela. Neither

are they willing to eliminate corporate profits at home in order to achieve social equality or combat environmental decay. The working man labors all day to make a profit for the factory owner and no amount of reform can change that. The citizens' taxes are used to overpay for an entirely unnecessary new weapons system in order to bolster a favored aerospace company that happens to have an effective lobbyist in Washington. The Black Panther Party is the target of organized genocide.

The Cambodia protests have shown us how far we have come in the six years since students at Berkeley first staged militant "student power" demonstrations. But Cambodia also demonstrated how far we have yet to go if there is to be a revolutionary change in America. For the student movement is still basicly isolated from the black and working class revolutionaries in the society.

The national student strike was called from New Haven, Connecticut, on May 1, 1970 where 15,000 radicals had gathered to protest the trial of Black Panther chairman Bobby Seale. The repression of the black community and the Panthers in particular was intended by its organizers to be a prime issue in the strike along with the invasion of Cambodia. But at nearly every campus where a strike was organized, the plight of the black colony in America was practically ignored. Even the wholesale attempt to exterminate the Panthers was forgotten. Yet two days later the killing of four white, middle-class students at Kent State University sent thousands of college youths into the streets.

This insensitivity of the student movement to black concerns threatens to split the revolutionary movement in America. For the Black Panthers and others are saying, either we are going to have a race war in America or we are going to have a class war, and that the difference is up to white radicals. Blacks are skeptical about our seriousness and our courage.

The murders of black students at Mississippi State College by state police, and the killing of Black Panthers in police ambushes must not go unnoticed. We cannot tolerate the use of loaded weapons by National Guardsmen against blacks while protesting their use on the campuses of predominantly white schools.

To win, we must convert a large proportion of the youth into full-time permanent social revolutionaries. This must be done if the radical movement in America is to grow and succeed, for student movements are notoriously ineffective in terms of changing the society. Student movements can act as a catalyst, but the wage laborers have the ultimate power to bring about a revolution.

For the first time since the Depression, there is now a significant minority of youth who openly advocate revolution in America. We are growing all the time, while developing an alternative life style from which our political agitation is continuing.

It is the building of this hard core of committed revolutionaries that is the most significant result of the kind of protest which resulted from the invasion of Cambodia and the Kent State killings. For, of the hundreds of students who were arrested in those protests, a few will stay on the battle front, but with even greater understanding and determination. They leave behind them a highly politicized and tense educational structure which will continue to blunder in its attempts to restore order.

The ratio of revolutionaries to radicals and of radicals to liberals is clearly increasing, and each new radical is capable of influencing many others. But it is easy to deceive oneself as to the strength of the revolutionary elements of the society. We are still a tiny minority, despite the illusions of strength caused by the success of actions like the Cambodia strike.

We are still too weak to win "military" victories against our enemies for they have at their disposal incredibly powerful tools of repression (as the Kent students found out). The more effective we become, the tighter the net of repression that surrounds us. Our struggle is going to take a long time—even longer if we cannot resist the temptation to prematurely employ terrorism and bombings rather than serious above ground organizing.

The elements of a revolutionary movement are all there. The working class is facing severe economic hardships and intolerable inflation. Black people are suffering from increasing unemployment and rising despair. Much of the youth is receptive to our analysis although not yet convinced that it is correct. And possibly most important, the peoples of the Third World are rising up against U.S. domination and thus exposing the fallacies of our "democratic" system.

In the meantime, we have an excellent opportunity within our own movement to present a structural alternative to the phoney democracy of the government. This is absolutely essential if we are going to survive and win the coming battle of ideologies. In place of elitism and ruthless competition we must model our organization and life style on a cooperative ethic.

Frustration and overconfidence are paradoxically the movement's greatest enemies. Frustration leads to terrorism which drives some of our best people underground where they can do little real organizing. Overconfidence stems from misinterpreting our own strength as a result of the apparent success of actions like the November Washington March and the Cambodia campus strikes.

We are capable of capturing the youth of the nation to add to the revolutionary movement. This is what is necessary to win, but it is not going to happen overnight. As Eldridge Cleaver put it:

The only way that the world is ever going to be free is when the youth of this country *moves* with every principle of human respect and with every soft spot we have in our hearts for human life, in a fashion that lets the pig power structure know that when people are racistly and Fascistly attacked, the youth will put a foot in their butts and make their blood chill.